THE UNIVERSITY OF
LONDON 1836 – 1986

THE UNIVERSITY OF LONDON
1836–1986

An illustrated history

NEGLEY HARTE

with a Foreword by HRH The Princess Anne, The Chancellor

THE ATHLONE PRESS
London and Atlantic Highlands, NJ

BUCKINGHAM PALACE

It is natural to indulge in some drum
beating at so major a mile-stone as a sesquicentennial. But
this is particularly understandable for an institution so
remarkable as the University of London, unique as it is among
universities in its scale, its federal structure, and its
external degree provision and its role in establishing new
universities in this country and the Commonwealth. The
University of London has an unrivalled record of 'firsts': in
awarding degrees without religious tests, in promoting
teaching and research in laboratory science, engineering and
modern languages, in admitting women to degrees and in
appointing women professors. The University also provides a
significant proportion of the nation's needs for skilled
manpower, as well as an established primacy in the field of
medical education.

It would require a very large volume indeed
to relate the University's long and complex history. The
present book seeks rather to record some of the highlights and
to capture a sense of the abiding ethos. A large number of
well-chosen illustrations throw light on many aspects of the
various different colleges and institutes which form the
University, all of which have impressive histories of their
own, some of them older than the University itself. The
threads connecting the past and the present are fascinatingly
teased out making this work a lively survey of the history of
a great University rather than a dull, formal record. I
commend it to all members of the University as well as to all
those interested in the development of education, research and
scholarship, throughout the world.

Anne

First published 1986 by The Athlone Press Ltd
44 Bedford Row, London WC1R 4LY
and 171 First Avenue,
Atlantic Highlands, NJ 07716

British Library Cataloguing in Publication Data

University of London
  The University of London, 1836–1986:
  an illustrated history
  1. University of London—History
  I. Title   II. Harte, Negley
  378.421   LF411

    ISBN 0–485–11299–X
    ISBN 0–485–12052–6 Pbk

Library of Congress Cataloging in Publication Data

Harte, N. B.
  The University of London, 1836–1986.

  Bibliography: p.
  Includes index.
  1. University of London—History.   I. Title.
LF411.H37   1986   378.421′2   86–10819
ISBN 0–485–11299–X
ISBN 0–485–12052–6 (pbk.)

Designed by Roger Davies
Typeset by August Filmsetting
Haydock, St Helens
Printed in Great Britain at the University Press,
Cambridge

Contents

1 The old and the new juxtaposed at Guy's Hospital Medical School, re-united since 1982 to form part of the United Medical and Dental School of Guy's and St Thomas's Hospitals: the 32 storeys of Guy's Tower opened in 1975 at the time of the 250th anniversary of the Hospital seen above the statue of the founder Thomas Guy (1644?–1724) erected in 1739.

The Federal University

Every University worthy of the name at all is an embodiment of optimism, of belief in youth and in progress, of a certainty that man does not live by bread alone, of a trust in the continuity of the human spirit and human life throughout the ages. What else makes it seem worthwhile to grub so dustily in the records of the past in order to hand on what is learned generation by generation to the future?

Sir William Beveridge, *The Physical Relation of a University to a City* (1928), p.2.

You mean the *so-called* University of London.

Comment made to the author by the then Director of the London School of Economics, Professor Ralf Dahrendorf, on being told that this history was being undertaken.

All universities are different, but some are more different than others. The University of London is the most different of them all. The forty-seven universities which now exist in the United Kingdom can be regarded as falling into four broad categories. There are, first, the six universities which are older than the University of London – the two ancient provincial English universities at Oxford and Cambridge, both dating back to the twelfth century, and the four ancient Scottish universities at St Andrews, Aberdeen, Glasgow and Edinburgh, all founded between 1411 and 1583. Secondly, there are the civic or 'redbrick' universities established in the aftermath of the University of London in many of the provincial centres of population in the later nineteenth and early twentieth centuries. Then there are two types of more recent 'new' universities established in the 1960s – the 'green fields' universities like Sussex and York, and the technological universities with pre-university antecedents like Strathclyde and Brunel. These groupings are somewhat blurred; British universities are characteristically British institutions and cannot be easily categorized.[1] But broadly they fall into these four groups, with two major exceptions.

The two biggest universities cannot be constrained into these categories at all. The Open University and the University of London are both *sui generis*. The Open University was established by the government in 1969 with nation-wide functions well-known to be distinct from those of the other universities. The University of London, established by the government in 1836, must be in a category all of its own for more complex reasons. Its uniqueness arises from its size, its federal structure, its metropolitan role, and, above all, the course of its historical development.

The University of London is essentially characterized by its federal structure, its existence in a variety of different institutional forms variously called 'colleges', 'schools' and 'institutes'. Spread out all over London – and beyond – are the present total of the

2 A diagrammatic map attempting to show the distribution of the sites of the schools and institutes which make up the federal University of London in 1986. In its sesquicentenary year, the University consists of 24 independent schools (one of which consists of 12 institutes) and 13 separate institutes – a total of 37 different institutions, some of them federal in themselves, besides six others having recognized teachers.

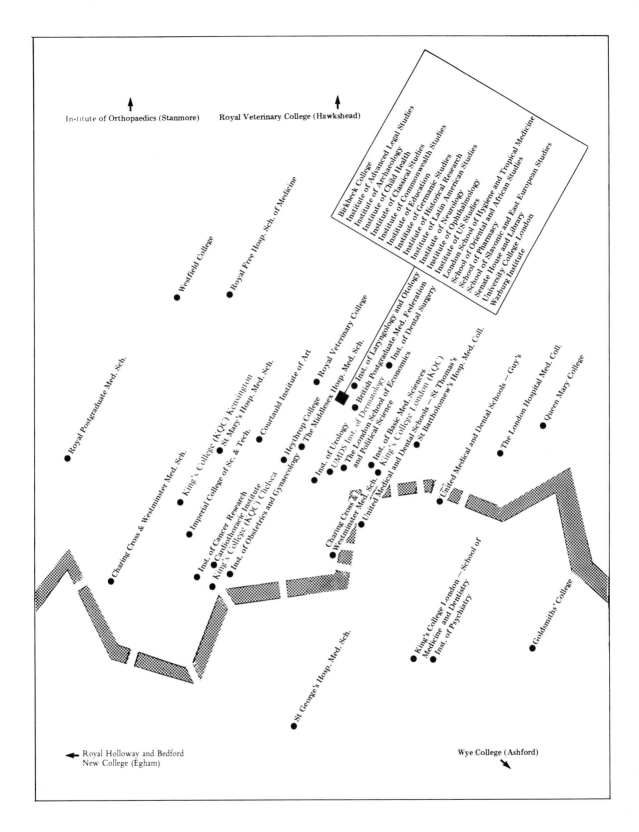

Institute of Orthopaedics (Stanmore)

Royal Veterinary College (Hawkshead)

Birkbeck College
Institute of Advanced Legal Studies
Institute of Archaeology
Institute of Child Health
Institute of Classical Studies
Institute of Commonwealth Studies
Institute of Education
Institute of Germanic Studies
Institute of Historical Research
Institute of Latin American Studies
Institute of Neurology
Institute of Ophthalmology
Institute of US Studies
London School of Hygiene and Tropical Medicine
School of Oriental and African Studies
School of Pharmacy
School of Slavonic and East European Studies
Senate House and Library
University College London
Warburg Institute

Westfield College

Royal Free Hosp. Sch. of Medicine

Royal Postgraduate Med. Sch.

King's College (KQC) Kensington
St. Mary's Hosp. Med. Sch.
Courtauld Institute of Art
Royal Veterinary College
Heythrop College
The Middlesex Hosp. Med. Sch.
Inst. of Laryngology and Otology
British Postgraduate Med. Federation
Inst. of Dermatology
Inst. of Dental Surgery

Chating Cross & Westminster Med. Sch.
Imperial College of Sc. & Tech.
Inst. of Cancer Research
Cardiothoracic Institute
King's College (KQC) Chelsea
Inst. of Obstetrics and Gynaecology

Inst. of Urology
UMDS
The London School of Economics and Political Science
Inst. of Basic Med. Sciences
King's College London (KQC)
King's College London — St Thomas's
United Medical and Dental Schools — St Thomas's Hosp. Med. Coll.
St Bartholomew's Hosp. Med. Coll.

United Medical and Dental Schools — Guy's
The London Hospital Med. Coll.
Queen Mary College

Chating Cross &
Westminster Med. Sch.
United Medical and Dental Schools

St George's Hosp. Med. Sch.

King's College London — School of
Medicine and Dentistry
Inst. of Psychiatry

Goldsmiths' College

Royal Holloway and Bedford
New College (Egham)

Wye College (Ashford)

11

thirty-seven distinct and separate institutions which constitute the University of London. Some of them are very distinct and separate. Some are federations in themselves. All of them treasure their own identity and individuality. All have their own history, and the history of several of them is older than that of the University itself. The separate institutions of the University of London are not at all comparable with the colleges of the universities of Oxford or Cambridge, or the other universities having some sort of collegiate system. The only other British university that has a remotely comparable federal structure is the University of Wales, with its seven constituent colleges situated in Aberystwyth, Bangor, Swansea, Cardiff and Lampeter. But the University of Wales is much smaller and much less complex, though its federal workings are not easily understood by outsiders. The complexities of the workings of the University of London are not easily understood even by insiders.

More especially than is generally the case with large institutions, the structure of the University of London can only be comprehended in terms of its history. Though it is the third oldest university in England, it is not a university of the 'ancient' type. It originates from an entirely new departure created in 1836. It is not a 'civic' university, lacking intimate connections in its origins with either the ancient corporation of the City of London or with the London County Council or the Greater London Council or with any of the metropolitan boroughs. It does not have a single founder or a single benefactor who was responsible for shaping or re-shaping it. The University of London grew not from one root, but from several. It cannot, however, be regarded as a natural growth. Its development has been seminally shaped by government policy at various times over the hundred and fifty years of its existence in various ways, and shaped too by a variety of other interest groups of a very disparate and often conflicting sort. Conflict indeed has been a continuing theme in the history of the University of London. This book has been produced to mark the hundred and fiftieth anniversary of the award of the first royal charter in November 1836. It attempts to portray some of the peculiar complexity of the University's history and to assess — to use an appropriately Benthamite word — the 'utility' of the University as a whole.

Two figures have long haunted attempts to describe the University of London: the taxi-driver and the foreigner. The one can rarely identify where it is and the other can never understand what it is. 'The acidly impartial cab-driver test of renown and public importance', one distinguished member of the University has recently stated, 'reveals that barely one driver in three knows instinctively

3 The University of London is not to be confused with its largest constituent part, University College London, though from its foundation in 1826 until 1836 the College was the University of London Mark I. Its main quadrangle, begun when the Duke of Sussex laid the foundation stone in February 1827, was declared to be complete by the Queen in November 1985 when Sir Hugh Casson's extensions on either side of the main entrance in Gower Street were added to the handsome neo-classical building originally designed by William Wilkins.

and without further instruction where and how to find the various colleges and buildings of the University.'[2] It used to be even more difficult. In 1922 Sir Gregory Foster, Provost of University College and a future Vice-Chancellor of the University, noted that 'if you ask a cabman, whether one of the old Jehu type or the modern taxi-driver, to drive you to the University of London, he either says he does not know where it is or he brings you to University College.' Soon after becoming Director of the London School of Economics in 1919 Sir William Beveridge had occasion to visit the head-quarters of the University, then situated in the Imperial Institute building in South Kensington. 'The cab-driver, when I asked for the University of London, looked blank. As I explained, a light broke on him. "Oh, you mean the place near the Royal School of Needlework." I discovered that this was what I did mean. There was in Imperial Institute Road an institution devoted to the art of needle-work, and advertising itself by a notice-board of exceptional size. Turning off at this notice, one came in due course to a flight of steps at the head of which, in a good light, one could read, on one side only, the name of the University of London.'[3]

For its first hundred years, the University was housed in a suc-cession of unsatisfactory locations which encouraged an obscurity about its existence. It was first accommodated in modest apartments at Somerset House from 1836 to 1853; then temporarily at

Marlborough House; then from 1855 in Burlington House, and after another period temporarily in a house in Savile Row, its first purpose-built accommodation was provided in a new building in Burlington Gardens in 1870. In 1900 these premises were given up when the University took an unhappy tenancy of part of the Imperial Institute. Not until the building of the Senate House in 1933–8 did the University acquire a freehold of its own, achieved by the efforts of Beveridge in particular to ensure that Londoners could not so easily overlook the University in their midst.

Since the 1930s the University has been associated with Bloomsbury. University College had been there since the 1820s, and the British Museum (entirely rebuilt in 1823–47) since its opening in 1759. The University rejected an early opportunity of moving to Bloomsbury in 1853, and between 1912 and 1927 much energy was devoted to raising indecision on the site question to a consummate art. Bloomsbury, created in the late eighteenth and early nineteenth centuries by the town planning policy of the Dukes of Bedford, was described by Henry James as 'an antiquated ex-fashionable region' when Vanessa and Virginia Stephen moved to Gordon Square in 1904 to escape from Kensington after the death of their father, Sir Leslie Stephen. The subsequent lives and friendships of Vanessa Bell and Virginia Woolf, as they became, were to associate the area indelibly with the 'Bloomsbury Group', that linking of literary and artistic lions in the early twentieth century who lived in squares and loved in triangles. Transport improvements led to the drift of the upper middle classes to more distant suburbs, and Bloomsbury had become unfashionable and decayed: 'more of the "bury" than the "bloom", my dear'. After the University itself escaped from Kensington, the Senate House was built on the Bloomsbury site in the 1930s, with architecture designed to put the University of London permanently on the map. Subsequently more and more property in the area was acquired, creating the long-desired 'University quarter' for London. In an increasingly conservation-minded age, many of the new University buildings in the 1950s and 1960s were controversial and vociferously criticized. But 'Bloomsbury' took on a new meaning, one that was not outmoded or purposeless.[4]

The Senate House is not the University of London, and only a proportion of the University is to be found in Bloomsbury. In London the term 'the University' is used confusingly in a double sense. Sometimes the federal body as a whole is intended, and sometimes only the central organization symbolized by the Senate House. Both meanings have been used in the last few paragraphs. The most commonly used meaning in most parts of the University (in the former sense) is the latter sense. It is a usage which im-

4 King's College, chartered in 1829 and opened in 1831, the Establishment response to 'the Godless institution in Gower Street', was affiliated to the new degree-giving University of London Mark II in 1836 along with what then became University College. The rival colleges, very different in ethos, were similar in character. The gateway of King's was demolished in 1966 to make way for a new building fronting the Strand opened by the Queen in 1972.

5 A cartoon at the time of the centenary in 1936 paid tribute to the University's path-breaking role in opening higher education to all regardless of religious belief or sex. The University's role in expanding the range of subjects taught, and in the extension of knowledge as well as its diffusion, has been equally pioneering.

6 After prolonged controversy between 1912 and 1927, the University's Bloomsbury site was acquired and developed as a University quarter or precinct, dominated by the Senate House built between 1933 and 1938. To the left, across what used to be called the University garden, is the School of Oriental and African Studies, begun but only partially completed before the outbreak of war in 1939, its new building added in 1973, and one of the few remaining Georgian houses of the former Torrington Square. Birkbeck College, which specializes in part-time education, is to the right.

A WORLD TRIBUTE

The University of London, which celebrated its centenary last week, was the first University to remove the bars of creed and sex in university education. Its students have come from all over the world. It has always made special provision, too, for external students.

7 The University of London Union – ULU to all students – was founded in 1921 and housed in various temporary locations until the permanent building in Malet Street was opened in 1957. 'Café ULU', 'Waves' and 'Mergers Bar' are recently added attractions, besides the fine swimming-pool provided through the generosity of Lord Nuffield.

mediately reveals the tensions between the centre and the constituent bodies of the federal organization. The University contains at the present time a total of twenty-four independent 'schools', as they are known. 'We class schools, you see, into four grades,' Evelyn Waugh's character Paul Pennyfeather was informed by Church and Gargoyle in *Decline and Fall*: 'Leading School, First-rate School, Good School, and School. Frankly ... School is pretty bad.' The schools of the University of London are less easy to classify. They vary considerably in size, range and ethos. None would rank itself at less than first-rate, and many are truly leading. The University of London is not easily likened to any other social institution, except perhaps the Courts of Heaven which, it may be recalled, were said to contain many mansions.[5]

The twenty-four schools can perhaps be seen as falling into three groups. There are, first, five colleges which are 'multi-faculty' institutions, each covering in their teaching and research concerns almost the whole range of academic disciplines. A rough-and-ready indication of their size can be given by citing the numbers of undergraduates and postgraduates registered at them in 1984–5 (including 'part-time' as well as 'full-time' students, ignoring the complicated sophistications of 'full-time equivalents').

	Under-graduates	Post-graduates	Total
King's College London	5119	1964	7083
University College London	5070	1842	6912
Queen Mary College	3067	502	3569
Royal Holloway & Bedford New College	2323	391	2714
Birkbeck College	1268	1421	2689

The two biggest colleges, UCL and KCL, both include medical schools. At UCL, the Faculty of Clinical Sciences has since 1980 contained the former University College Hospital Medical School, a separate body from 1907, and King's College School of Medicine and Dentistry has since 1983 again formed part of KCL, from which it was separated in 1909. Since 1985, KCL has also subsumed Chelsea College and Queen Elizabeth College, both formerly independent schools of the University. Queen Mary College has been enhanced since 1983–4 by the transfer of fifty-three academic staff and about 350 science-based students from other colleges, particularly Westfield College. Royal Holloway and Bedford New College was formed in 1985 by the amalgamation of Royal Holloway College (opened in 1887) and Bedford College (opened in 1849), originally women's colleges which both admitted men as students from 1965. Birkbeck College, developing from its original foundation as the London Mechanics' Institution in 1823, spec-

8 The massively flamboyant building of Royal Holloway College on Egham Hill built in 1879–86. In 1985 as part of the 're-structuring' of the University, Bedford College was moved out and amalgamated with it to form Royal Holloway and Bedford New College, one of the five University centres into which science teaching is being concentrated.

ializes uniquely in the education of mature students, especially on a part-time basis.

Second, there are eight colleges which specialize in particular academic disciplines or groups of disciplines. They vary considerably in size.

	Under-graduates	Post-graduates	Total
Imperial College of Science and Technology	3273	1731	5004
London School of Economics	2271	1965	4236
School of Oriental and African Studies	718	338	1056
Westfield College	763	98	861
Wye College	394	177	571
School of Pharmacy	330	82	412
Royal Veterinary College	346	65	411
Heythrop College	10	49	59

The two largest, the Imperial College of Science and Technology and the London School of Economics and Political Science are stars in the firmaments of the natural and applied sciences and the social sciences respectively. Both contain a high proportion of research students. The others have more specialized concerns. Westfield College, a women's college begun in 1882 which became co-educational in 1964, has since 1982 been stripped of its sciences, becoming a small college in the Faculty of Arts with an unsettled future. Heythrop College, the one school of the University (since

9 The Director of the Courtauld Institute of Art, Professor Michael Kauffmann, photographed recently at Somerset House, showing on the right what was the entrance to the original premises of the University of London from its foundation in 1836 until 1853. Accommodation in the now empty northern wing of Somerset House has been offered to the Courtauld Institute for its teaching and for display of its renowned art collection, and an appeal for the necessary £3M is currently in progress.

1970) not in receipt of a UGC grant, teaches theology in a Roman Catholic context.

Third, there are eleven separate medical schools.

	Under-graduates	Post-graduates	Total
United Medical and Dental Schools of Guy's and St Thomas's Hospitals	1658	234	1892
London Hospital Medical College	908	271	1179
Charing Cross and Westminster Medical School	965	95	1060
London School of Hygiene and Tropical Medicine	–	879	879
St Bartholomew's Hospital Medical College	651	91	742
St George's Hospital Medical School	606	123	729
Middlesex Hospital Medical School	490	122	612
St Mary's Hospital Medical School	528	45	573
Royal Free Hospital School of Medicine	504	63	567
Royal Postgraduate Medical School	–	455	455
British Postgraduate Medical Federation			

10 The main entrance to LSE, perhaps the most widely-known abbreviation of any academic institution in the world. Since its foundation in 1895, the London School of Economics and Political Science – strategically placed between the City, Fleet Street and Whitehall – has been famous (sometimes notorious) as a power-house of teaching and research in the social sciences. Over the door can be seen the symbol of the beaver and the School's motto: *Rerum Cognoscere Causas*.

Six of them in their origins antedate the foundation of the University of London, and two more date from the later nineteenth century (St Mary's, 1854, and the Royal Free Hospital School of Medicine, 1874). All have close relations with the hospitals with which they are connected. Three are entirely concerned with post-graduate research, the result of successive attempts to rationalize medical education in London: the London School of Hygiene and Tropical Medicine (opened in 1929), the Royal Postgraduate Medical School (opened in 1935) and the British Postgraduate Medical Federation (opened in 1947).

The last, constitutionally a school of the University, consists of twelve separate institutes, as well as having central activities concerned with postgraduate study for hospital doctors and general practitioners in the four Thames Health Regions. The Hunterian

Institute (formerly the Institute of Basic Medical Sciences) is connected with the Royal College of Surgeons; the Institute of Cancer Research with the Royal Marsden Hospital; the Cardiothoracic Institute with the National Heart Hospital, the Brompton and London Chest Hospitals; the Institute of Child Health with the Hospital for Sick Children, Great Ormond Street; the Institute of Dental Surgery with the Eastman Dental Hospital; the Institute of Laryngology and Otology with the Royal National Throat, Nose and Ear Hospital; the Institute of Neurology with the National Hospital for Nervous Diseases, Queen Square; the Institute of Obstetrics and Gynaecology with the Hammersmith Hospital and Queen Charlotte's and Chelsea Hospitals; the Institute of Opthalmology with the Moorfields Eye Hospital; the Institute of Orthopaedics with the Royal National Orthopaedic Hospital; the Institute of Psychiatry with the Maudsley and Bethlem Hospitals; and the Institute of Urology with St Peter's, St Paul's, St Philip's and the Shaftesbury Hospitals.

Beside the 'schools' of the University, there are thirteen separate 'institutes' coming under the direct control of the Senate. They fall into two categories. There are those which directly admit students to read for degrees in particular fields.

	Under- graduates	Post- graduates	Total
Institute of Education	–	2719	2719
Courtauld Institute of Art	82	286	368
School of Slavonic and East European Studies	285	39	324
British Institute in Paris	259	6	265
Institute of Archaeology	142	91	233
Warburg Institute	–	36	36

The largest of these, the Institute of Education, is in the process of becoming a 'school', while retaining its present title. It will be noted that the School of Slavonic and East European Studies is an 'institute'. The Institute of Archaeology is about to amalgamate with University College. The British Institute in Paris, the Courtauld and the Warburg remain unique establishments in their different ways.

Seven institutes do not normally have students directly registered at them. They constitute nuclei of research interests in their respective fields, bringing together the academic staff and research students of the various schools, as well as forming national and international centres for their disciplines. The oldest of them, the Institute of Historical Research, founded in 1921, has been described by one of its many visiting American scholars as 'the best club in England'.

11 The entrance to the building in Woburn Square which since 1958 has housed the unique Warburg Institute, an institutional refugee from Nazi Germany: above the door is the Institute's 'signet' taken from a work published in Germany in 1472, describing the interrelation of the four elements of which the world was conceived to be made, earth, air, fire and water, and linking them to their related qualities of hot, cold, moist and dry, as well as to the seasons of the year and to the four humours of man, in an image of cosmic harmony.

12 Other symbols above the fine 1929 entrance to the London School of Hygiene and Tropical Medicine in Keppel Street, designed by Verner O. Rees and provided by the Rockefeller Foundation. The London School of Tropical Medicine, founded by the Seamen's Hospital in 1899, was amalgamated in 1924 with a new School of Hygiene concerned with 'the maintenance of health and the prevention of diseases in their widest application, not only in temperate but also in tropical and arctic climates'.

Institute of Advanced Legal Studies
Institute of Classical Studies
Institute of Commonwealth Studies
Institute of Germanic Studies
Institute of Historical Research
Institute of Latin American Studies
Institute of United States Studies

Besides the institutions in these five listings, there are also six 'institutions having recognized teachers', an elastic category linking varied institutions each having a role of its own. The largest is Goldsmiths' College, an institution with a status of Byzantine complexity, having 2282 undergraduates and 221 postgraduates as 'internal students' of the University, besides other students not coming under this description. There are also the London Graduate School of Business Studies, as the London Business School is officially called, the Jews' College, and the three leading music colleges: the Royal Academy of Music, Royal College of Music and Trinity College of Music. Besides the schools, the institutes and the institutions having recognized teachers, there are a number of central activities working for the federation as a whole, among which are the University Library, the Department of Extra-Mural Studies, the

13 The former Queen Elizabeth College in Campden Hill, Kensington, is the part of the University which has been most affected by various bouts of re-constituting and re-structuring policies. Originating in the 'lectures for ladies' given by King's College in 1878, becoming the 'Ladies' Department' in 1885 and the 'Women's Department' in 1902, in 1908 it became King's College for Women, in 1915 the Department of Household and Social Science, in 1928 King's College of Household and Social Science, in 1953 the co-educational Queen Elizabeth College, and in 1985 the Kensington campus of 'KQC', the enlarged King's College incorporating both Queen Elizabeth College and Chelsea College – eight different names and five fundamental changes of direction in just over a century.

Schools Examinations Department, the Audio-Visual Centre, the Careers Advisory Service and the University Computer Centre. They too have to be taken into account.

Enough has been said of the fifty-five different institutions mentioned in this outline description of the University in its sesqui-centenary year – without reference to the distinctive parts of some of them – to indicate that the University of London is of peculiar complexity. It cannot be said to be an uncontroversial grouping of institutions. Some members of the University do not disguise their view that it is too large and diverse a collection of institutions to be plausibly united. A more perceptive view of the totality would stress the flexibility of the arrangements which enable so various a group of institutions to be brought together into one overall London-wide framework, including some that would hardly be viable on their own. A static description of so embracive a federation is difficult to render comprehensible; it can only be grasped once the historical dimensions are added, especially at a time when

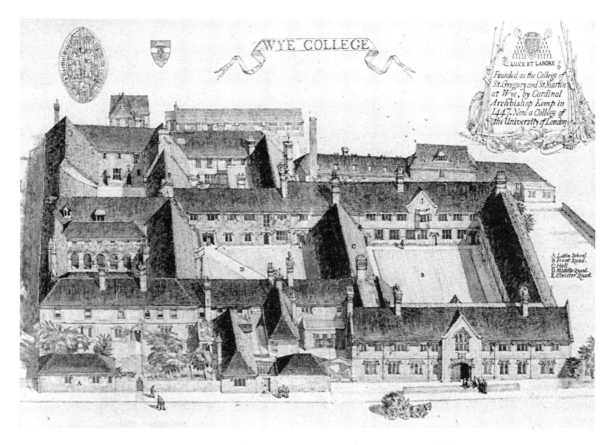

WYE COLLEGE

LUCE ET LABORE

Founded as the College of St.Gregory and St.Martin at Wye, by Cardinal Archbishop Kemp in 1447. Now a College of the University of London.

A *Latin School*
B *Front Quad.*
C *Hall*
D *Middle Quad.*
E *Cloister Quad.*

14 In the Kent countryside between Ashford and Canterbury is Wye College, founded in 1894 as an agricultural college in premises originally built as a secular college for priests established in 1447 by John Kempe (1380–1454) soon before he became Archbishop of Canterbury. The old collegiate buildings, carefully renovated, and other new premises, provide a University of London but non-London location for studies in agriculture, horticulture and various aspects of the rural environment, besides the Centre for European Agricultural Studies established at the time of joining the EEC in 1973.

the University is undergoing a painful process of 're-structuring', coincidental with its sesquicentenary.

The University of London did not begin as a federal organization. The University was never made to order. It was formed in stages out of institutions which came into existence in various historical contexts. Some of the early proposals for a University in London are referred to in the next chapter. The first proposal to achieve realization was made in a famous letter published in *The Times* written by Thomas Campbell in February 1825. It resulted in what can be called the University of London Mark I. Founded in 1826 with the legal status of a limited liability company, the self-proclaimed University of London opened in Gower Street in 1828. It attracted much attention for eliminating religious affiliation from the entrance requirements and sectarian theology from the syllabus. It attracted too an Establishment rival in the form of King's College which opened in 1831, having obtained in 1829 a charter, a form of official recognition denied to the 'University of London'. The two new aspirant university institutions in London in the 1830s clashed not only with the reactionary opposition of Oxford and Cambridge, but also with the more genuine objections of the various medical teaching institutions of London, especially those connected with the long-established hospitals. The result – after much controversy – was the foundation in 1836 by the government of a new University, the University of London Mark II as it might be identified. It was an examining body chartered to award degrees to candidates produced by what then became University College, as well as by King's College, the medical schools, and other institutions which could be recognized for the purpose. The University of London Mark I, a unitary university on a Scottish and German model, gave way to the University of London Mark II, a new concept which made a virtue of compromise by opening the way to wider aims.

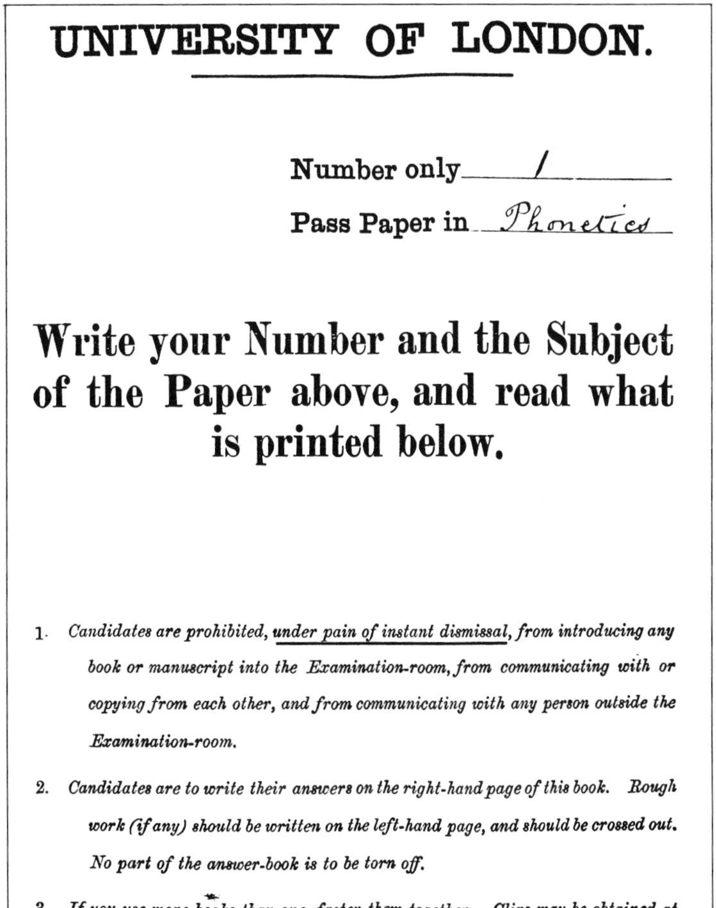

15 Examinations have always been a central feature of the University of London; indeed, between 1836 and 1900 the University in its Mark II form was notoriously a 'mere examining board'. Generations of candidates have been familiar with exam answer books in one form or another, all officially destroyed after being marked and checked. One that has happened to survive is this example dating from 1890, part of a batch of 60,000 printed in that year.

UNIVERSITY OF LONDON.

Number only_____ / _____

Pass Paper in__ *Phonetics*

Write your Number and the Subject of the Paper above, and read what is printed below.

1. *Candidates are prohibited, <u>under pain of instant dismissal</u>, from introducing any book or manuscript into the Examination-room, from communicating with or copying from each other, and from communicating with any person outside the Examination-room.*

2. *Candidates are to write their answers on the right-hand page of this book. Rough work (if any) should be written on the left-hand page, and should be crossed out. No part of the answer-book is to be torn off.*

3. *If you use more books than one, fasten them together. Clips may be obtained at the Examiners' table.*

4. *The answers of Candidates must be legibly written.*

16 Plenty of pictures exist of students taking degrees, but very few of them actually taking exams. This rare example shows an MB examination being held in 1949 in the Great Hall of St Bartholomew's Hospital, built in 1732 by James Gibbs, with the walls lined by the names and pictures of benefactors, prominently including Henry VIII who re-founded the Hospital in 1544.

Awarding degrees on this basis remained the basic purpose of the University of London for the rest of the nineteenth century. The proto-federal link with the teaching institutions, established in 1836, was broken in 1858 in the way discussed in chapter 3. Out of the great late nineteenth-century controversies (discussed in chapter 4) emerged the reconstitution which produced in 1900 what can be called the University of London Mark III. The University was transformed into a federal university, including University College, King's College, the medical schools and a variety of other constituent parts. Having been 'that august negation of the very idea of a University', as Arnold Bennett called it, the University of London after 1900 became a new body, albeit one that could be described by H.G. Wells in 1903 as something which 'does not exist in political thought. It is an acephalous invertebrate in the political world.'[6]

Nevertheless, the thraldom of examinations gave way to a university concerned with teaching and research. A major constitutional change in 1929 (discussed in chapters 5 and 6) gave more power to the centre. Less fundamental but important constitutional changes resulting in the University of London Act of 1978 and the consequent new statutes adopted in 1983 (chapter 7) have brought about the present structure. The special link between the University of London and the government, financial in its basis, was removed in 1901 and ended in the 1920s with the government contribution towards the provision of Senate House. Since then the University has stood in the same relationship to the government as the other universities; the government was increasingly the paymaster of them all, and in London the Court of the University became a sort of sub-UGC, distributing government funds to the various parts of the University. What was founded as a national university became the University of London in the twentieth century in fact as well as in name, notably maintaining some of its former functions.

The nineteenth-century University of London was, in modern terms, an amalgam of an Open University and a Council for National Academic Awards. It had neither the technology of the one, nor the system of inspection of the other, but its functions were perceived as a sort of cross between the two. The increase in the output of its graduates is shown in figure 1. The University of London Mark II has considerable achievements to its credit. The matriculation examination was increasingly used as the first national school-leaving certificate, the origin of the School Certificate

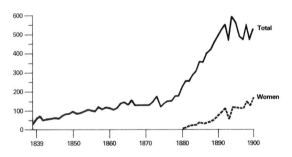

Fig 1   Number of Graduates, 1839–1900

17 One of the special glories of the University of London is that it was the first British university to award degrees to women. In 1878 sex discrimination in the examinations was ended, and the first women graduates were produced in 1880. By contrast, women were not permitted to graduate at Oxford until 1920, or at Cambridge until 1923. In 1885, the *Graphic* devoted a whole page to 'a lady BA of London University'.

and the General Certificate of Education. The London syllabus brought a range of new subjects into the scope of university education for the first time, particularly laboratory science and the modern languages. Degrees were awarded from the start without discrimination on religious grounds, and in 1878 the examinations were thrown open to women for the first time. The removal of religious, social and sexual barriers to higher education was an achievement that must command admiration. Many features of the University of London became the model for the provincial universities as they developed in the late nineteenth century, and for universities overseas in the Empire too. When the universities of

Oxford and Cambridge were reformed in the 1850s and after, their revitalization revealed the influence of London. The University's modernizing influence was immeasurable, but pervasive, in the United Kingdom and in many other parts of the world.

The University of London Mark III continued to play a pioneering role in a variety of ways. The enormous growth in its size is evident from the numbers of students both 'internal' and 'external' graphed in figure 2. From 2004 internal students when they were first counted in 1902–3, the number grew to a peak of 55,628 in 1981–2. A special feature has been the way in which London degrees have remained open to all through the external system, the continuation of the central characteristic of the University of London Mark II. Prior to 1932–3, external candidates for degrees –

Fig 2   Number of Students, 1900–85

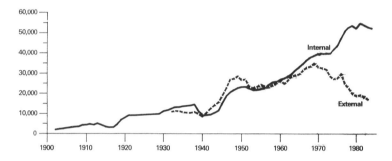

whether studying privately or at a range of other educational institutions – were not required to register as students of the University, so statistics for them are not available until that year.

In size, however measured, the University of London stands in a class apart from every other British university, just as London itself has always towered above every other English town in terms of

18 Two of the earliest women students in their 'prettily furnished rooms' at College Hall soon after it opened at Byng Place in 1882 (see **123**). The first women's hall of residence offered 'the social amenities of collegiate life', and a private room and full board for between 57 and 75 guineas per session of 33 weeks.

19 The 'Senior Student' at Westfield College in her 'pleasantly furnished room' photographed in 1922.

20 The resonances of several generations of social change are encapsulated in a photograph of Lucinda Neal with another student in her room in 1985 at International Hall, an intercollegiate hall of residence opened in 1962 and expanded to offer accommodation to some 480 men and women students.

21 Dame Mary Scharlieb, one of the first women to graduate in medicine in 1882, lecturing in the 1890s to students at the London School of Medicine for Women, founded in 1874 and for long the only medical school in the country which admitted women.

22 Professor Ruth Bowden lecturing in the same room in 1967 to students at the Royal Free Hospital School of Medicine; the School's name was changed in 1947 when, along with the other medical schools, it became co-educational.

23 A meeting of the Mycenaean seminar at the Institute of Classical Studies in 1985 listening to a paper by a visitor from the University of Paris on Minoan town planning, with Professor Nicholas Coldstream in the chair. Such seminars, the life-blood of research in the humanities, are held in various of the institutes of the University, those at the Institute of Classical Studies having been outstandingly creative and cathartic since its foundation in 1953.

24 The British Institute in Paris since 1969 has been a full institute of the University of London, the only part of the University entirely based abroad. Begun in 1894 as the *Guilde Franco-Anglaise*, becoming the *Institut Britannique à Paris* in 1928, the Institute has been housed since 1976 with the British Council's British Cultural Centre in the rue de Constantine. It is a centre of English studies for French students, and of French studies for English students.

25 The Queen Mother as Chancellor of the University of London in 1959 opening the new library of Makerere University College in Uganda, one of the Commonwealth university colleges helped by being in 'special relation' with London while they were achieving full university status. With the Queen Mother is Arthur Tattersall, then the Secretary of Makerere University College, later the Secretary of University College, 1964–78, and Public Orator of the University, 1975–8.

26 The Courtauld Institute Galleries in Woburn Square contain a superlative collection of French Impressionist and post-Impressionist paintings presented to the University by Samuel Courtauld. Among the many masterpieces is Edouard Manet's *Un bar aux Folies-Bergère* (1882). 'If one lacked time or strength to visit more than one London gallery, the Courtauld would be the one to choose. It is small, beautifully arranged, and every painting in it is important.'

27 The Picture Gallery at Royal Holloway College displays the remarkable collection of pictures acquired by Thomas Holloway in 1881–3 reflecting high Victorian taste. One of the many famous works is the narrative painting of Paddington Station by W.P. Frith, *The Railway Station* (1862), one of the central works of art of the nineteenth century.

28 Another collection of unexpected treasures is contained in the Petrie Museum of Egyptian Archaeology at UCL, which includes many of the fascinating discoveries made by Sir Flinders Petrie, FRS, FBA, the pioneering Professor of Egyptology, 1892–1933. They include the recently-cleaned relief from Koptos showing Senusret I (*c.* 1971–50 BC) dancing ceremonially before the ithyphallic fertility god Min.

29 Professor Sir Alexander Fleming, FRS (1881–1955), seen in his bacteriological laboratory at St Mary's Hospital Medical School around the time when he discovered penicillin in 1928, a discovery of major potential for which he later received a Nobel Prize.

30 Opposite the Courtauld Institute Galleries is the Percival David Foundation of Chinese Art in Gordon Square, a treasure-house by any standards. Among the hundreds of magnificent Chinese ceramics presented to the University in 1950 by Sir Percival David is a brilliant blue and white temple vase dating from 1351, one of a pair unequalled in quality.

31 On the occasion of the laying of the foundation stone of the Wolfson Institute at the Royal Postgraduate Medical School in 1959, Sir Isaac Wolfson, a generous donor to the University, was shown the heart-lung machine by its inventor, Professor Denis Melrose. The machine enabled the heart and lungs to be by-passed for operation purposes, opening the way to open-heart surgery.

32 An aerial view of the area north of Geneva showing the sites of the European Organization for Nuclear Research (CERN). The dotted line shows the route of the tunnel beneath the farmland between Geneva and the Jura mountains to accommodate the Large Electron-Positron Collider, which will enable the acceleration of electrons and positrons to the highest energies ever achieved. The Departments of Physics at several London colleges are deeply involved in this research programme. Professor Ian Butterworth, FRS, the Research Director at CERN, will become Principal of Queen Mary College in 1986.

33 The most far-flung of all elements connected with the widely-dispersed University of London has been the Giotto space probe, which was sent 90 million miles to collect data on Halley's Comet in the University's sesquicentenary year. Built by British Aerospace, the probe contained scientific instruments designed by the Mullard Space Science Laboratory of UCL.

34 The Hutton Tension Leg Platform
erected in the North Sea by Conoco in 1984,
a major advance in oil production platforms
achieved through the research of the London
Centre for Marine Technology, an initiative
in the underlying principles of the design of
offshore structures established in 1976 by
Imperial College and University College
acting jointly.

35 Professor Roland Levinsky, Hugh
Greenwood Professor of Immunology at the
Institute of Child Health, one of the
institutes grouped together to form the
British Postgraduate Medical Federation,
seen examining a child patient who has
undergone a successful mismatched bone-
marrow transplant at the Hospital for Sick
Children in Great Ormond Street, a
technique which has benefited from intensive
laboratory-based research at the Institute of
Child Health in recent years.

36 The *VCH* – the Victoria History of the
Counties of England – is a major long-term
research project, begun in 1899 and taken
over by the University of London in 1932.
Organized by the Institute of Historical
Research in partnership with the local
authorities of many English counties, large
volumes based on systematic research into
the records relating to particular localities are
painstakingly produced, nearly two hundred
of them so far.

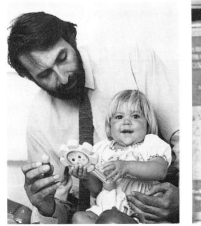

37 The Chancellor of the University, HRH The Princess Anne, flanked by the Vice-Chancellor, Lord Flowers, FRS, and the Principal, Peter Holwell, opening a presentation ceremony at the Albert Hall in January 1986. Graduates have been formally presented to the Chancellor since 1849, and for long 'Presentation Day' was the University's only formal occasion. Over 15,000 graduates are now produced every year, and several such ceremonies are needed.

38 Since 1930 a highly select number of honorary degrees have been presented each year at the Foundation Day ceremony held to commemorate the award of the University's first Charter on 28 November 1836. Here Princess Anne, Chancellor since 1981, is seen hooding Sir John Sainsbury, the Chairman of Sainsbury's, with the honorary degree of DSc(Econ) in November 1985, watched by the Vice-Chancellor, Lord Flowers.

39 On the same occasion Princess Anne is seen congratulating Iris Murdoch, the well-known novelist and philosopher, on the award of her honorary DLit. The Foundation Day ceremony is now held in the Logan Hall, opened in the new Institute of Education building in 1977 and named in honour of Sir Douglas Logan, the great Principal of the University from 1948 to 1975.

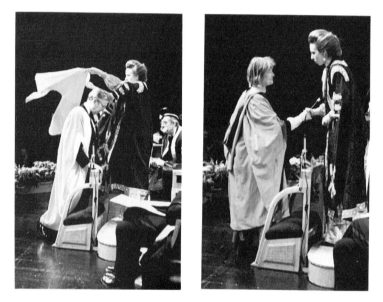

population and influence. With well over 50,000 students, the University of London is very substantially larger than the next biggest universities, Oxford with over 13,000 students, Cambridge with nearly 13,000, followed by Manchester with over 12,000.

A good 15 per cent of all the country's university students are London students, and the proportion is significantly higher for certain important particular groups: 21 per cent of all full-time post-graduates, 23 per cent of all overseas (i.e. non-EEC) students, and 25 per cent of all part-time students. These figures exclude the 17,455 students (9034 at home and 8421 overseas) registered as external students for first degrees, and a further 804 registered for higher degrees. They exclude too the 19,341 individuals signed up for the

40 The Senate – 'the supreme governing and executive body of the University in all academic matters' – in November 1985 being addressed by the Vice-Chancellor, Lord Flowers, with the Chairman of Convocation, Professor J.P. Quilliam, the Clerk of the Senate, Peter Taylor, and the Principal, Peter Holwell, also on the platform. The much enlarged size of the Senate since the new statutes came into effect in 1981 means that meetings can no longer be held in the Senate Room, and the 117 members have to be accommodated in the Beveridge Hall. They sit in alphabetical order at desks familiar to examination candidates.

41 The Court of the University, which controls all matters relating to finance, meeting in October 1985 with Lord Scarman, the senior Law Lord, well-known for his inquiry into the Brixton disorders in 1981, in the chair. To his right is Sir Peter Parker, and to the right of the Vice-Chancellor and the Principal is Sir Michael Clapham, two of the wise men appointed to the Court by the Crown. In the foreground is another, Sir Peter Matthews, former Chairman of Vickers and Chairman of the Council of University College, with next to him Dr I.G. Patel, Director of the LSE since 1984. On the right is Nicola Rossi, the current President of ULU, and Sir Frank Hartley, formerly Vice-Chancellor, 1976–8.

42 A chart showing the development of the scientific disciplines taught at Imperial College and its antecedent institutions, produced at the time of the centenary of the foundation of the Royal College of Chemistry in 1945. Many important London names in the advance of science are identified. *Overleaf.*

nearly 900 courses offered by the Department of Extra-Mural Studies. Of the £1,225M which the University Grants Committee distributed to British universities in 1983–4, £235M came to the University of London – some 20 per cent of the total.

The University of London forms about a fifth of the entire British university sector. There are nearly 1000 professors, over 600 readers and nearly 5000 recognized teachers. The research staff brings the number of full-time academic employees of the various parts of the University to nearly 8000. The total number of persons employed by the University easily exceeds 20,000. Convocation has about 90,000 members. The sheer size of the University of London is its most conspicuous feature.

ADMINISTRATION	MINING	METALLURGY	GEOLOGY	NATURAL HISTORY	PHYSICAL SCIENCE

Director — At the Museum of Practical Geology. Jermyn Street

1851 — GOVERNMENT SCHOOL OF MINES AND OF SCIENCE APPLIED TO

Sir Henry de la BECHE (1851-55) | Sir Warington W SMYTH (1851-91) | John PERCY (1851-79) | Sir Andrew RAMSAY (1851-76) | Edward FORBES (1851-54) |

1853 — METROPOLITAN SCHOOL OF SCIENCE APPLIED TO MINING AND

Sir Roderick I. MURCHISON (1855-71)

BIOLOGY
The Rt. Hon. Thomas H. HUXLEY (1854-85)

Robert HUNT (1853-54)
PHYSICS
Sir George STOKES (1854-60)

1857 — GOVERNMENT SCHOOL OF MINES

John TYNDALL (1860-68)

1863 — ROYAL SCHOOL OF MINES

Frederick GUTHRIE (1868-86)

Dean of the N.S.S. (R.C.S) and R.S.M.

Sir W Chandler ROBERTS-AUSTEN (1879-1902) Dept transferred to S.Kensington 1880

J.W. JUDD (1876-1905) Dept transferred to South Kensington 1877

— Departments of the Royal School of Mines transferred to South Kensington

AGRICULTURE

PHYSICAL ASTRONOM

1881 — ROYAL SCHOOL OF MINES — NORMAL SCHOOL OF

The Rt Hon Thos. H. HUXLEY (1881-95)

Transfer of Dept to South Kensington completed 1890

J W WRIGHTSON (1882-97)

BOTANY | ZOOLOGY

Sir Arthur RÜCKER (1886-1901)

Sir Norman LOCKYE (1881-1901)
Astronomical Physics

1890 — ROYAL SCHOOL OF MINES — ROYAL COLLEGE OF

J.W. JUDD (1895-1905)

Sir Clement LE NEVE FOSTER (1891-1904)

Wm. GOWLAND (1902-09)

Dept closed 1897

Sir John FARMER (1895-1929) | G. B. HOWES (1895-1905)

H.L. CALLENDAR (1801-30)

S.H. COX (1904-12)

W.W. WATTS (1905-30)

Sir Wm TILDEN (1905-08)

1907 — IMPERIAL COLLEGE OF

ROYAL SCHOOL OF MINES | ROYAL COLLEGE OF

Rector of the Imperial College
T.W. BOVEY (1908-10)
Sir Alfred KEOGH (1910-22)

W.A. CARLYLE (1909-13)

Technology of Woods and Fibres
Percy Groom (1911-31)

Plant Physiology and Pathology
V.H. Blackman (1911-20)

Adam SEDGWICK (1909-1913)
E.W. Macbride (1909-13)

Lord Rayleigh (1908-20)

Wm. FRECHEVILLE (1912-19)

Wm GOWLAND (1913-14)
Sir Harold CARPENTER (1914-40)

Economic Mineralogy C G Cullis (1915-38)

Comparative Pathology
H.G. Plimmer (1915-18)

Entomology
M. Lefroy (1912-25)

BIOLOGY

E.W. MACBRIDE (1913-34)

W.Watson (1915-20)

Astro-Physics A. Fowler (1915-34)

S. J. TRUSCOTT (1919-35)

Biochemistry
S. Schryver (1920-29)

TECHNICAL OPTICS
F.J. CHESHIRE (1917-26)

Optical Design
A.E.Conrady (1917-31)

A.O.Rankine (1920-37)

Mine Surveying L.H.COOKE (1919-29)

Instrument Des" A.F.Pollard (1920-43)

Sir Thos HOLLAND (1922-29)

Plant Physiology W. Brown (1928-37)

F.Balfour-Browne (1925-29)

A.O.RANKINE (1925-31)

Sir Henry TIZARD (1929-42)

V.H.BLACKMAN (1929-37) J.W.Munro (1920-34)

Incorporated in Physics Meteorology (transferred from Aeronautics)

Sir George THOMSON (1930-)

J.A.S RITSON (1935-)

P.G.H BOSWELL (1930-58) Mining Geology

Biochemistry A.C.CHIBNALL (1936-43)

Zoology and Applied Entomology J.W. MUNRO (1934-)

Sir Gilbert Walker (1932-34)

Oil Technology V.C.Illing (1936-)

Botany W.BROWN (1937-)

D.Brunt (1934-38)

Natural Philosophy H.Dingle (1937-)

S.J.TRUSCOTT

Plant Physiology F.G.Gregory (1937-)

J.A.S RITSON

Mining Geology W.R.Jones (1941-)

H.H.READ (1938-)

D.BRUNT (1939-)

R. V. SOUTHWELL (1942-)

Technical Optics L.C. Martin (1948-)

ADMINISTRATION	MINING	METALLURGY	GEOLOGY	BIOLOGY	METEOROLOGY	PHYSICS
IMPERIAL COLLEGE	ROYAL SCHOOL OF MINES			ROYAL COLLEGE OF		

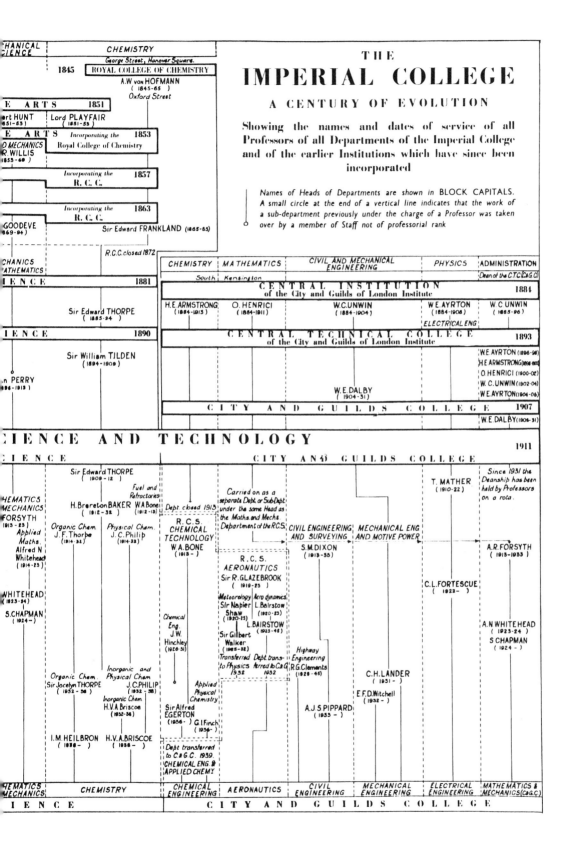

43 Convocation, the body of graduates, has been an important component of the University since being constituted in 1858. It has frequently been a force for useful change, and frequently a source of irritation. Graduates in the nine faculties of the University elect the Standing Committee, here shown assembled in 1985 around the Chairman (since 1973), Professor J.P. Quilliam, Emeritus Professor of Pharmacology at St Bartholomew's Hospital Medical College. Convocation elects the Chancellor and twenty 'lay' members of the Senate, who volunteer experience from many walks of life in the counsels of the University.

44 For one hundred and fifty years medicine has been a major concern of the University, which now produces a third of the country's doctors. One of the most fascinating small museums in London has been created by the renovation of the operating theatre and herb garret of St Thomas's Hospital constructed in the 1820s in the loft of St Thomas's Church (later Southwark Cathedral Chapter House), and abandoned when the Hospital and its Medical School moved in the 1860s. The early nineteenth-century operating theatre is a unique survival.

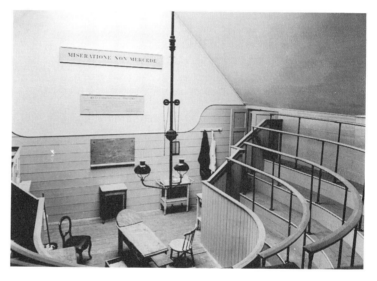

The scale of the University of London combined with its federal nature makes the task of writing a complete history virtually impossible. This work attempts a selective overview. An illustrated history can easily be a distorted history. Pictures tend to be taken of formal occasions rather than everyday ones, of the unusual rather than the usual, of the untypical rather than the typical. The University of London indulges little in ceremonial, but ceremonial occasions create a visual record while the normal activities of study and research tend to go unillustrated. A bias is thus introduced into the nature of the sources which the historian has to use. Great openings, royal visits and other grand events inevitably figure large in a

45 The Nobel Prize awarded in 1971 to Dennis Gabor, FRS (1900–79), the great scientist of Hungarian origin who worked in London from 1934, becoming Professor of Electron Physics at Imperial College. The prize was awarded for his invention and development of holography.

history drawing upon visual sources, but can easily give a misleading and superficial impression of the history of an institution, especially one that is essentially an interconnected series of separate institutions. Much as the historian tries to seek illustrations which illuminate the reality of changing situations, the potential to distort must be explicitly recognized alongside the potential to encapsulate.

Many important themes are inevitably squeezed out. Any intelligent history of the University would focus on academic developments rather than on the constitutional superstructure. The whole point of the University is its work in diffusing knowledge and in extending knowledge. Teaching and research should be at the core. It seems an impossible task to attempt to survey the development of the whole range of institutionalized disciplines covered by the University. Some fifty-nine different subjects are now represented by Boards of Studies, from 'Aeronautical Engineering' to 'Zoology and Comparative Anatomy (including Palaeo-Zoology)', and sixteen more are represented by Special Advisory Committees, from 'Area Studies' to 'Sociology as Applied to Medicine' — a total of seventy-five different fields of academic endeavour. Illustration **42** shows the sort of thing that should be at the centre of such an academic history: it covers only fourteen subjects at one college for only part of its existence.

Such an approach could neglect critical changes in context. H.G. Wells, for example, wrote of his period as a student at the Royal College of Science in the 1880s as follows: 'the professors . . . being preoccupied by the keen competition in research, lecture a minimum of lectures, talk a text-book that is, and never come into personal contact with their students at all. During my three years of instruction, save for a rare "good morning", I never spoke to my professors at South Kensington — Professors Huxley, Guthrie and Judd —

46 'Where else in London can you find Karl Marx, Milton Friedman, William Shakespeare, Marilyn Monroe and 20,000 penguins?' Dillon's Bookshop began as a partnership between the University and Una Dillon in 1956 and steadily expanded to occupy the whole of the Edwardian Gothic building between Malet Street and Gower Street. Owned since 1977 by Pentos plc, the premises are presently being remodelled to create what is claimed will be 'Europe's finest bookstore'.

except in the case of the latter. And most of my conversations with Professor Judd were devoted to points of discipline.'[9] The nature of personal relationships has been transformed during the last century; the quiet rise of small-group teaching has replaced the bleak lectures of the nineteenth century; 'discipline' of students has come to be perceived in radically different terms; student life outside the lecture-room has been revolutionized. The history of institutions, however unwhiggishly written, can all too easily miss out such fundamental dimensions of change.

Novels may supply a corrective. Three works by David Lodge, a student at University College in the 1950s, now Professor of Modern English Literature at Birmingham, speak clearly: *The British Museum is Falling Down* (1965) captures the excitement and the despair of being a research student in London in the 1950s; *How Far Can You Go?* (1980), a truly historical novel, brilliantly traces the lives of a group of London students from the 1950s to the 1970s; *Small World* (1984) is farce, but reveals much about academic life in the 1980s. In some ways works like these say more about the University as it has affected the lives of people involved in it than the many reports and memoranda and minutes and official letters and statistics on which most of this book is based. Yet these sources can be made to reveal much. The past is not dead. It lives, and it lives on.

47 The University of London Boat Club has been in the top bracket of the rowing world since the 1960s. Its oarsmen figure large in the Henley Regatta, the Club having won more Henley medals than any other since 1961 when the Thames Cup was first won. Since 1973 twenty-one crews have been national champions. An impressive eight are seen here at Henley in 1984.

48 In 1981 the number of internal students of the University reached a peak of over 55,000. Student activity took a great variety of forms, one of them being demonstrations against government-imposed increases in overseas students' fees made before the cuts in higher education expenditure announced in the summer of that year. The Senate House was briefly 'occupied', an activity generally considered by the 1980s to be left over from a previous period.

49 An alternative image of student life was provided by sporadically continuing 'rag stunts', an activity generally thought to be left over from an even more previous period. Westfield College students enjoyed a *fin de siècle* luncheon in Whitestone Pond in 'rag week' in 1982, just before Westfield College began to be shrunk.

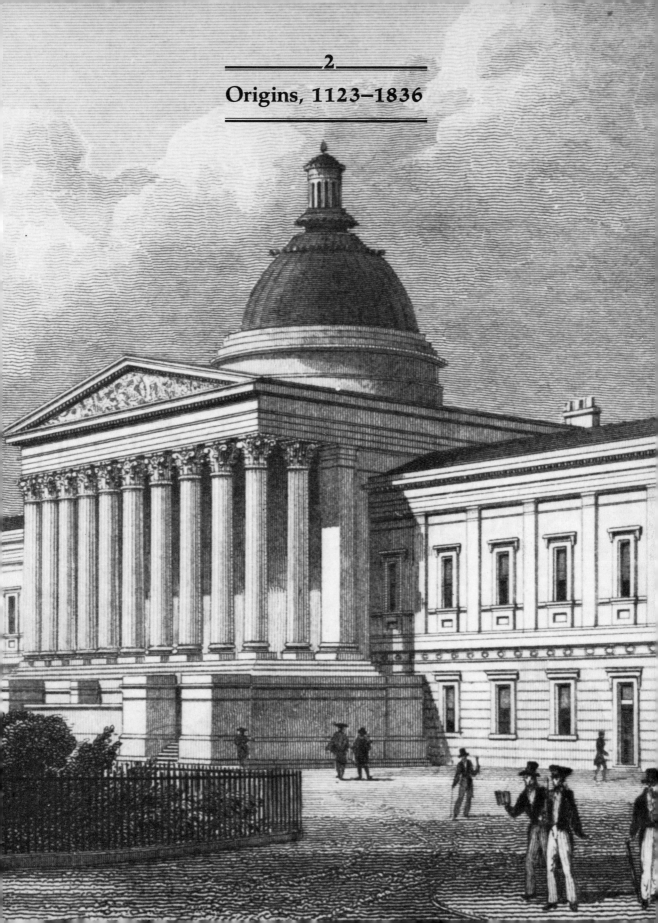

Why should such a Metropolis as London be without a University? Would it not save considerably the expense we are at in sending our young gentlemen so far from London? Would it not add to the lustre of our state, and cultivate politeness among us? What benefits may we not in time expect from so glorious a design? Will not London become the scene of science? ... Knowledge will never hurt us, and whoever lives to see a University here will find it give quite another turn to the genius and spirit of our youth in general.

DANIEL DEFOE, *Augusta Triumphans: Or, the Way to make London the most Flourishing City in the Universe* (1728), p. 5.

There is one matter which I beg you to bring to the King's notice yet again before your departure; this is the proposed foundation of a university of London. You have my authority to tell His Majesty of my absolute conviction that the implementation of this plan would bring about England's ruin.

Metternich's instructions to the Austrian Ambassador in London, 8 September 1825; G. de Bertier de Sauvigny, *Metternich et son Temps* (1850), p. 187.

London was the biggest city in the world long before it had a university. London became the biggest city in Europe in the late seventeenth century when its population grew to exceed the half-million or so of Paris, seat since the twelfth century of one of the great mother universities of the Middle Ages. By the beginning of the nineteenth century, London had grown to contain about a million people, constituting a good tenth of the total population of Britain. London was not only the capital of the United Kingdom of Great Britain and Ireland, but also the political, economic, and social centre of the 'first industrial nation' and of an almost literally world-wide empire. It was the metropolis. London had everything, but it was almost alone among the capitals of Europe in not having a university. The obvious first question is: why not? Why was there no university in so large, rich, long-established and powerful a city?

The implications of Metternich's point quoted at the head of this chapter take us some way towards an answer. The only two universities in England prior to the Industrial Revolution were situated at Oxford and Cambridge, both small and relatively controllable towns some fifty-odd miles to the north-west and north of London respectively. The traditional assumption was that there was a sort of division of labour: London was where careers and fortunes were made, while Oxford and Cambridge found their secluded specialized niche in being the centres of godliness and good learning. London money flowed regularly to investment in higher education

50 The neo-Grecian design for the University of London Mark I in Gower Street by William Wilkins (1778–1839), showing one of the wings as originally planned, but never built for lack of funds. Pugin regarded the architecture as pagan, adding acidly that it was 'in character with the intentions and principles of the institution'. *Previous page.*

51 The canopied effigy of Rahere (d.1143) added in the fifteenth century to his tomb at St Bartholomew the Great, the oldest parish church in London. Rahere, a courtier of Henry I, sometimes described as a jester or minstrel, founded the church and its accompanying hospital, the earliest institution so to be named, in 1123. St Bartholomew's Hospital has remained on the original Smithfield site since then.

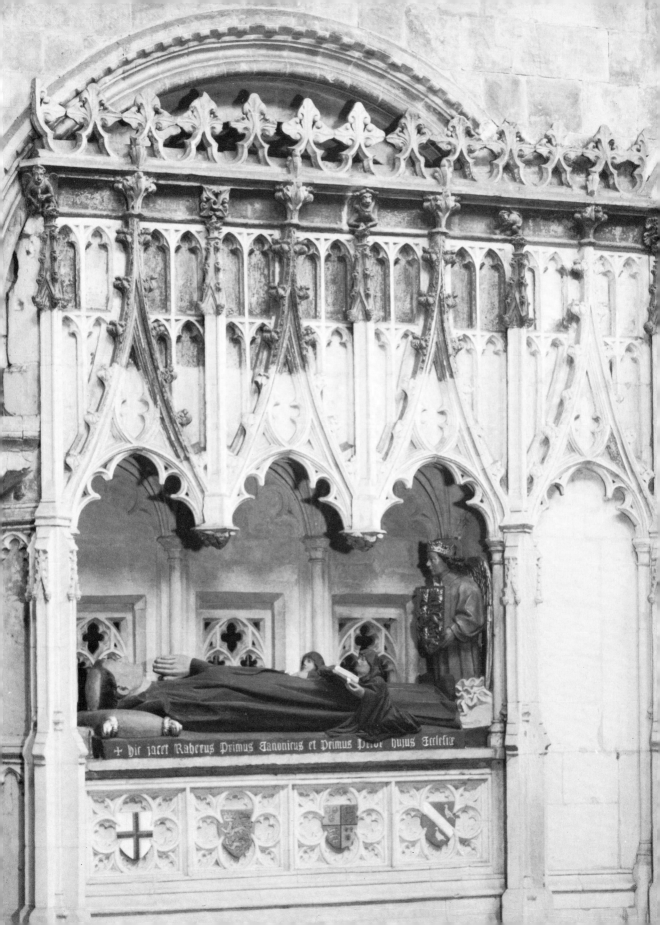

+ hic jacet Raherus Primus Canonicus et Primus Prior hujus Ecclesiæ

in the two universities in the provinces. Some 10 per cent of all charitable giving by Londoners in the period 1480–1660, it has been calculated, was directed to Oxford or Cambridge, mostly in the form of a rich stream of additions to college endowments, improvements to buildings and funds for scholarships and fellowships. Some donations or bequests were substantial. Sir Thomas White, for example, the great merchant tailor who was Lord Mayor of London in 1553 spent the latter part of his life and most of his fortune on single-handedly founding St John's College at Oxford, and coincidentally at the same time Dr John Caius began to devote the wealth accumulated from his successful and fashionable medical practice in London to refounding what became Gonville and Caius College in Cambridge.[1]

Oxford and Cambridge long had a monopoly on what for centuries passed as higher education in England, though not in Scotland, where the situation was quite different. The substantial growth of London began in the sixteenth century, and the earliest of a tepid stream of proposals for establishing a university in London date from that period. Sir Humphrey Gilbert, the navigator and colonizer of Newfoundland in the 1580s, suggested to Queen Elizabeth I the need to found an 'Academy' in London. About 1570 he pointed out that 'the greatest nomber of younge gentlemen within this Realme are most conversant abowte London' and that there ought to be provision 'for their better educacions'. Oxford and Cambridge were both 'drawn to licentiousness and Idleness', and his proposed 'Queen Elizabeth's Academy was to be on a new plan: 'whereas in the universities men study onely schole learninges, in this Academy they shall study matters of accion meet for present practize, both of peace and warre.'[2]

Sir Thomas Gresham (1519–79), the great merchant and royal financial agent in Antwerp, was successful in establishing a college in the City of London. In his lifetime he founded the Royal Exchange, opened by Queen Elizabeth in 1570, on the model of the Bourse at Antwerp. His will provided that after his wife's death the palatial mansion he built in the 1560s in Bishopsgate should become the seat of a collegiate establishment in which seven professors of divinity, astronomy, music, geometry, law, physic and rhetoric should give lectures, one on every day of the week, 'for the gratuitous instruction of all who chose to attend'. The professors were to be paid the generous remuneration of £50 per annum, and the College was to be controlled by the City Corporation and the Mercers' Company as trustees. After the death of Gresham's widow in 1596, these provisions were put into effect. The Royal Exchange, Fuller said in his *Worthies of England*, was 'a kind of college for

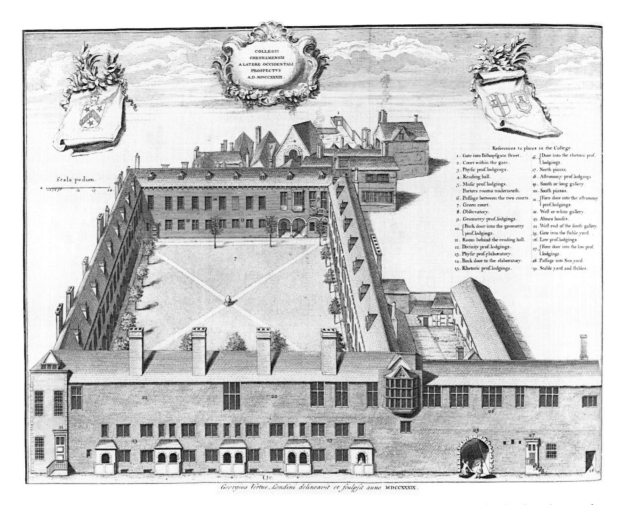

Within the image, legend text:

References to places in the College.

1. Gate into Bishopsgate street.
2. Court within the gate.
3. Phyfic prof. lodgings.
4. Reading hall.
5. Mufic prof. lodgings.
   Porters rooms underneath.
6. Paffage between the two courts.
7. Green court.
8. Obfervatory.
9. Geometry prof. lodgings.
10. Back door into the geometry prof. lodgings.
11. Room behind the reading hall.
12. Divinity prof. lodgings.
13. Phyfic prof. elaboratory.
14. Back door to the elaboratory.
15. Rhetoric prof. lodgings.
16. Door into the rhetoric prof. lodgings.
17. North piazza.
18. Aftronomy prof. lodgings.
19. South or long gallery.
20. South piazza.
21. Fore door into the aftronomy prof. lodgings.
22. Well or white gallery.
23. Almes houfes.
24. Well end of the fouth gallery.
25. Gate into the ftable yard.
26. Low prof. lodgings.
27. Fore door into the low prof. lodgings.
28. Paffage into Son yard.
29. Stable yard and ftables.

Scala pedum.

Georgius Vertue, Londini delineavit et fculpfit anno MDCCXXXIX.

52 Gresham College, seen here in George Vertue's engraving of 1739, was founded in 1596, in the Bishopsgate mansion built in the 1560s by the great merchant and financier Sir Thomas Gresham (1519–76). For a time a series of lectures given by seven professors flourished, and the first meetings of the Royal Society were held in the 1660s in the room marked 11 on the plan. The Royal Society moved away in 1710, and the College declined; the premises were pulled down in dubious circumstances in 1768.

merchants' and Gresham College was 'a kind of exchange for scholars'. The lectures were well-attended and Gresham College soon became a 'favourite resort of learned men'. It was at Gresham College that the first meeting of the Royal Society was held in 1660, and following a lecture by Sir Christopher Wren, 'something was offered about a design of founding a Colledge for the Promoting of Physico-Mathematicall Experimentall Learning'.[3]

The Royal Society continued to meet at Gresham College until 1710, apart from a break after the Great Fire of 1666. After 1710 Gresham College went into a decline and was so decayed by 1768 that the building was disposed of by the trustees, who even paid the government to pull the building down. The lectures continued in an obscure room at the Royal Exchange, until a new Gresham College on a modest scale was built in 1842. For a time in the 1890s a link with the University of London, then attempting reconstitution, was considered, but it was not forged, and the Gresham heritage drifted on until it was attached to the new City University in 1966.[4]

53 A college at Chelsea was founded by James I in 1609 'intended for a spiritual garrison, with a magazine of all books for that purpose; where learned divines should study and write in maintenance of all controversies against the Papists'. Only one side of the first quadrangle was built and despite being given to the Royal Society in 1669, the building and the College collapsed in 1678.

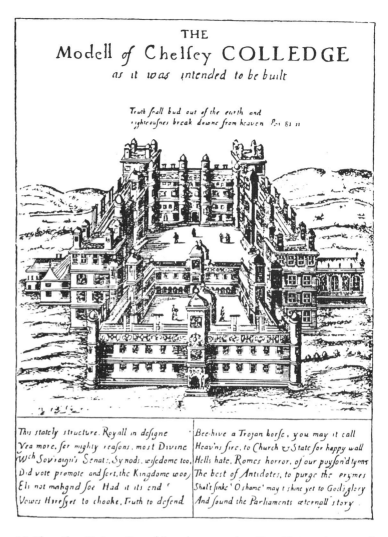

THE Modell of Chelsey COLLEGE as it was intended to be built

Truth shall bud out of the earth and righteousnes break downe from heaven Ps: 81 11

This statly structure. Royall in designe
Yea more, for mighty reasons. most Divine
Wch Soveraigns Senat: Synods. wisdome too,
Did vote promote and sett, the Kingdome woo)
Els not mahqnd foe Had it its end
Vowes Hirefyer to chooke, Truth to defend

Beehive a Trojan horse, you may it call
Heav'ns fire, to Church & State for happy wall
Hells hate. Romes horror, of our puyson'd tymns
The best of Antidotes, to purge the erymes
Shal't sinke 'O shame' may t shine yet to Gods glory
And found the Parliaments æternall story.

Neither the University of London nor the City University owed anything in their origins to Sir Thomas Gresham's imaginative but squandered foundation. It had flourished for a time, but Gresham College was to be a precursor rather than an origin of a university in London.

The Royal Society's promising discussion of 'a Colledge for the Promoting of Physico-Mathematicall Experimentall Learning' in 1660 did not lead to anything, nor did a number of other seventeenth-century proposals. Abraham Cowley's project in his *Proposition for the Advancement of Experimental Philosophy* (1662) envisaged twenty professors, sixteen fellows and two hundred scholars, all researching and teaching in a truly Baconian manner. They were 'never to write anything ... but what, after very diligent examination, they shall fully believe to be true, and to confess and recant it as soon as they find themselves in error.' This institution was never more than an idea. The College established by James I at Chelsea, referred to by Archbishop Laud as 'Controversy College', never fully took off.[5] There remained an occasional dream that, as Sir William Petty put it in 1687, 'an Universitas' would lead to 'the emprovement of London'.[6]

The dream was embroidered by Daniel Defoe in the 1720s. Gresham College's design was laudable, he wrote, 'but it smells too much of the *sine cure* ...'. With characteristic optimism, Defoe argued that 'an Academical Education is so much wanted in London, that everybody of ability and figure will readily come to it; and I dare engage the place need but be chosen, the tutors approved of, to complete the design at once.' Defoe's vision was ahead of its time: 'As London is so extensive, so its University may be compos'd of many colleges, quarter'd at convenient distances; for example, one at Westminster, one at St James's, one near Ormond Street (that part of town abounding in gentry); one in the centre of the Inns of Court; another near the Royal Exchange; and more if occasion and encouragement permit.'[7] An extravagantly conceived but short-lived 'London University' may have operated for a fortnight in 1742 in rented accommodation in the Strand, with a few lectures – according to the *Daily Advertiser* at the time – beginning with one on 'a rational View of the Nature, Reality, Origin, Extent, past and present State, of all Liberal Arts and Sciences; with Means of Improving them.'[8] It was either absurdly over-ambitious, or it was a joke. It led to nothing.

From the late sixteenth century it nevertheless came to be accepted that in some sense there were three universities in England, the third being in London. 'In my time', wrote William Harrison (1534–93) in his *Description of England*,

> there are three noble universities in England, to wit, one at Oxford, the second at Cambridge, and the third in London; of which the first two are the most famous, I mean Cambridge and Oxford, for that in them the use of the tongues, philosophy, and the liberal sciences, besides the profound studies of the civil law, physic, and theology, are daily taught and had; whereas in the latter the laws of the realm are only read and learned, by such as give their minds unto the knowledge of the same.

In London the Inns of Court and of Chancery – 'sundry famous houses' – produced 'many scholars of great fame': 'They have also degrees of learning among themselves and rules of discipline, under which they live most civilly in their houses, albeit that the younger sort of them abroad in the streets are scarce able to be bridled by any good order at all.'[9] The origins of the Inns of Court are obscure, since they were careful to avoid being hampered by charters or by any statutory basis. By the fifteenth century they were established

MOTIVES
GROUNDED
Upon the Word of God, and upon
Honour, Profit, and Pleasure for the
present Founding an University
in the Metropolis

LONDON:
With Answers to such Objections
as might be made by any (in their
incogitancy) against the same.

Humbly Presented(in stead of Hea-
thenish and Superstitious New-yeares
Gifts) to the Right Honourable the Lord Major,
the Right Worshipfull the Aldermen his Brethren,
and to those faithfull and prudent Citizens which
were lately chosen by the said City to be of the
Common Counsell thereof for this
yeare insueng, viz.
1647.

By a true Lover of his Nation, and especially
of the said City.

Printed at _London._ 1647.

54 A pamphlet in 1647 proposed the foundation of a university in London that would supply the nation's needs in a way unfulfilled at Oxford or Cambridge. Its author was possibly Samuel Hartlib, a prolific proposer of improvements in education and in husbandry and 'a conduit pipe for things innumerable'.

as legal locales, and they had acquired a teaching function for the legal profession. In 1470 they were described by Sir John Fortescue as 'the academy of the laws of England'. The number of students at them increased at least four-fold in the course of the sixteenth century, and by the beginning of the seventeenth century the Inns could be collectively described by Sir Edward Coke as 'the most famous university, for the profession of law, or any one humane Science, that is in the world'.[10]

John Stow's _Annales, or Generall Chronicle of England_ in 1615 contained an account of 'the three most famous universities of England, viz. Cambridge, Oxford and London'. Sir George Buck (1560?–1623) contributed the description of 'the Third Universitie

55 The Inns of Court in London offer the closest physical resemblance to the colleges of Oxford and Cambridge. Lawyers took over the former premises of the Knights Templar in the fourteenth century, and the fine hall of the Middle Temple was built in 1570, seen here in Joseph Nichols's painting of 1738, with the late seventeenth-century fountain in the foreground.

of England' under the title 'A Treatise of the Foundations of all the Colledges, Auncient Schooles of Priviledge and of Houses of Learning, and Liberall Arts, within and about the most famous Cittie of London.' He chronicled all the 'Arts and Sciences proper and fit for ingenious and liberal persons which were and are in this city professed, taught and studied' at a miscellany of different institutions. He claimed that 'it followeth consequently that London may not only challenge justly the name and style of a University, but also a chief place in the catalogue of universities'. To Buck it was 'clear that unto London belongeth duly not only the style and title of a university, but also of a chief and principal university, having no complement thereof but one, and that is the government and protection of an honorable chancellor . . .'.[11]

This view, dating from 1615, was triumphantly cited by those who campaigned for the reconstitution of the University of London in the late nineteenth century and by those who sought to establish the federal University of London in the early twentieth century. It provided some historical legitimization for what was, in reality, an

A CATALOGVE, OR TABLE OF ALL THE ARTS, AND
SCIENCES READ, AND TAVGHT IN THIS *VNIVERSITIE OF* LONDON.

Theologie
Grammar
Rhetorike
Poetry
Arithmetike
Logike
Philosophie
Municipall, or common Law
Law of Conscience
Ciuill Law
Cannon Law
Phisike
Chirurgery
Astronomy
Geometry
Musike
Mathematikes
Hydrographie

Geographie
Nauigation
Languages
Cosmographie
Calligraphie
Brachygraphie
Steganographie
Art Gladiatorie
Hippice, or the art of Riding
Polemice, or art Millitary
Pyrotechnie
Artellerie
Art of swimming
Orchestice, or art of Dancing
Graphice, or the art of Paynting
Heraldica
Art of Reuels
Art Memoratiue, And others.

56 By the early seventeenth century some considered that the various 'houses of learning' in London together formed an unconstituted university. In 1615 Sir George Buck provided a list of all the subjects taught in what he explicitly regarded as the University of London.

entirely new vision of the structure of higher education in London. Even so, the creators of the University of London in its Mark I form in 1826, its Mark II form in 1836 and its Mark III form in 1900 all had a good deal of history to contend with. Ante-dating the University was a range of pre-existing institutions, some of them important enough for it to be plausibly held that there already existed an unformed university in London.

The longest roots of the University of London in its twentieth-century form are to be sought not so much in the teaching of law in London as in the teaching of medicine. The date 1123 in the title of this chapter is perhaps contrived, but it is not spurious. It was in 1123 that St Bartholomew's Hospital was founded on its present site by Rahere, a courtier of Henry I and canon of St Paul's Cathedral. The story is told that it was the result of a vision. While on a pilgrimage to Rome, Rahere fell ill and promised that if he recovered he would found a hospital for the poor and sick in London. He did recover and on the way back to England he had a vision of St Bartholomew, who told him that the promised foundation should be in Smithfield and should be dedicated to St Bartholomew. The Priory and the Hospital were duly dedicated in 1123, and Rahere became the first Prior. From the start, the Hospital was more than an almshouse, and for many generations it became an important centre for the care of the sick and of foundlings and stray children.

The origins of St Thomas's, the other great medieval London hospital, are more obscure. It appears to originate in the infirmary of the Priory of St Mary Overy in Southwark, an ancient foundation which itself originated, as S. Gordon Wilson romantically but pointedly claimed, 'when Oxford was an obscure Saxon village and Cambridge noted only for eels'.[12] The sick were possibly treated there before the foundation of St Bartholomew's Hospital and before the canonization of Thomas à Becket in 1173 enabled a new dedication. A new hospital was built in 1215, and from then on the Priory and the Hospital developed separately.[13] The separate existence of both St Bartholomew's and St Thomas's as hospitals enabled them to survive the Reformation, though not without difficulty. When all monastic possessions were confiscated by the Crown in 1539, their future was uncertain for a time, but St Bartholomew's was re-founded by Henry VIII in 1544 and in 1546 the Lord Mayor and the Corporation of the City of London became its rulers, as they did of St Thomas's also in 1551. The constitutional position of the two hospitals changed with the coming of the National Health Service in 1948, but their historical development has been continuous since the middle of the sixteenth century.

St Bartholomews Hospital

We the Principal Surgeons of this HOSPITAL Certify that Mr Robert Watts has diligently attended ye Practice thereof 12 Months

March 13th, 1776

Percivall Pott
Stafford Crane
Robt Young

57 A certificate of attendance awarded in 1776 to a medical student by the surgeons of St Bartholomew's Hospital, showing the hospital as completely rebuilt in 1730–69 by James Gibbs, with the central square which has been described as one of the greatest outdoor rooms in England.

It is difficult to identify the period when they can first be properly regarded as hospitals with a teaching function. By the 1170s there were, according to William Fitzstephen, several 'famous schools' in London, where some scholars 'are exercised in disputation for the purpose of display, which is but a wrestling bout of wit, but others that they may establish the truth for the sake of perfection. Sophists who produce fictitious arguments are accounted happy in the profusion and deluge of their words; others seek to trick their opponents by the use of fallacies.'[14] Teaching in London can recognizably be traced back to the twelfth century, but it would be fanciful to claim that medical education began in the early years of St Bartholomew's and St Thomas's. There is no evidence concerning the training of doctors in the Middle Ages. Yet it must have gone on. Physicians studied at universities, while surgeons gained practical knowledge

58 St Thomas's Hospital, founded as the infirmary of the Priory of St Mary Overy in Southwark, was re-endowed and named after Thomas à Becket following his martyrdom in 1170, and re-founded after the dissolution of the monasteries by the City of London in the 1550s. Medical teaching of a sort took place for centuries, but it was not systematized until the eighteenth century when the hospital appeared as it was shown in Maitland's *History of London* (1756).

59 The earliest of the 'voluntary' hospitals of the eighteenth century was Westminster Hospital, the first to be founded in addition to the two medieval hospitals, St Bartholomew's and St Thomas's. The 'Public Infirmary for the Sick and Needy' was opened in 1720 by trustees who included Henry Hoare, the banker. Medical students were recorded from the 1730s, and the 'Westminster Medical School' was established in 1834.

by apprenticeship, regulated after 1540 by the company of Barber-Surgeons. At St Thomas's the first apprentice to a surgeon is recorded in 1561, and the first regulation concerning students was made in 1699: 'no Surgeons' Cubs or persons in that nature do keep their hats on before the Physicians and Surgeons of this house when they are in the wards of this Hospital.' Further regulations about 'cubs' (or 'surgeons' young men') were laid down in 1703, and the conditions under which certificates could be awarded after examination were determined in 1737. At St Bartholomew's 'the young men that are apprentices to the three Chirurgions' were first explicitly mentioned in 1664, and in 1669 a library was formed for the use of 'young university schollers'. Percivall Pott (1714–88), surgeon at the Hospital from 1749 to 1787 began to deliver lectures on anatomy, and under John Abernethy (1764–1831), surgeon from 1787, a distinct medical school began to be formed, with various lectures and definite teaching arrangements, though it was some years before the term medical school or medical college was used. By 1795 a special lecture theatre had been built.[15] At both St Thomas's and St Bartholomew's Hospitals, the institutional arrangements for medical teaching evolved gradually between the late seventeenth and the late eighteenth centuries from the old practice of 'walking the wards' with the appointed surgeons.

In eighteenth-century London five new hospitals were established, different in origin from the two old monastic and royal foundations. The first of the 'voluntary' hospitals based upon the raising of private subscriptions was the Westminster Hospital (founded in 1716 and opened in 1720); Guy's Hospital was the next (opened in 1726 alongside St Thomas's as the result of Thomas

60 The memorial to Thomas Guy (1644?–1724) in the chapel of Guy's Hospital, established at his 'sole costs and charges'. Guy's fortune was based on publishing cheap editions of the Bible and on dealing in government securities in the early days of the National Debt in the 1690s. He prudently sold his South Sea Company stock just before the bubble burst in 1720. Above can be seen the motto: *Dare quam Accipere* – Give rather than receive – taken by the students to refer to the medicine dispensed.

61 A splinter group from the Westminster Hospital founded St George's Hospital in 1733, originally at the former Lanesborough House in Knightsbridge – shown here on a pupil's certificate of 1787 – before being rebuilt at Hyde Park Corner in 1827–34. The Medical School was formalized in 1831.

62 John Hunter, FRS (1728–93), surgeon at St George's Hospital from 1756 until his sudden death during a heated meeting at the Hospital in 1793; the couch on which he died is still to be seen in the library of the new St George's Hospital Medical School at Tooting. It was said of him that he 'found surgery a craft and left it a science'. His museum of specimens, later acquired by the Royal College of Surgeons, was famous.

63 Guy's Hospital was opened in 1726, soon after Thomas Guy's death, and subsequently extended on land leased from St Thomas's Hospital. From 1768 until 1825 medical teaching was jointly undertaken with St Thomas's as the United Hospitals of the Borough. Since 1982 the two medical schools have again been united.

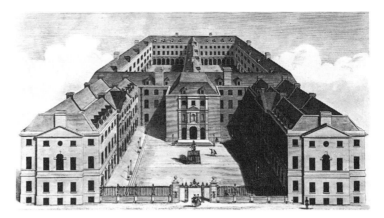

64 A plaque at Guy's records the time when Keats was a student there. Somerset Maugham's first novel, *Liza of Lambeth* (1897), drew upon his experiences as a medical student at St Thomas's. Robert Bridges, later Poet Laureate, wrote a Latin poem describing his colleagues at St Barts in 1877 when he was a casualty physician there. Also at St Barts can be seen the very spot where it is believed Sherlock Holmes on New Year's Day in 1881 spoke the deathless words, 'You have been in Afghanistan, I perceive', to Dr Watson at their first meeting.

Guy's benefaction); St George's Hospital was begun in 1733 by splitting away from the Westminster (opened in 1734); the London Hospital was opened in 1740 as the London Infirmary (becoming the London Hospital in the 1750s), and in 1745 the Middlesex Infirmary was opened (becoming the Middlesex Hospital in 1746). The new foundations, all established within twenty-five years of one another, each began to contribute towards medical education. At the Middlesex Hospital students were recorded as 'walking the Hospital' from the start, and from 1757, when a new building was opened, there were 'resident surgical pupils' and it was resolved that 'the physicians and surgeons have liberty to read lectures in physic and surgery at this Hospital'. Guy's Hospital claims to have been the first to organize systematic lectures on both clinical and pre-clinical subjects, which it did in conjunction with St Thomas's Hospital from 1768. It was then resolved that 'for the future all such persons as shall be chosen surgeons of this Hospital shall occasionally give practical lectures on surgery to the pupils that shall be entered at this Hospital.' A lecture theatre was built in 1770. The first to establish a medical school as such was the London Hospital, where a register of students had been kept since 1741. In 1785 a Medical College was opened in conjunction with the Hospital, but constitutionally separate and in its own building.[16] It was a major step forward.

Another new hospital was founded as the West London Infirmary in 1818, opened as the Royal West London Infirmary and Lying-in Institution, Charing Cross, in 1821, and renamed the Charing Cross Hospital in 1827. From the start it was the intention to combine the practice and the teaching of medicine, though the Medical School was not identified separately by name until 1834.[17] In that year the teaching at the Westminster Hospital, which had been carried on since the 1730s, was organized into the Westminster Medical School. Around the same time, the extensive teaching

65 One of the most well-known of the private medical schools in London was that run in Great Windmill Street by William Hunter, FRS (1718–83) – the brother of John Hunter – shown here in his anatomy theatre with the recombined persons of his anatomical subjects.

66 The Charing Cross Hospital, originally built in 1831, and its Medical School (to the right) in 1881. The institution was founded in 1818 with the intention from the start of providing a 'hospital to administer to the sick poor of a densely-populated district' together with 'a school of theoretical and practical instruction in medicine and surgery, including all the branches of science relating to the healing art'.

In as much as ye have done it unto one of the least of these my Brethren, ye have done it unto me. St Matt. XXV. v. 40.

The London Hospital
For Charitably Relieving Sick & Wounded
Manufacturers
and Seamen, in Merchants Service, Their Wives & Children
These are to Certify that Mr Francis Hay Child
hath Diligently attended the Practice of Surgery as
a dressing Pupil in this Hospital for Nine Months
last past Witness our Hands this 5th Day of October
in the Year of our Lord 1782.

Ri: Grindall.
Jas. Rondeau Chairman
Geo. Neale
William Blizard

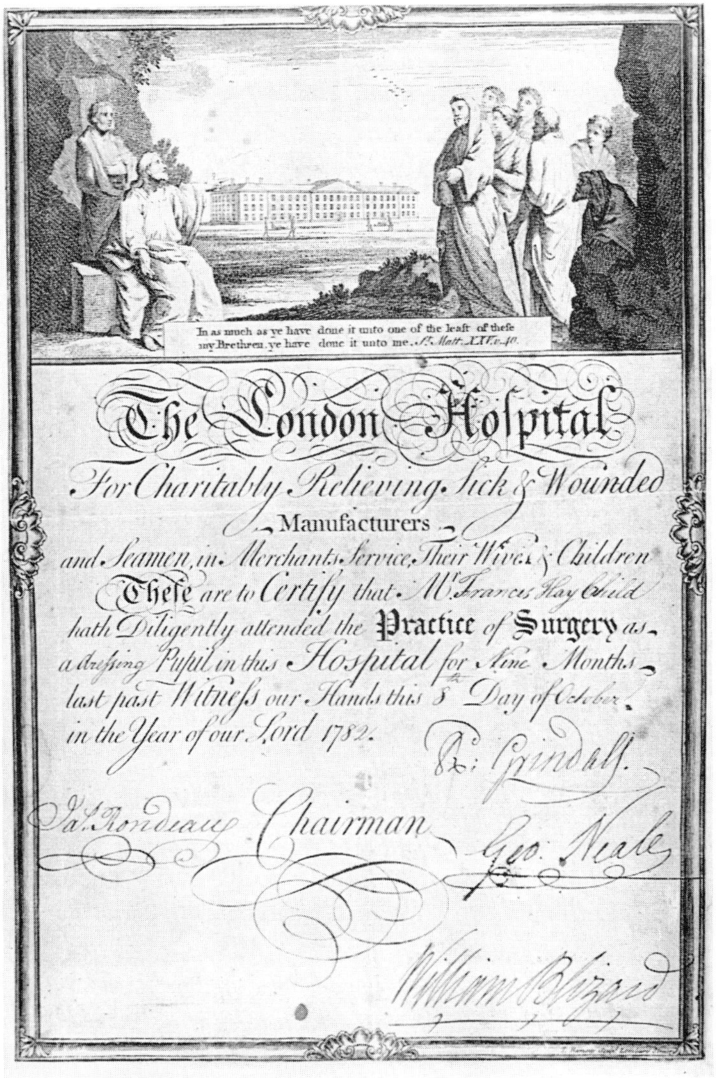

67 A certificate of attendance awarded to a dressing pupil at the London Hospital, founded in 1740, showing the Hospital as built in Whitechapel in 1759. The first complete Medical School was opened in 1785 next to the Hospital, but independent of it and controlled by the body of teachers.

provision at St Bartholomew's Hospital came to be regarded as forming a Medical School or College. The Middlesex Hospital Medical School was formalized in 1835. At St George's, where teaching had been slower to develop, the Medical School had been established in 1831. These developments represented something more than changes of name; they were a response to the opening of the University of London Mark I in 1828, its establishment of a Faculty of Medicine, and the building of its own hospital in 1833–4.

Until the 1830s medical education in England was fundamentally detached from universities. Teaching evolved in connection with the work of the different hospitals, and there was no equivalent of the university medical schools and the university hospitals of continental Europe, or of the powerful Medical School established

68 The Middlesex Hospital was opened in 1745 'for the Sick and Lame and Lying-in Women'. From the start there were students 'walking the Hospital', but the Medical School as such was not established until 1835, when the buildings shown here were erected alongside the Hospital. 'You cannot imagine a prettier thing than that School', wrote Sir Charles Bell.

69 The Royal College of Physicians was chartered by Henry VIII in 1518, and its authority was extended to the whole country in 1523. It was based first in the City house of its founder, Thomas Linacre (1460?–1524) and then in Warwick Lane where these handsome premises were erected after the Great Fire. In 1825 the College moved to Pall Mall, and in 1964 to new buildings in Regent's Park.

70 Benjamin Golding (1793–1863), the founder (at the age of 26) of the Charing Cross Hospital and the Medical School. His aims were ambitious: 'the want of a University, so far as Medical Education is concerned, will be fully supplied, and the branches of instruction in which those places are defective, namely, the Practical, will be here amply made up, and no advantages which they furnish excepting the honorary distinction of degrees will be unpossessed.'

Collegium Regale
Medicorum LONDINENSIUM.

71 Sir William Blizard, FRS (1743–1835), the great surgeon, twice President of the Royal College of Surgeons, who was largely responsible for founding the London Hospital Medical College in 1785, which grew into 'the most convenient, salubrious and handsome school in the metropolis'.

at the University of Edinburgh in 1736. The medical profession in England was divided, formally and socially, into three classes of medical practitioner licensed by different bodies. The élite, the physicians, belonged to the Royal College of Physicians, chartered in 1518, the fellows of which had to have degrees from Oxford or Cambridge. The surgeons, whose training was originally purely practical, belonged to a guild linked with barbers from 1540 to 1745; the Royal College of Surgeons did not emerge until 1800. The Society of Apothecaries, chartered in 1617, also provided their own path to a medical qualification. Between 1840 and 1858 there were no fewer than seventeen bills introduced in Parliament in an effort to introduce a standardized licence to practise medicine, and the resulting Act of 1858 which established the General Medical Council and the Medical Register left intact the powers and privileges of the existing corporations and the old hierarchical disorder. The result was a very haphazard system of medical education in London, in which a large number of unregulated private medical and anatomy schools played a necessary part.[18] There were many vested interests ready to oppose the establishment of any university in London which attempted to meddle in medicine.

London had hundreds of 'penny universities', as the coffee houses were known, and there were a good number of teaching institutions concerned with aspects of what later came to be called 'higher education', but before 1828 London had no university in a sense any foreigner would understand. The University of London, long contemplated in a variety of vague forms, was born in the pages of *The Times* newspaper on 9 February 1825. It was conceived in Germany, and its parentage was Scottish.

The open letter published in *The Times* was addressed by Thomas Campbell to Henry Brougham. Campbell, the Glasgow-educated poet whose *Pleasures of Hope* (1799) had brought him popular fame and a rapid entrée into London literary society, first conceived the idea of a new metropolitan university while visiting Bonn University in 1820. 'The Germans', he wrote, 'had at one time a strong prejudice against the existence of an university in a capital town, but they now find the students of Berlin and Vienna the most regular-living youth in all Germany.' He considered that 'London contains the greatest assemblage in the world of those small comfortable trading fortunes which place their owners in a station where intellectual accomplishments can too easily be dispensed with.' What he suggested was the establishing of a University 'for effectively and multifariously teaching, examining, exercising, and rewarding with honours in the liberal arts and sciences, the youth of our middling rich people, between the ages of 15 or 16 and 20, or later if

72 The Barbers' Company and the Guild of Surgeons were amalgamated by Act of Parliament in 1540; they separated in 1745, the Surgeons building their own hall (next to Newgate prison) where the bodies of murderers were taken for dissection. In 1800 the Company was chartered as the Royal College of Surgeons, moving to new premises in Lincoln's Inn Fields. Their examinations, according to this cartoon of 1800 showing Roderick Random's experience, witnessed much dissension among the examiners.

73 The original building of the Royal Veterinary College was opened in 1791 on its present site in Camden Town, where horses for the metropolis were in good supply. The first Principal, Charles Vial de St Bel, came from Europe's foremost veterinary college at Lyons to establish the first veterinary college in England. He died of glanders two years later, but the College survived and grew as an independent institution, eventually joining the University in 1949.

you please.' It was a diffuse letter, but what enabled this proposal to become the first effective proposal for a university in London was the involvement of Brougham. Campbell indulged in the pleasures of hope; Brougham got things done.

Brougham, one of a brilliant generation of students at the University of Edinburgh in the 1790s, became an MP in 1810 and espoused various campaigns for reform, especially in the field of education. He brought together various interest groups excluded from the universities of Oxford and Cambridge, where it was necessary to belong to the Church of England for entrance to the one and for graduation from the other. The Jews were involved through Sir Isaac Lyon Goldsmid, the Catholics through the Duke of Norfolk, and many nonconformist interests through people like Zachary Macaulay and F.A. Cox, the wealthy Baptist minister of Hackney. In 1825–6 many meetings both public and private were arranged by Brougham, with the result that by 11 February 1826 it was possible to bring the University of London into formal existence by an elaborate Deed of Settlement. The repeal in 1825 of the Bubble Act prohibiting company formation enabled the body in the absence of a charter to take the legal form of a limited liability company, a status that brought much obloquy in the resulting period of financial speculation. It was, nevertheless, the obvious way to raise the necessary finance. Shares of £100 each were offered to people willing to become 'proprietors' of the proposed university. A site of nearly eight acres in Bloomsbury on the edge of the built-up area of London, previously intended to be developed as 'Carmarthen Square', was bought in August 1825 for £30,000 by three of the richest promoters. By the time of the first meeting of the 'proprietors' in October 1826, only 1300 shares had been taken up, 200 fewer than the minimum deemed necessary, but plans for the building were being pressed ahead and the foundations were being dug. William Wilkins's fashionable design was accepted, and by October 1828 the University was ready to open its doors. 'It seems so short a time', wrote Zachary Macaulay's daughter, 'since the whole scheme has been planned and executed that it reminds me of Aladdin's enchanted palace which sprung up in a single night. . . .'

One of the members of the original Council of twenty-four elected by the 'proprietors' to run the University was George Birkbeck, another Scotsman, the founder in 1823 of the London Mechanics' Institute which was intended to appeal to 'respectable mechanics', skilled craftsmen in particular. What was offered there was not technical instruction but general education, with lectures on such subjects as electricity and optics in which scientific principles and practical implications were identified. The fare was varied by

74 What became the University of London Mark I was proposed in a letter to Henry Brougham published in *The Times* in February 1825 written by the then well-known poet Thomas Campbell (1777–1844), after a visit to Germany where he was particularly impressed by the religious toleration of the refounded university at Bonn.

75 Campbell's dream of a university in London became effective largely through the efforts of Henry Brougham (1778–1868), one of the founders of the *Edinburgh Review* in 1802, who moved to London to seek commanding outlets in the law and politics for his versatility and dynamism, becoming an MP, a campaigner for reform especially in education and Lord Chancellor, as Lord Brougham, in 1830. Brougham regarded himself as a Benthamite, as a believer in the utilitarian principle of the 'greatest happiness of the greatest number' – though it was claimed that in his view the greatest number was number one.

lectures on phrenology, bump by bump, and courses on arithmetic, memory training, drawing and music. The University of London was to appeal to a superior social group. 'By the middling rich', said Campbell, 'I mean all between mechanics and the enormously rich.' The University was to be for the middle class, an increasingly prosperous group in the period of enormous expansion in commercial and managerial occupations when London was the hub of the 'workshop of the world'. Many new professional skills were needed, and neither Oxford nor Cambridge showed any signs of relaxing their social or religious exclusivity or adapting the narrow basis of their syllabus. 'The exclusion', pronounced the first *Prospectus* of the University of London in 1826, 'of so great a body of intelligent youth, designed for the most important occupations in society, from the highest means of liberal education, is a defect in our institutions, which, if it were not become familiar by its long prevalence, would offend every reasonable mind.'

What offended many, in the period between Campbell's letter to *The Times* in 1825 and the opening in 1828, was the University's firm intention to have no religious entrance requirements and to have no teaching of religion. It became known as 'the godless institution of Gower Street'. Edward Irving called it 'the Synagogue of Satan'.

76 The Royal Institution of Great Britain was founded in Albemarle Street in 1799, the precursor of several other institutions demonstrating the value of 'useful knowledge' in a society witnessing social and economic change on an unprecedented scale. It did much to focus attention on a new approach to science.

77 A cartoon by Robert Cruikshank of Brougham hawking shares in the projected University of London round Lincoln's Inn in July 1825.

The POLITICAL TOY-MAN.

78 The University of London Mark I was founded by what Jeremy Bentham (1748–1832) called 'an association of liberals' rather than by Bentham himself as is often erroneously believed. This myth is sustained in a bizarre manner by University College's possession of the clothed skeleton of the great philosopher of jurisprudence, 'in the attitude', as he himself instructed before his death, 'in which I am sitting when engaged in thought'. The 'Auto-Icon' is seen here as it was displayed from 1850 to 1948, with Bentham's actual mummified head at its feet. The head – perhaps the most extraordinary possession in the entire University – is now kept in the College safe.

79 Sir Charles Bell, FRS (1774–1842) moved from Edinburgh to London in 1804 to practise and to teach medicine, taking over William Hunter's School of Anatomy and linking it to the Middlesex Hospital where he became a surgeon. In 1828 he became the first Professor of Surgery at the University of London Mark I, giving the first inaugural lecture there, but the affiliation he proposed between the new University and the Middlesex Hospital was rejected by the governors of the Hospital, obliging the University to build its own hospital. Bell resigned from the University to establish the Medical School at the Middlesex, but soon returned to Edinburgh. The unity he hoped for between University College and the Middlesex Hospital Medical School is to be achieved, in new circumstances, in 1987.

> Birkbeck, and Brougham, and Gregory,
> And other wicked people,
> Had laid a plan to undermine
> The Church; if not the Steeple!
> The London University!
> O what a shocking notion;
> To think of teaching any thing
> But Church and State devotion!

The Tory press contained many clever attacks, such as this in *John Bull* in July 1825:

> Come bustle, my neighbours, give over your labours,
> Leave digging and delving, and churning:
> New lights are preparing to set you a staring,
> And fill all your noddles with learning.
> Each Dustman shall speak, both in Latin and Greek,
> And Tinkers beat Bishops in knowledge –
> If the opulent tribe will consent to subscribe
> To build up a new Cockney College.

Here the social groups being appealed to were quite mistaken. Besides extending the social appeal of university education, the important development was the extension of the syllabus of higher education. 'The course of instruction', said the *Prospectus*, 'will at present consist of Languages, Mathematics, Physics, the Mental and the Moral Sciences, together with the Law of England, History, and Political Economy; – and the various branches of knowledge which are the objects of Medical Education.' The teaching of English, the modern languages and the laboratory sciences, were to be notable innovations. Among the twenty-four founding professors were many men of outstanding promise, several of them the products of the Scottish universities, like many of the founders.

That the University of London, despite all the sarcastic attacks on it, was meeting a new need, is evident from the founding of a rival institution which soon followed. Even before the University opened in 1828, a meeting chaired by the Duke of Wellington and attended by three archbishops, seven bishops and 'the principal nobility', decided that 'a college for general education be founded in the metropolis, in which, while the various branches of literature and science are made the subjects of instruction, it shall be an essential part of the system to immure the minds of youth with a knowledge of the doctrines and duties of Christianity as inculcated by the United Church of England and Ireland.' The most active founder of what was by permission of George IV called 'King's College' was the Revd Dr George D'Oyly (1778–1846), the devout and energetic Rector of Lambeth. The College obtained a Charter in 1829, its building next to Somerset House was erected, and in October

80 One of the original share certificates as issued in 1826. It was hoped to raise the substantial sum of up to £300,000 by selling shares at £100 each to the 'proprietors' of the new University, but less than half this amount was raised and it was virtually all spent on the building. The founding Council heroically declared that it chose 'a great design suited to the wants, the wealth and the magnitude of the population for whom the Institution is intended' rather than 'one commensurate with its present means'.

81 An invitation to the ceremony for laying the foundation stone of the University of London Mark I in April 1827. The stone was laid by the Duke of Sussex, the only member of the royal family with any intellectual pretensions.

1831 it opened. Despite the religious differences with the University of London, the two new institutions were remarkably similar.

London now had two rival putative universities, one chartered but calling itself a College, the other unchartered, but calling itself a University. From the outset, the Gower Street institution sought incorporation, first by attempting to promote parliamentary bills, and then after the Whigs came into government in 1830, by seeking a charter. One was on the point of being sealed in 1831, when Oxford and Cambridge weighed in to demand inclusion of a clause restraining the University from granting degrees. This was a power the University was keen to obtain. The resulting controversy lasted for four years. Apart from the reactionary opposition of Oxford and Cambridge, there was the problem of the more genuine objection of the various London medical schools. They naturally thought it presumptuous of the new *soi-disant* University to claim the right to

82 The London Mechanics' Institution was founded in 1823 and opened in Southampton Buildings in 1824 (the Building Society and Deposit Bank was a later development, taking the ground floor in 1851). It became the Birkbeck Literary and Scientific Institution in 1866 and Birkbeck College in 1907.

83 George Birkbeck (1776–1841), a student at Edinburgh in the 1790s along with Henry Brougham, began the 'mechanics class' at Anderson's Institution in Glasgow (later Strathclyde University) before moving to London to practise as a doctor and to establish the London Mechanics' Institution. He observed the 'intelligent curiosity' of artificers, and: 'the question was forced upon me, Why are these minds left without the means of obtaining that knowledge which they so ardently desire, and why are the avenues of science barred against them because they are poor?'

KINGS COLLEGE VERSUS LONDON UNIVERSITY
or Which is the Weightiest

84 A cartoon portraying the antagonism between the University of London Mark I and the rival King's College founded in 1828: a clutch of bloated bishops, including the Archbishop of Canterbury and the Revd Dr George D'Oyly, with the added weight of Money and Interest, are pitted against Brougham (waving the broom) and Bentham (clad in dressing-gown), supported by Sense and Science.

85 Another cartoon attacking King's College at the time of its foundation in 1828: the Patron, George IV, 'royally extends his snuff-box to the professors as a token of his approbation. The grand entrance is a stupendous arch; on the key-stone is a cherubic head of the Patron, and on each side are colossal statues. On the right is Justice, with one of her eyes open, to denote that whoever entered the College should be regarded with favour. The left is Equity with the hands in the pockets, to express the indolence with which it decides ... The wings contain the apartments of the Professors of the College. The windows are small, as no *new light* is required.'

award degrees, including degrees in medicine, when they had no such power. There might as well, argued the *London Medical Gazette*, be 'Masters of Medicine and Surgery' 'in the *University* of St Bartholomew's – in the United Colleges of Guy and St Thomas – or, what would come nearer the mark, in the London *University* at Mile-End Road.' There was 'nothing intrinsically more ridiculous' in even the private medical schools awarding degrees 'than in a joint-stock company taking the appellation of an University ...'. In 1834 the University's petition for a charter, and the counter-petitions of Oxford and Cambridge and several medical bodies, came before the Privy Council. 'Pray', asked Brougham as Lord Chancellor, 'what is to prevent the London University granting degrees *now*?', to which the reply was given: 'The universal scorn and contempt of mankind.' Brougham, for once in his life, could think of no reply.[19]

86 King's College as it actually appeared after its opening in 1831. The two-acre site on the eastern side of Somerset House was provided by the government for the erection of 'a college in which instruction in the duties and doctrines of Christianity as taught by the United Church of England and Ireland shall be for ever combined with other branches of useful knowledge.' The building was designed by Sir Robert Smirke (1781–1867) to harmonize with Somerset House.

The University continued to award 'Certificates of Honours', but drew back from awarding degrees until it could obtain a charter properly entitling it to do so. In March 1835, after a long debate on the subject in the House of Commons, the short-lived Tory government of 1834–5 was defeated and a motion was passed requesting the King to grant 'His Royal Charter of Incorporation to the University of London, as approved in the year 1831 by the then Law Officers of the Crown, and containing no other restriction than against conferring degrees in divinity and in medicine.'[20] When the Whig government under Lord Melbourne resumed office in April 1835 it was realized that the matter would have soon to be settled. Further convoluted Privy Council discussions were held, and the issue was discussed several times by the Cabinet, which at a Saturday meeting in June 1835 finally decided upon a compromise plan.[21] It was explained as follows to the Duke of Somerset and the other members of the Council of the University:

It is intended by the Government to take the following steps with a view to provide a mode for granting Academical Degrees in London to persons of all religious persuasions, without distinction and without the imposition of any test or disqualification whatever:

1 The Charter sought for by the Duke of Somerset and others will be granted, incorporating the parties by the title of 'London University College'.

2 Similar Charters will be granted to any Institution of the same kind which may be hereafter established.

3 Another Charter will be granted to persons eminent in literature and science, to act as a Board of Examiners, and to perform all the functions of the Examiners in the Senate House of Cambridge; this body to be termed the 'University of London'.

4 Pupils from University and King's College to be admitted, on Certificates of having gone through a course of study at those establishments, and having obtained a proficiency to pass for a Degree, and having conducted themselves to the satisfaction of the Governing Bodies of those Colleges, to be examined, and to be classed according to their relative merits.

5 Any other Bodies for Education, whether corporated or uncorporated, may from time to time be named by the Crown, and their pupils to be admitted to examination for Degrees.

6 The same principles to be applied to Degrees in Medicine.

7 The Degrees to be granted to be, A.B., A.M., B.L., D.L., B.M., D.M.

8 The Crown to have the power of appointing new and additional Examiners from time to time.

9 All By-Laws and Regulations for the conduct of the University of

87 In March 1829 Battersea Fields witnessed a remarkable duel between the Duke of Wellington, Prime Minister at the time, and the Earl of Winchilsea, an ultra-Protestant who published an accusation that Wellington's espousal of Catholic emancipation would undermine the Anglican principles of King's College. Wellington demanded withdrawal of the charge of irreligion and perfidy, and then, when apology was not forthcoming, 'reparation'. In the resulting duel, the Earl fired into the sky and the Duke's shot missed. Winchilsea apologized and honour was satisfied.

88 Two houses in the Strand were demolished to make way for the entrance to the awkwardly-shaped site of King's College. Smirke's gateway was surmounted by the College's coat of arms and its motto: *Sancte et Sapienter*.

89 The North London Hospital was opened in 1834 and extended in 1838–46 after it became University College Hospital in 1837, seen here across what was to be the front quad of UCL. The hospital was established by the Faculty of Medicine at the University of London Mark I since 'the Medical School cannot ... satisfy the anticipations of the Council and the Proprietors of the University, or the hopes of the Professors to make it the first Medical School in Europe, without the aid of an Hospital.' The hospital was the first in London to be the product of a medical school, rather than the other way round.

90 King's College Hospital opened in 1840 in the former workhouse next to St Clement Dane's church and alongside the slaughterhouses of Butcher's Row. The *Medical Times* commented: 'Its locality is fine – shambles on one side and a churchyard on the other – butchers within and without – prayers for the living and the dead.' It was entirely rebuilt in 1861.

London to be submitted to the Secretary of State, and thus made subject to parliamentary responsibility.
10 The King to be Visitor.
11 Fees to be taken on Degrees for the purpose of paying the expenses of the Examiners, but to be regulated and approved of by the Treasury.

The University of London proposed in 1835 was to be established and financed by the government on an entirely new basis. The Chancellor of the Exchequer, Thomas Spring Rice, played the leading role in creating it, supported by Lord John Russell, the Home Secretary. Melbourne himself contributed to the drafting of the proposals. 'It seems to me well-conceived', he wrote, 'but I would omit the words which I have underlined in the preamble and in the first enacting clause. There is no need to point so precisely to its being a measure for the benefit of Dissenters. All persons will be entitled to take advantage of it under the words as they will stand after the omission.'[22]

The existing University saw that it would have to accept the proposals. The Senate, the body of the professors, decided to make the best of it by recommending to the 'proprietors' that they should:

consent without reluctance to the change of name which will be suggested to them. It is manifest that the superior body, by which academical honours are to be bestowed, will be the body most fit to be designated as 'The University of London'. It would be weak in us to wish to retain the name when we consent to waive the exclusive claims which it implies. The name of 'University College' will sufficiently mark our precedence among the Colleges associated with the University, and point us out as the germ which has given life to the whole body. Indeed, if the proposed University is to be established, we ought strongly to desire that it should be established under our present name, that it may appear to all the world to be what it really is, not an original creation, but merely an extension of our system and a consequence of our principles.

The University of London Mark II, new in concept but comparable in some ways to the University of France, was to be a quite different creation from the University of London Mark I with its Scottish and German models. The continuation of the University of London Mark I as University College London after 1836 was frequently to be a source of friction.

Metropolitan Degrees, 1836–1870

... we will venture to cast the horoscope of the infant Institution. We predict, that the clamour by which it has been assailed will die away, – that it is destined to a long, a glorious, and a beneficent existence, – that, while the spirit of its system remains unchanged, the details will vary with the varying necessities and facilities of every age, – that it will be the model of many future establishments, – that even those haughty foundations which now treat it with contempt, will in some degree feel its salutary influence, – and that the approbation of a great people, to whose wisdom, energy and virtue, its exertions will have largely contributed, will confer on it a dignity more imposing than any which it could derive from the most lucrative patronage, or the most splendid ceremonial.

T.B. MACAULAY in the *Edinburgh Review*, XLIII (1826), p.340.

I protest to you, gentlemen, that if I had to choose between a so-called University which dispensed with residence and tutorial superintendence, and gave its degrees to any person who passed an examination in a wide range of subjects, and a University which had no professors or examinations at all, but merely brought a number of young men together for three or four years ... if I must determine which of the two courses was the more successful in training, moulding, enlarging the mind ..., I have no hesitation in giving the preference to that University which did nothing, over that which exacted of its members an acquaintance with every science under the sun.

J.H. NEWMAN, *On the Scope and Nature of University Education* (1850), pp.137–8.

The University of London of 1836 was established by direct government action, in contrast to the University of London of 1826 which was an entirely private enterprise. The paradox of being a state educational foundation in the age of laissez-faire was both a source of strength and a source of difficulty. The difficulties were to become more evident as time passed but the potentialities of the new institution were apparent in 1836. That year was, as it transpired, one of the years of the lowest 'social tension' in the nineteenth century according to W.W. Rostow's correlation of low grain prices and low unemployment. It was the first year in which investment in the new railway system approached mania.[1] The reasons for the chartering of the University of London in 1836 were not more deep-seated than the political considerations weighed by the Whig government in the way discussed at the end of the last

91 'Darwin's bulldog': T.H. Huxley, FRS (1825–95), lecturer at the Royal School of Mines from 1854 and creator of the 'Normal School of Science', later the Royal College of Science. One of the giants of nineteenth-century science, he was an examiner for the University from 1856, and one of the architects of the first science degrees in 1860, long before he served as a member of the Senate from 1883 to 1895.

92 The first Charter granted to the University of London by King William IV, sealed on 28 November 1836. Immediately before on the same day a Charter was granted to the body previously known as the University of London giving it the new name 'University College London'. The seeds of the great federal University of London were thus planted, but great difficulties were stored up by the separation of the functions of teaching and examining.

chapter. The University of London Mark II was born in compromise, but it was given aspirations which were undeniably high.

The aims of the new University were laid out in the Charter granted on 28 November 1836[2]. 'Whereas', William IV declared,

for the advancement of Religion and Morality, and the promotion of useful knowledge, to hold forth to all classes and denominations of Our faithful subjects, without any distinction whatsoever, an encouragement for pursuing a regular and liberal course of Education; and considering that many persons do prosecute or complete their studies both in the Metropolis and in other parts of Our United Kingdom, to whom it is expedient that there should be offered such facilities, and on whom it is just that there should be conferred such distinctions and rewards as may incline them to persevere in these their laudable pursuits...

The University of London was thus constituted:

for the purpose of ascertaining, by means of examinations, the persons who have acquired proficiency in Literature, Science and Art, by the pursuit of such course of education, and of rewarding them by Academical Degrees, as evidence of their respective attainments, and marks of honour proportioned thereunto...

The 'entire management of, and superintendence over the affairs, concerns and property' of the University was to be in the hands of a Senate. The Senate was to determine the policy of the new University, and to make the necessary by-laws and regulations, but the power of approval was firmly kept within the government's ultimate control: 'all such Bye-laws and Regulations having been first submitted to one of Our Principal Secretaries of State, and approved of, and countersigned by him'.

The members of the Senate – the Fellows of the University, as they were called – were all appointed by the government. In 1835–6, the Chancellor of the Exchequer addressed various distinguished persons in the manner in which he wrote the following letter to George Airy, the Astronomer Royal, worth quoting in full for what it reveals about the official thinking behind the foundation.[3]

Downing Street
Sept. 24. 1835

My dear Sir

In order to carry into full effect the intentions of His Majesty, as communicated in His gracious answer to an Address of the House of Commons, on the subject of the Grant of Academical Degrees, in the Metropolis – the Government have it in contemplation to incorporate by Charter a central board under the title of the Royal University of London. To this body will be entrusted the duty of examining persons duly qualified by Education at the London University College, King's College, and such other establishments as may from time to time be named by the Crown, and of granting to such persons, as may appear duly qualified, degrees in Arts, Law, & Medicine.

His Majesty's Government are extremely desirous that the persons named in the Royal Charter should be such as to give to the public the fullest security for the effectual & impartial discharge of their new and most important duties, & it will be peculiarly gratifying to me if I am permitted to submit your name to my Colleagues as one of those who we may be enabled to recommend to the Crown as willing to undertake this important & most honourable trust. The duties will be confined to the period of the examination only, and therefore will not require any very considerable portion of your time, on which I am aware there are many other claims.

But when it is considered how great is the object to be attained in giving a useful direction, as well as affording new encouragement to the intellectual improvement of a numerous class of the King's subjects, who,

93 Thomas Spring Rice (1790–1866), Chancellor of the Exchequer from 1835 to 1839 in Lord Melbourne's government and, in this capacity, the effective founder of the University of London as constituted in 1836. Too lively and warm-hearted to be a successful politician for long, he was raised to the peerage in 1839 as Lord Monteagle of Brandon, and subsequently served as a member of the Senate of the University from 1850 until his death.

94 Lord John Russell (1792–1878), Home Secretary from 1835 to 1839 and later twice Prime Minister, 'the arch-whig of the nineteenth century'. He was one of the founders of the University of London Mark I in 1826, and one of the main influences behind the state-funded University of London Mark II in 1836; as Home Secretary he had to give his approval to the proposals for the syllabus of the first examinations.

without any distinction or exclusion whatever will be admitted under the proposed system to the honor of Academical degrees, I trust that you may be induced to give to the Government your zealous & valuable co-operation.

I have the Honor to be
My dear Sir
with sincere regard & esteem
Yours very faithfully.
T. Spring Rice

The thirty-eight who accepted the invitation put in these terms were men of notable distinction and promise. No fewer than thirty of those chosen to constitute the founding members of the Senate came to command a place in the *Dictionary of National Biography* (though a significant proportion of their entries do not mention the University of London). The most striking characteristic of the original Senate was the large number of its members who occupied leading positions in medicine or in the front rank of the contemporary scientific world.

The person appointed as the first Chancellor, Lord Burlington, and the nominee as the first Vice-Chancellor, Sir John William Lubbock, were leading examples of the type of figure selected to plan the University of London. As a student, William Cavendish had carried off most of the glittering prizes Cambridge offered before becoming MP for the University at the age of 21 in 1829. His support for Parliamentary reform in 1831 led to the University rejecting him and he sat for other seats until he succeeded his grandfather as the second Earl of Burlington in 1834. He thereupon abandoned politics and devoted the rest of his life to intellectual and public concerns. In 1858 he succeeded his cousin as the seventh Duke of Devonshire, and left a recognized mark on the country as the developer of Barrow-in-Furness, Eastbourne and Buxton. The twenty years during which he presided over the infant University of London deserve more recognition. He was a commanding Chancellor when the growth of the University in the public mind was as much in need of nurture as the growth of the activities of the University itself. Burlington remained a member of the Senate longer than any of the other founding Fellows, up to the time of his death in 1891, though he retired as Chancellor in 1856. After the death of the Prince Consort in 1861, he became Chancellor of the University of Cambridge, attempting to redress the balance of intellectual trade with that University by spreading some of the London spirit in presenting the Cavendish Laboratory to Cambridge. John William Lubbock, the first Vice-Chancellor, like Burlington, had been a student at Trinity College, Cambridge, and he inherited a place in his family bank, succeeding as the third

95 William Cavendish, 2nd Earl of Burlington and later 7th Duke of Devonshire (1808–91), portrayed in his robe of office as the first Chancellor of the University of London. He was Chancellor for twenty years after the foundation in 1836, serving subsequently as a member of the Senate until the time of his death – an unrivalled period of service of fifty-five years.

96 Sir John William Lubbock (1803–65), the first Vice-Chancellor from 1836 until 1842, and subsequently a member of the Senate until the time of his death. A banker as well as Treasurer and Vice-President of the Royal Society, he was the author of *Remarks on the Classification of Different Branches of Human Knowledge* (1838).

baronet in 1840. He also maintained the serious scientific interests which led to him becoming Treasurer and Vice-President of the Royal Society, offices which he occupied for many years after 1830. He took what was in effect a comparable position as Vice-Chancellor for the University's first six years. At the time of the foundation, the Chancellorship was much more active a position than it was to become, and the Vice-Chancellorship rather less so, but both Burlington and Lubbock were actively and keenly involved in the shaping of the University of London in its refounded form after 1836.

As many as sixteen members of the Senate were professional medical men. They included some of the leading figures in the field, such as Sir Stephen Love Hammick, Surgeon Extraordinary to William IV as he had been to George IV, Sir James Clark, FRS, who was to be Queen Victoria's first physician, Sir Philip Crampton, FRS, Surgeon-General to the forces in Ireland and President of the Dublin College of Surgeons, General Sir James MacGrigor, FRS, the Director of the Army Medical Department who had earned Wellington's admiration as chief of the medical staff in the Peninsula, and Sir Charles Locock who long had the best obstetric practice in London and who was to attend at the birth of all Queen Victoria's children. There were some notable teachers of medicine, apart from Cornwallis Hewett, who was Professor of Medicine at Cambridge. Archibald Billing, FRS, who was to remain a member of the Senate up to his death in 1881 – the second longest period of service after Lord Burlington's – was an outstanding teacher at the London Hospital Medical College. He was the first to combine a course of clinical lectures with regular bedside teaching. His *First Principles of Medicine* grew into a bulky textbook. Thomas Hodgkin taught at Guy's Hospital and had wide Quakerly philanthropic concerns. Jones Quain came from Ireland to teach anatomy in London, wrote his *Elements of Anatomy*, for long the standard work, and for a time between 1831 and 1835 was Professor of Anatomy at the University of London Mark I.

Other medical members of the Senate were men of wide scientific interests. Neil Arnott, FRS, a former student at St George's Hospital, had a lucrative medical practice in Bedford Square; he was also an inventor (of the water-bed, for example, in 1832), and he was well known in scientific circles. Peter Mark Roget, FRS, 'physician and savant' as the *DNB* characterizes him, took his MD at Edinburgh in 1798 at the age of 19, and 'pursued a career of almost unexampled activity for nearly half a century engaging with indomitable energy in scientific lecturing, in work connected with medical and scientific societies, and in scientific research'. At the time of the foundation of the University, Roget was Secretary of the Royal Society, an office he was to hold from 1827 to 1849. He was to achieve eternal fame as the compiler of the famous *Thesaurus*, which first appeared in 1852 and went into twenty-eight editions during his lifetime.

The second largest professional group after the medical men was drawn from the law. There was Lord Brougham, the former Lord Chancellor and prime mover in the foundation of the University of London Mark I. Two others had been among the original professoriate at that establishment. Andrew Amos had been Professor of English Law, and was later to be Professor of Law at Cambridge. John Austin, even more celebrated as a jurist and law reformer, had been Professor of Jurisprudence. William Empson, another barrister, was Professor of the Laws of England at the East Indian College, Haileybury, and a frequent contributor to the *Edinburgh Review* of which he was to become editor. Nassau William Senior was also a lawyer and Master in Chancery, as well as having been the first Professor of Political Economy at Oxford. Sir John Shaw Lefevre's start in the law was the basis for a distinguished career as a public servant in which he became Clerk of the Parliaments. The width of

97 Archibald Billing, FRS (1791–1881), whose outstanding teaching at the London Hospital Medical College was succeeded in 1836 by his devotion to the University of London's aspirations to set the highest standards in medical education after he became one of the most influential of the members appointed to the original Senate.

98 Thomas Hodgkin (1798–1866), a member of the Quaker family which made such notable contributions to science and to social reform: another physician with a concern to make the University of London a force for the improvement of medical education. Like Billing, Arnott and Roget, he remained a member of the Senate from 1836 until the end of his life.

99 Neil Arnott, FRS (1788–1874), a medical practitioner rather than a teacher of medicine, but one with wide scientific interests of the sort strongly represented on the new Senate. In 1869 he gave the University enough money to found scholarships in chemistry and physics, the first non-state-funded awards to candidates performing well in the examinations.

100 Peter Mark Roget, FRS (1779–1869), one of the most active of the original members of the Senate, active in his capacity as the chairman of the committee to plan the Faculty of Medicine, and active too in a remarkable range of medical, scientific and literary activities.

the interests of both Senior and Shaw Lefevre is shown by the fact that both were Fellows of the Royal Society.

In fact, no fewer than eighteen of the original members of the Senate were Fellows of the Royal Society. Besides those already mentioned as medical men or as lawyers, there was Sir George Airy, FRS, a future President of the Society, who for forty-six years from 1835 served as an Astronomer Royal of extraordinary energy, reforming Greenwich after having been Lucasian Professor of Mathematics at Cambridge at the age of 25. There was Admiral Francis Beaufort, FRS, Hydrographer to the Navy and in himself a synonym for nautical science. There was William Thomas Brande, FRS, the leading chemist of the metropolis, who attended Sir Humphrey Davy's lectures at the Royal Institution and succeeded him as professor there. Michael Faraday, FRS, had been Davy's assistant at the Royal Institution and developed into one of the most brilliant and influential scientists of the century. John Dalton, FRS, lived eccentrically and modestly in Manchester, but his work on atomic theory brought him a European reputation. He first visited London in 1792

101 William Thomas Brande, FRS (1788–1866), the leading practitioner and teacher of chemistry, and editor of the *Dictionary of Science and Art* (1842). He was one of the members of the original Senate who acted also as an Examiner in the early years of the scheme of examinations.

102 John Dalton, FRS (1766–1844), at 70 the oldest of the members of the Senate appointed in 1836, and one of the three never to attend a meeting (besides Lord Brougham and one R.R. Pennington). Improbably portrayed in classical form when the British Association for the Advancement of Science held its twelfth meeting in Manchester in 1842, he was unassuming in the Quaker manner, but a brilliant scientist.

for a Quaker meeting and described the city as 'the most disagreeable place on earth for one of a contemplative turn to reside in constantly'. The Revd Richard Sheepshanks, FRS, was by contrast a more polished gem, who took holy orders but never pursued a clerical career, preferring a scientific vocation and his work as Secretary of the Royal Astronomical Society. John Stevens Henslow was Professor of Botany at Cambridge for thirty-four years from 1827; Charles Darwin was to be his favourite pupil.

Only a small number of those appointed as members of the Senate were neither medical men, scientists nor lawyers. Thomas Arnold came from a strikingly different milieu. Since 1828 he had been Headmaster of Rugby, beginning the regeneration of the public school. J.H. Jerrard, a former Fellow of Caius College, Cambridge, was the first Principal of Bristol College. The Revd Connop Thirlwall, the most liberal of divines, had in 1834 launched a memorable attack on the Anglican exclusivity of Cambridge. Later Bishop of St David's (from 1840 to 1875), he was a former Fellow of Trinity College, Cambridge, one of the group of 'liberal-minded clergymen, ardent educationalists, solid in character and learning, versed in mathematics and in classical scholarship' who gave that College its nineteenth-century ethos.[4] The Senate in 1836 also included two Whiggish bishops – the Bishop of Durham, the first whose palatinate jurisdiction was separated from the ecclesiastical, and the Bishop of Chichester, William Otter, who from 1830 to 1836 had been the first Principal of King's College. Henry Warburton, FRS, could almost count among the scientists; he was a radical MP who had been one of the founding Council of the University of London Mark I.

It should also be noted that Warburton had been a student at Trinity College, Cambridge, intellectually the leading Oxbridge college of the day. At least ten of the founding Fellows of the University of London shared membership of the same Cambridge college with Spring Rice, MP for Cambridge, himself also a Trinity College man. Only two (Arnold and Senior) had any connection at all with Oxford. If the University of London Mark I was Edinburgh on the Thames, the University of London Mark II was Trinity College, Cambridge, writ metropolitan.

Taken as a whole, the thirty-eight members of the founding Senate were a very impressive group. Spring Rice had chosen an able range of men, varied, but not so diverse as to lack a strongly progressive theme. Many of them were men of enduring distinction. Some of them had names which were to virtually enter the language: Hodgkin's disease and the Beaufort scale are still with us, though Arnott's stove – a smokeless grate for which he was awar-

103 The northern front on the Strand of Somerset House, built in the 1770s by Sir William Chambers to house the Royal Society, the Royal Academy and the Society of Antiquaries, with large statues above the Corinthian columns representing Truth, Justice, Valour and Temperance. When the Royal Academy moved out in 1836, accommodation was provided for the University of London on the first floor to the right of the entrance.

ded the Rumford Medal of the Royal Society in 1854 – has gone the way of the brougham, Lord Brougham's favoured vehicle. (His own stylish carriage carried his coroneted monogram: there may be a 'B' on the outside, it was said, but there is a wasp inside.) There were potential connections with the personnel of the University of London Mark I through the inclusion of Brougham himself, and Warburton, as well as Amos, Austin and Quain, while the interests represented had been widened considerably.

In some ways the task of the newly appointed members of the Senate in November 1836 was evidently easier than that facing the founding fathers of most universities. There were no buildings to be constructed, no teachers to be chosen, no students to be registered. They faced nevertheless a great challenge: they had to shape the syllabus for modern education.

The Senate did not meet until March 1837 owing to difficulties in fitting up temporary accommodation for the University in the apartments at Somerset House formerly occupied by the Royal Academy. The northern block of Somerset House facing on to the Strand, built to house the Royal Academy, the Royal Society, and the Society of Antiquaries from 1780, had subsequently been the home of the Royal Academy and its famous exhibitions until 1836 when the Academy moved to what later became the National Gallery building in Trafalgar Square. Its rooms were divided between two newly established government educational bodies, the School of Design and the University of London, with the School of Design needing the greater part. From the School was to grow the Royal College of Art, the Victoria and Albert Museum and the many municipal art schools, but its beginnings in 1836 were modest. The first students were admitted in the summer of 1837, when B.R. Haydon found 'nine poor boys drawing paltry patterns' – 'And this', he expostulated, 'is the School of Design, the Government of Great Britain has founded in its capital! I felt my cheeks crimson . . .'[5] The colour has not been recorded of the cheeks of early visitors to the University's premises, its four rooms on the first floor of Somerset House, with other rooms borrowed when needed from the School of Design. Even by February 1838 the furnishings can be taken to be materially incomplete, since in that month the Vice-Chancellor was moved to write to Spring Rice himself as Chancellor of the Exchequer to seek assistance in the matter of acquiring enough chairs.[6]

At its first meeting on 4 March 1837, the Senate addressed itself immediately to a theme that was to be a recurrent one over the ensuing 150 years. The very first line of the minutes concerns finance: 'Resolved – 1. That immediate application be made to the Government for the sum of £1000 to defray the various expenses which must be incurred at the outset, in order to enable the Fellows to hold their meetings and to commence their functions . . .' The government's response was one that was not so usually to recur: an account was opened at the Bank of England and the full amount claimed was paid before the end of the month. Funding for the first year of the University's operations was provided out of 'civil contingencies'. In subsequent years, an estimate was to be presented annually and specifically voted by the House of Commons. In the event, the University managed to spend only £364 13s 10d up to the end of 1837, leaving a balance of £635 6s 2d to be carried forward. The eternal problems of finance and accommodation were evident right from the start, but they were not the only causes of the debilitating controversies which overshadowed the first two years and which threatened to abort the life of the infant institution.

104 Andrew Amos (1791–1860), a brilliant lawyer, one of the central group of members of the Senate who were products of Trinity College, Cambridge. He also belonged to the smaller group who were connected with the University of London Mark I, where he had served as Professor of English Law from 1828 to 1833.

105 William Otter (1768–1840), Bishop of Chichester when he became a member of the Senate, but before that the Cambridge friend of Malthus and the first Principal of King's College from 1830 to 1836.

106 Nassau William Senior, FRS (1790–1864), a lawyer more famous as an economist, the only Oxford graduate on the original Senate besides Thomas Arnold. He had been the first Professor of Political Economy at Oxford in 1825, and in 1834 was the effective author of the *Report* that led to the New Poor Law.

107 Henry Warburton, FRS (1784–1858), the only MP among the original members of the Senate, another Trinity College, Cambridge, man; a leading reformer and 'philosophical radical'.

The trouble began with the decision at the Senate's second meeting to appoint a Registrar to conduct the business of the University at a salary of £1000 per annum, a sum equivalent to the University's entire annual income. Spring Rice, as Chancellor of the Exchequer, objected; 'no-one', he wrote, 'can be more deeply interested than I am in your complete success . . .', but he insisted that so high a salary was extravagant and would not approve more than £500 for the purpose. The Senate was 'anxious that the foundations of our Institution be laid on a scale commensurate with the magnitude of the design'; 'we cannot', they declared, 'but regard our University as calculated eventually to attain an important station among similar institutions in this Empire, and as destined to give a powerful impulse to the advancement of learning and science'. It was necessary, therefore, that the Registrar should 'in addition to an unimpeachable moral character possess the manners and feelings of a gentleman, enlarged and liberal views, a sound judgment and discretion, active habits, experience in conducting business, as well as various literary and scientific attainments'. So highly qualified an administrative

108 The coat of arms as granted to the University in April 1838: 'Argent, the Cross of St George, thereon the Union Rose irradiated and ensigned with the Imperial Crown proper, a Chief Azure, thereon an open Book also proper, Clasps gold.'

officer must be paid appropriately. While the government continued to refuse to sanction a salary of £1000 a year, there was discussion within the Senate about who should be appointed as Registrar. Some members wanted the appointment of James Craig Somerville, a doctor and Inspector of Anatomy, while others held that he would be 'a most improper person' and raised charges of grave professional misconduct against him. This double dispute blighted the efforts to set the University up throughout 1837.

At the end of that year there was a development which more than one member of the Senate thought would be fatal to the new University. The original Charter had by oversight been drawn up in such a way that it expired on the death of William IV in June 1837. A second Charter was necessary, and it was duly issued in the name of Queen Victoria in December 1837. It was identical with the first Charter, except that Lord Brougham who had never attended a meeting was dropped and two new members of the Senate were added – the Bishop of Norwich and James Craig Somerville, the very man to whom there had been such strong objections when his name was put forward for the office of Registrar. There had been no consultations at all about the membership of the Senate in the second Charter, and deep dissatisfaction was caused. The medical men on the Senate were taken aback, since reports injurious to Somerville's moral character prevailed extensively in medical society. Sir Charles Locock, for example, considered him 'obnoxious' and 'unfit to associate with gentlemen'. Representations were made to Lord Burlington and to the government, as a result of which Somerville threatened actions for libel and slander. Lord John Russell, as Home Secretary, was obliged to conduct an inquiry into the charges against Somerville, who initially refused the opportunity of 'retiring quietly without exposure'. For some time the business of the Faculty of Medicine was entirely suspended and several

109 A high proportion of the members of the original Senate were themselves graduates of Cambridge, but it is significant that one of the first things they undertook after they first met in March 1837 was an investigation into the universities of France and Germany. Oxford and Cambridge were not to provide the model for the University of London.

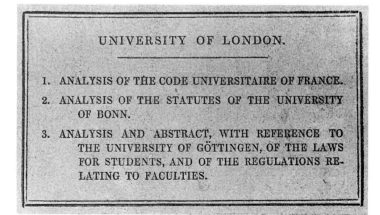

UNIVERSITY OF LONDON.

1. ANALYSIS OF THE CODE UNIVERSITAIRE OF FRANCE.

2. ANALYSIS OF THE STATUTES OF THE UNIVERSITY OF BONN.

3. ANALYSIS AND ABSTRACT, WITH REFERENCE TO THE UNIVERSITY OF GÖTTINGEN, OF THE LAWS FOR STUDENTS, AND OF THE REGULATIONS RELATING TO FACULTIES.

110 Thomas Arnold (1795–1842), Headmaster of Rugby and the member of the Senate least in sympathy with the direction taken by the Senate as a whole after 1837. He was the first member to resign on a point of principle (in 1838), after attending several meetings of the Senate in London, visits he combined with sittings for his portrait by Thomas Phillips.

members of the Senate threatened to withdraw from the University before eventually Somerville was obliged to resign in July 1838.

By then, the Senate had managed to agree on the appointment of a Registrar (at a compromise salary of £600 a year). Richard Wellesley Rothman was appointed in April 1838. Like others concerned with the new University, Rothman (1800–56) was a product of Trinity College, Cambridge. He became a Fellow of that College in 1825, and served as Junior Bursar in 1834–6. He continued to hold his life lay Fellowship there, becoming Senior Fellow after 1843. He took a Cambridge MD in 1840, but seems not to have practised medicine. He was a man of wide scientific sympathies, writing a *History of Astronomy* for the 'Library of Useful Knowledge', and acting for a time in the 1840s as Secretary of the Royal Astronomical Society, a neighbour of the University in Somerset House.[7] Only with his appointment was the University of London able to get down to serious business.

The first steps towards drawing up a scheme of examinations had been taken in April 1837, before the issue concerning the Registrar had been settled, when the Senate divided itself into committees to organize the three Faculties of Arts, Laws and Medicine. They began by seeking detailed reports on the structure of foreign universities, getting Lord Palmerston as Foreign Secretary to require a number of British ambassadors to furnish information. In November 1837 the University made its first purchase of a book: Victor Cousin's *Rapport sur l'État de l'Instruction Publique dans quelques Pays de l'Allemagne et particulièrement en Prusse*. Foreign models were being tentatively digested when another problem hit the struggling University, the problem of religion and its role in education.

Thomas Arnold abhorred 'Education without Christianity', and he had agreed to become a member of the Senate in order to give a religious influence to its proceedings. He was conscious that 'the advancement of Religion and Morality' was listed ahead of 'the promotion of useful knowledge' in the Charter. 'I hold myself bound to influence', he wrote, 'the working of a great experiment, which will probably in the end affect the whole education of the country'. He feared that Unbelief was making a cat's paw of Dissent. The University College view was that sectarian religion should be firmly excluded, and all religion as far as possible avoided. In January 1838 the College made representations to Lord John Russell about the manner in which the University might examine the Greek Testament and Church History: 'such examinations, while seemingly confined to a knowledge of the Greek language and of historical facts, might be so pursued as to force a scholar to a defence or apology for his religious faith'. At the same time, Arnold found that

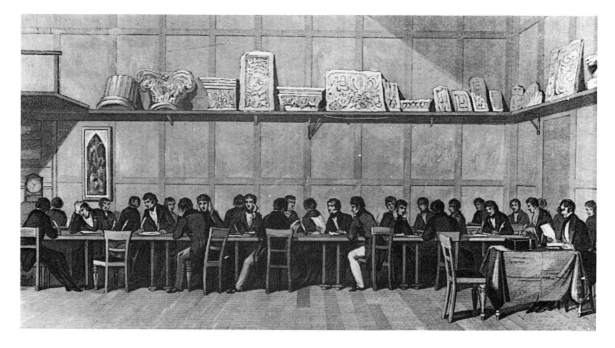

111 The Matriculation examination taking place in July 1842 in the University's original premises at Somerset House shared with the School of Design, to whom the antique casts belonged. The average age of the candidates at this examination was twenty years and ten months.

he was the only member of the Senate who did not believe it right to award degrees to Jews. Before the end of 1838 he felt obliged to resign from the Senate.[8]

The problems connected with Somerville and with Arnold were very different in character, but they were none the less problems which meant the University got off to a sluggish start. The Bishop of Durham wrote to Lord Burlington as Chancellor in July 1838 to acknowledge 'the judgment and temper with which you have presided over our jarring deliberations' when 'the unhappy circumstances which have attended the composition of the Senate ... prevented the execution of any decided plan for conducting the examination of the University' and threatened to make the University a 'laughing-stock'. The beginnings of the University were hardly auspicious.

Sufficient progress, however, was made by November 1838 to enable the University to hold its first examination, that for Matriculation, the hurdle which the Senate decided must be cleared before candidates could present themselves for the degree examinations. Passes had to be obtained in four papers: classics; mathematics; natural philosophy; and in one of chemistry, botany or zoology. Twenty-two of the original twenty-three candidates passed, and were thus entitled to become the candidates for the University's degrees. The degrees of Bachelor of Arts, Master of Arts, Bachelor of Laws, Doctor of Laws, Bachelor of Medicine and Doctor of

PASS EXAMINATION.

COMMENCING NOVEMBER 5, 1838.

MONDAY MORNING, 10 *to* 1.

MATHEMATICS.

ARITHMETIC AND ALGEBRA.

Examiners, Mr. JERRARD and Mr. MURPHY.

1. GIVE the definition of a fraction, and explain the method of reducing fractions to a common denominator.
Of the fractions $\frac{2}{3}$, $\frac{5}{7}$, which is the greater?

2. Add together the fractions $\frac{11}{17}$, $\frac{31}{31}$, $\frac{266}{337}$, $\frac{5}{13}$, $\frac{24}{30}$; and divide $43\frac{7}{7}$ by $7\frac{5}{8}$.

3. Reduce the fraction $\frac{4015}{6503}$ to its lowest terms and transform it to a decimal.

4. Prove the rule for the multiplication of decimals. Multiply ·576 by 83·4, and divide 222·027 by ·0013.

5. Extract the square root of 9,512,295,961.

6. Find the simple interest on £207. 12s. 6d. for $21\frac{1}{4}$ years, at 3 per cent. per ann.

7. Prove that $a\,b = b\,a$. State and demonstrate the truth of the rules for the signs in algebraic multiplication and division.

8. Multiply $x^5 + a^5 - a\,x\,(x^3 + a^3)$ by $(x^3 + a^3) + a\,x\,(x + a)$.

MONDAY, May 27.—AFTERNOON, 3 *to* 6.

CHEMISTRY, ANIMAL PHYSIOLOGY, VEGETABLE PHYSIOLOGY AND STRUCTURAL BOTANY.

CHEMISTRY.

Examiner, Mr. BRANDE.

1. State the composition of the atmosphere and of water, and enumerate the different compounds which result from the union of their respective elements.

2. State the composition and define the properties of the binary compounds which carbon forms with oxygen.

3. What are the leading characters of the principal combinations of hydrogen and carbon, how are they analysed, and what are their usual sources?

4. What are the substances which usually occur in the spring waters of London and its immediate vicinity, and what are the tests by which such substances are most readily detected?

5. What is chlorine? How is it obtained? What is the result of its combination with hydrogen? What is the probable cause of its disinfectant powers? What are the best means of evolving and applying it as a disinfectant?

6. In cases of poisoning by oxalic acid, by hydrocyanic acid, by sulphuric acid, and by corrosive sublimate, what are the best chemical antidotes, and what are the principles upon which they are administered?

---

112 The first exam paper ever set by the University of London, a paper in mathematics sat on 5 November 1838 inaugurating the Matriculation examination.

113 The first degree examinations took place in May 1839; this paper was sat on the afternoon of the first day, the examiner being the distinguished chemist W.T. Brande (see **101**).

Medicine were specifically mentioned in the Charter. The first degree examinations were held in May 1839 for the BA, and all seventeen candidates passed. The examinations for the LLB, the MB and the MD took place later in the year, producing a further fourteen graduates. The first MAs followed in 1840 and the first LLD in 1843.

In forming the scheme of examinations, the Senate from the start firmly rejected any selective à la carte menu. What was offered was sternly table d'hôte. Criticisms of the range of subjects insisted upon, and of the innovatory stress on scientific subjects, were soon heard. In 1841 St Patrick's College, Carlow, petitioned the University that the number and variety of compulsory subjects for examinations imposed too great a burden, and the teachers at St Cuthbert's College, Ushaw, declared that 'if the students of so many of our

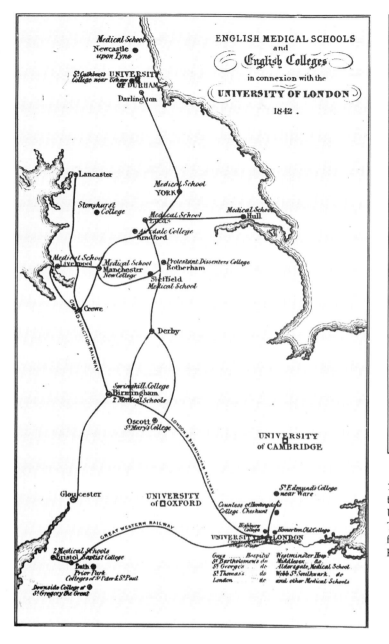

PASS EXAMINATION.

First Division.

Barnes	....	University College.
Brown	....	University College.
Griffith	....	University College.
Jennings	....	University College.
Lee	....	University College.
O'Loghlen	....	University College.
Pocock	....	King's College.
Reed	....	University College.
Ridley	....	University College.
Spalding	....	University College.
Tennent	....	University College.
Waley	....	University College.

Second Division.

Ball	....	King's College.
Blakiston	....	University College.
Butterworth	......	King's College.
Case	....	University College.
Crump	....	King's College.

CHEMISTRY.

Ridley	....	University College.

ANIMAL AND VEGETABLE PHYSIOLOGY.

Arranged in the order of proficiency.

Barnes	....	University College.
Spalding	....	University College.

115 The first degree pass list published after the BA examinations in 1839 listing the University's first seventeen graduates. Thirteen of them, it will be observed, were from University College and four from King's College.

114 That the University of London Mark II was the national university of the railway age is evident from the map produced by R.W. Rothman, the first Registrar, in 1842.

University of London

This is to Certify.

that Mr F. W. Mackenzie obtained the Degree of Bachelor of Medicine in this University at the Annual Examination for the same in 1839. and that he was placed in the Second Division at the Pass Examination.

Burlington
Chancellor.

University of London.

This is to Certify.

that Henry Marsland Matriculated as a Student in the University of London in the year 1840: and that he was placed in the First Division at the Pass Examination.

5th November, 1840.

Registrar.

116 The other degree examinations later in 1839 also led to three LLBs and nine MBs; this is one of the original degree certificates awarded.

117 One of the earliest surviving Certificates of Matriculation. More modest than the degree certificates, it was signed by the Registrar rather than the Chancellor and does not bear the University's seal.

leading Colleges and Institutions be compelled to distract their minds by such a multiplicity of pursuits, the knowledge of a great majority of the graduates of the University of London will prove to be but superficial on the whole'. In 1843 several nonconformist colleges also stated that they found that the requirements were 'excessive'. The Professor of Medicine at St Andrews was reported as claiming in 1847 that 'not a single professor in any university in the United Kingdom could answer the questions put by your Examiners'. The University stuck to its guns, and refused to relax the demanding standards that it insisted upon. It would be very unwise, the Senate rightly thought, for the new national university to be an easy touch for degrees in an increasingly qualifications-conscious society needing a mould in which to set its education system.

The Charter required candidates for its degrees to present 'a Certificate ... to the effect that such Candidate has completed the course of instruction' at either University College or King's College 'or from such other Institution, corporate or unincorporated, as now is, or hereafter shall be established for the purposes of Education, whether in the Metropolis or elsewhere within Our United Kingdom . . .' The first institution which sought recognition was the Royal Belfast Academical Institution, and they were told that the power to recognize institutions for this purpose rested with the government rather than with the University.[9] The first institution for which the government in 1838 approved a royal warrant enabling certificates of study to be issued to candidates as the Charter empowered University College and King's College to do was the University of Durham, by then the only other university in England besides Oxford, Cambridge and London. The University of Durham had been founded as an offshoot of the wealthy Cathedral which obtained an Act of Parliament for the purpose in 1832 and a royal Charter enabling the award of its own degrees in 1837. It was an Anglican establishment on an Oxbridge model, without the wider aims of the University of London. The other new university objected to the subordination implied by the affiliation to the University of London, however loose, and the Bishop of Durham interceded with Lord John Russell to ensure that the naming of the University of Durham be 'expunged, in order to conceal from the world, if possible, that they have anything to do with that of London'.[10]

Other institutions were keen to have their affiliation with the University of London proclaimed. The schools of medicine at the London Hospital, the Middlesex Hospital, and St George's Hospital were among the first to do so, and by the beginning of 1840 as many as thirty-six medical schools throughout England, Scotland and Ireland had connected themselves to the University. By 1853, the number had grown to a total of sixty-eight medical schools, in addition to thirty-two non-medical institutions, including University College and King's College, but excluding the other universities which were all approved for the purpose. It could be claimed – and it was claimed – that the graduates of the University of London represented 'the élite of above a hundred institutions', but the institutions were, it has to be admitted, a pretty mixed bag. The line between secondary education and higher education, both as yet anachronistic terms, was still to be drawn, and alongside the varied catholic and nonconformist establishments were some institutions that were clearly schools. As early as 1841 hopes were expressed for an alteration to the Charter permitting the affiliation of institutions outside the United Kingdom. The Principal of Sydney College, New South Wales, in 1846 pointed out the needs of the Australian colonies and the difficulties involved in sending candidates on a journey of 17,000 miles in order to take the examinations. He hoped that the

118 The diversity of the educational institutions affiliated to the University from 1836 to 1858 is shown in the engravings heading the *University of London Almanac* for 1846. As well as University College (top left) and King's College (top right), there was Highbury College (bottom right), a dissenting academy, and Stonyhurst College (bottom left), the Catholic seminary in Lancashire.

119 That the University of London was not a university for London alone is even more evident from the *University Almanac* engravings of a year or two later, proclaiming the affiliation to the University of establishments as varied as Queen's College, Birmingham (top left), the Wesleyan Collegiate Institution at Taunton (top right), Huddersfield College (bottom right), and St Patrick's College, Carlow, Ireland (bottom left).

UNIVERSITY COLLEGE.

KING'S COLLEGE.

SPRINGHURST COLLEGE.

HIGHBURY COLLEGE.

QUEEN'S COLLEGE, BIRMINGHAM.

WESLEYAN COLLEGIATE INSTITUTION AT TAUNTON.

PATRICK'S COLLEGE, CAR.

HUDDERSFIELD COLLEGE.

Matriculation examination in particular could be opened to colonial candidates; 'it fixes a standard', he said, 'not left to the discretion of professors and masters but to the wisdom of a learned body in England'. In 1850 the University obtained a supplemental Charter enabling institutions throughout the British Empire to be recognized for the purpose of permitting candidates to offer themselves for London degrees. The metropolitan university was henceforth to be not only national, but also imperial, in scope.

The apparently ambitious superstructure was founded on what was a humble base. The essential peculiarity of the University is revealed in table 3.1, which lays out the finances of the University in its first year of actual operation. Expenditure took the form of the salaries of the examiners, almost all of them members of the Senate, and of the Registrar and the only other official, the Clerk to the Senate. There were the wages of the porter (shared with the School of Design), and a variety of small miscellaneous expenses. The modest income from the fees of the examination candidates was supplemented by a substantial grant provided directly by the government. The Treasury kept the University's expenditure under detailed observation, down to controlling an increase in the porter's wages by a shilling a week, and insisting in 1842 on reducing the examiners' fees. The government's detailed control of the University can be made vividly evident by quoting a passage in a letter from the Vice-Chancellor to Lord John Russell as Home Secretary after the first Matriculation examination: 'As the students Hargreave and Sargent and also Manning and Mason are reported by the Examiners to be equal in merit, I wish to ascertain whether in your Lordship's opinion we should divide the £30 per annum (line 185) or what course should be adopted in this and similar cases. The Senate will delay their decision until we know your Lordship's wishes.' The University of London – the metropolitan university, the national university, the imperial university – was the government university.

The growth of the University in the 1840s, after its uncertain start, witnessed a developing consciousness among the graduates of the need for some sort of corporate existence and recognition. An enquiry from one graduate, a clergyman, about the wearing of gowns and hoods led to the adoption of 'academical costume' in 1844. No occasions for the wearing of it were prescribed, but 'in those cases in which such graduates or undergraduates should think fit to wear an academical dress distinguishing them as connected with the University', styles were approved based on those of Cambridge, adding 'distinctive velvet facing' to the types of gowns used in that university. In 1844 too the first edition of the *University*

Table 3.1 Income and Expenditure of the University of London for the Year Ended 31 March 1840[11]

RECEIPTS

	£	£	s	d
BALANCE brought forward		24	14	3
GRANT from Her Majesty's Government		4700	0	0
FEES: at BA Examination	170			
at MB Examinations	125			
at MD Examination	20			
at Matriculation Examinations	60			
at LLB Examination	30			
		405	0	0
WASTE PAPER		2	1	4
TOTAL		£5131	15	7

EXPENDITURE

SALARIES

EXAMINERS		£	s
Classics	Dr Jerrard	200	0
	Rev C. Thirlwall	77	0
	T.B. Burcham	123	0
French	C.J. Delille	20	0
German	Dr Bialloblotzky	20	0
Logic &c.	Dr Jerrard	37	10
	Rev C. Thirlwall	37	10
Mathematics	G.B. Jerrard	200	0
	Rev R. Murphy	200	0
Chemistry	Prof. Brande	20	0
	Prof. Daniell	30	0
Natural History and Animal Physiology			
	Prof. Henslow	50	0
Hebrew Text of the Old Testament, the Greek Text of the New, and Scripture History			
	Rev W. Drake	37	10
	Rev T. Stone	37	10
Laws and Jurisprudence			
	W. Empson	37	10
Medicine	Dr Billing	187	10
	Dr Tweedie	187	10
Surgery	John Bacot	187	10
	Sir Stephen Hammick	187	10
Anatomy and Physiology			
	Francis Kiernan	187	10
	Dr R.B. Todd	187	10
Physiology and Comparative Anatomy			
	Dr Roget	187	10

		£	s			
Midwifery and the Diseases of Women and Infants						
	Dr Locock	75	0			
Chemistry (Medicine)						
	Prof. Daniell	75	0			
Botany	Prof. Henslow	37	10			
Materia Medica and Pharmacy						
	Jonathan Pereira	75	0			
REGISTRAR		600	0			
CLERK TO THE SENATE		212	10			
TOTAL SALARIES				3515	0	0
EXHIBITIONERS (Manning, Mason, Hargreave, Sargent, Todhunter, Ellis, Jones, Martineau)				62	5	10
SCHOLARS (Waley, Quain)				50	0	0
WAGES				108	2	6
MESSAGES				1	12	0
POSTAGE				55	18	5
BOOKS				86	17	8
STATIONERY				108	16	8
ENGRAVING				121	7	4
ADVERTISEMENTS				368	6	2
RATES				32	13	9
IRONMONGERY (Bishop, for Box)				3	13	0
COALS				15	10	0
OIL, GAS &c.				11	5	1
REFRESHMENTS				0	13	10
GRATUITIES				10	0	6
MISCELLANEOUS				11	6	1
TOTAL				4563	9	10
Balance				568	5	9

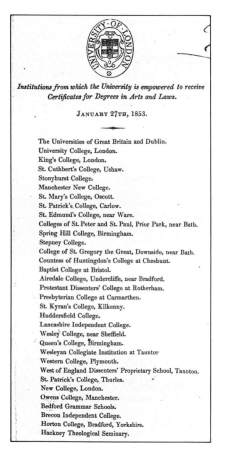

120 By 1853 no fewer than thirty institutions had received government approval to enable them to certify students as suitable to become candidates for University of London degrees alongside the students of University College and King's College; as many as sixty-eight medical schools throughout the country were also approved for the purpose.

Calendar was published, followed in 1846 by a *University Almanac.* A number of the graduates in 1845 proposed to form a London University Union in order to impart 'a more corporate spirit with a view of promoting the interests of the University and establishing and maintaining a friendly feeling and intercourse amongst all its members'. They sought rooms for meetings and a library, a request which the University in its limited accommodation at Somerset House had no means of supplying. A 'general meeting of graduates' was called by public advertisement and held at Freemasons' Hall in June 1848 with the hope of creating some sort of soul for the University that was effectively nothing more than a skeleton of an examining body.

There were, by then, over four hundred graduates and the resulting 'Committee of Graduates' began to press for their voice to be heard in the affairs of the University. The Senate at once adopted the Committee's first request that there be a ceremony at which the graduates could be presented to the Chancellor, and thus in May 1849 the University held its first reception in borrowed rooms in Somerset House. There was no funding for the refreshments required at such an event, and the expenses had to be shared by the Chancellor personally subscribing £30, the Vice-Chancellor £10 and the remaining £60 6s 8d distributed among the members of the Senate. The soirée was evidently a success, and the following year saw 'Presentation Day' becoming a public occasion, beginning a tradition of at least one ceremonial occasion for the University every year.

A university that took over twelve years to get round to holding a social occasion of any description was clearly an unusual university, but equally it was one that was not open to the charge of being totally unable to change. The 1849 soirée occasioned a realistic and favourable view expressed in a magazine which briefly flowered at University College.[12]

A first-floor lodging in Somerset House is not so aristocratic as a collection of stately buildings surrounded by trees and pleasant gardens, the bustle of the Strand is not so academical as the quiet of a College quadrangle, nor is an annual stipend from Government so delectable a thing as a rich endowment of landed estates; but it is a great thing to be gaining more and more of public opinion every day, to see the old universities reforming on our model . . .

The growing body of graduates, given confidence by the growing identity of the University, began to extend their campaign for formal recognition. They were instrumental in pressing for the recognition of London medical degrees as qualifications to practise medicine, an inequity righted by Act of Parliament in 1854. The prime object of the graduates was to have themselves formally constituted into a body recognized as Convocation, a body which would have an important place in the University's constitution. Ten years of careful argument and pressure brought the organized graduates what they sought in the major changes resulting from the third Charter granted in 1858.

By then, the University had been installed in new premises. The University had long been borrowing or hiring additional accommodation at examination time from the other learned and educational bodies in Somerset House. The 1847 examinations required the use of five rooms in two buildings, which created difficulties since the examiners themselves were expected to invigilate their own examinations. In the same year the Society of Antiquaries needed to borrow the Senate Room for a meeting, and noted how it seemed 'peculiarly bare and unadorned in its walls'. The University attempted vainly on several occasions to get the government to bestir itself in the matter of more extensive and more permanent accommodation, but nothing happened until 1853 when the expansion of the revenue departments in Somerset House required the rehousing of the Registrar-General's department in the University's premises. Somerset House was becoming 'the national beehive', and

121 The graduates being presented to the Chancellor, Lord Burlington, in the Hall of King's College in May 1850 at the University's first public 'Presentation Day'. The ceremony became an annual one, held the following year in the Donaldson Library at University College, and the year after that in a room borrowed from the Royal Society. Not until 1856 after the move to Burlington House could the University attempt to provide accommodation for its only occasion other than examinations and meetings of the Senate.

THE

LONDON

UNIVERSITY CALENDAR.

1844.

LONDON:
RICHARD AND JOHN EDWARD TAYLOR,
RED LION COURT, FLEET STREET.
1844.

122 The first edition of the *London University Calendar* was published in 1844, and has appeared annually since then (apart from 1940–7). It printed the examination regulations and the names of the examiners and other officials of the University, as well as the names of those who had passed the examinations in the previous year. From 1845 it also printed the previous year's exam papers and continued to do so until 1905–6, which ensured that the original slim early Victorian publication grew substantially into three fat Edwardian volumes.

the government was obliged to look around for new accommodation for its University. It first offered a large detached house near University College, recently vacated by Coward College, but the University did not yet feel a *Drang nach* Bloomsbury and turned the suggestion down out of hand on the grounds that the situation was 'so inconvenient and remote'. It settled for accommodation of a temporary character in a grander location at Marlborough House, where from the end of 1853 the University was housed in what was called 'a miserable garret'. In 1855–6 it was moved on again, this time to Burlington House, converted by the government to provide accommodation for the Royal Society and several other learned societies, which again became the University's neighbours in new premises. The east wing provided an appropriate room for the meetings of the Senate and offices for the Registrar, but the problem of providing space for the growing number of examination candidates remained unresolved.

While the University was moving to Burlington House, the death of R.W. Rothman meant that it had to select a new Registrar. Rothman had been of a quiet and retiring disposition; his successor, W.B. Carpenter, maintained a much higher public profile. A staunch Unitarian, he had been a student at University College and had practised medicine in Bristol in the 1840s before coming to London to serve as a professor at the Royal Institution as well as at University College and Bedford College.[13] A scientist and leading defender of science, he was the right man to administer the University in the second phase of its development. In 1863, in recognition of his 'watchful observation of the march of the University in detail', his salary was raised to the £1000 level disputed twenty-six years previously.

The first effect of the 1858 Charter was to add the graduates to the 'body politic and corporate' of the University, along with the Chancellor, the Vice-Chancellor and the members of the Senate, by creating Convocation and giving it 'the power of discussing any matter whatsoever relating to the University' and 'the power of accepting any new Charter for the University'. All graduates of a certain number of years' standing were entitled to become members on payment of 10s 6d per year, or 3 gns for life. Convocation was also made responsible for the nomination of up to a quarter of the members of the Senate, the remainder still to be appointed directly by the government.

The new Charter also made a second major change in the structure of the University, one that had not been campaigned for and which was much more controversial. The requirement that all

123 The building in Byng Place as built by Thomas Cubitt in 1832 for Coward College, a residential theological college in the tradition of dissenting academies. In 1850 Coward College moved away to Swiss Cottage, combining with Homerton College and Highbury College to form New College. In 1853 the premises were offered as the headquarters of the University of London, but rejected as too 'remote'. In 1882 the building became the original home of College Hall, the first hall of residence for women students, and now houses the Friends' International Centre, opposite the University of London Union.

124 By 1851 the total number of candidates offering themselves for the University's examinations had reached 355, of which 206 were candidates for Matriculation. A somewhat plaintive circular letter from the Registrar to the examiners touched on one of the problems.

125 Burlington House as it appeared in 1855–6 when the University moved there, having been temporarily accommodated in Marlborough House for over two years after being ejected from its original premises in Somerset House. The University's offices were in the east wing on the left, with the use of a hall in the west wing seating up to 180 exam candidates.

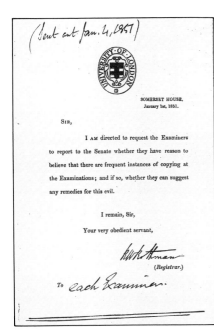

(Sent out Jan. 4, 1851)

SOMERSET HOUSE,
January 1st, 1851.

Sir,

I am directed to request the Examiners to report to the Senate whether they have reason to believe that there are frequent instances of copying at the Examinations; and if so, whether they can suggest any remedies for this evil.

I remain, Sir,

Your very obedient servant,

R.W. Rothman

(Registrar.)

To *each Examiner.*

126 William Benjamin Carpenter, FRS (1813–85), the University's second Registrar from 1856 to 1879. A scientist with a prodigious output of publications on physiology and zoology, he was 'perhaps the last complete naturalist'. His *The Microscope and its Revelations* ran into eight editions.

candidates should present a certificate of study at an affiliated institution was retained in the case of medicine, but it was abolished for all other examinations. The examinations were thrown open to all-comers. This decision was regretted by King's College, the teachers at which stated their opinion that 'mere examinations, without evidence that a regular curriculum of study has been followed, are a very insufficient test of education'. University College was even more deeply opposed. The ending of the requirement for collegiate education was deplored by the College as 'likely to be injurious to the cause of regular and systematic education, and as not only lowering the value but altering the very meaning of an English university degree'. In 1858 University College felt that the basis of the compromise of 1836 establishing the University as a separate body had been betrayed.

The University's defence of this apparently major change was couched in terms of the minor changes it made in practice. It was the government and not the University which determined the institutions deemed to be affiliated to the University, and the unregulated diversity of the resulting list was evident for all to see. Some of the institutions issued the necessary certificate on terms that were virtually fraudulent, and the University had no powers of inspection or control. The incipient collegiate system was, the Senate admitted, 'a mere name'. Far better, they felt, to proclaim 'the comprehensive principle' and declare Free Trade in education.

At the same time, significant alterations to the degree regulations were introduced by dividing the examinations for the BA into two parts. The 'First BA' was to be taken at least one year after Matriculation, and passes were required in each of four papers: Latin and Roman history; English language, literature and history; mathematics; and either French or German language. At least a further year later the 'Second BA' required passes in five papers: classics; Grecian history; natural philosophy; animal physiology; and logic and mental and moral philosophy. For the candidates who passed, further examinations were available for 'honours' (with the possibility of prizes and scholarships of £50 per annum for three years). The range of knowledge required remained extensive, though there was no longer any requirement concerning the means by which it had been obtained. The degree was open to all who could pay the non-returnable fee of £5 for each part of the BA examination, while the hurdles to be cleared were raised rather than relaxed.

After 1858, the University – the University of London Mark IIB, as it might be identified – also revised its regulations for Matriculation. Now offered twice a year, in January and July, candidates were required to pass in five subjects at the same examination: classics; English language, English history and modern geography; mathematics and natural philosophy; chemistry; and either French or German. The examination occupied twenty-eight hours, spread over five days. For those who passed, further examinations were available for honours (and the possibility of exhibitions of £30 per annum for two years) in mathematics and natural philosophy; classics; chemistry; and natural history. After 1861 the separate honours examination was abolished, and honours ('first division') were awarded to candidates achieving more than 1600 marks out of the total of 2800. A long list of teachers in 1862 claimed the requirements were too stiff: 'the number of subjects included in the examination is larger than either sound theory or experience would justify'. But the Senate – none of whom, of course, were teachers – maintained that the demanding standard was necessary. 'To obtain from students', they reported, 'as the condition and price of Academical Degrees, the greatest amount and the widest range of well-directed study, in Science as well as in Literature, – to keep up and, as far as

127 Sir John Shaw Lefevre, FRS (1797–1879), one of the members of the original Senate and the second Vice-Chancellor, serving judiciously in that capacity for the twenty years from 1842 to 1862. A lawyer, he sat on a great many royal commissions, becoming Clerk of the Parliaments and a Civil Service Commissioner.

105

may be, to elevate the actual Standard of liberal education – are the tasks confided to the University by its Charter.' The University was conscious that Matriculation was not only the first step to obtaining its degrees, but also the termination 'of the literary and scientific education received by large numbers of schoolboys who are prevented by circumstances from the farther presentation of systematic studies'. If the University did nothing else, it must insist upon high standards. Nearly half of all candidates were failed.

By 1858 the number of Matriculation candidates had mounted to 299 and the pressure on accommodation reached crisis point. A virtue was made of necessity by permitting the examination to be taken at a number of provincial centres, and in 1859 Queen's College, Liverpool and the recently established Owens College in Manchester were the first to be approved for this purpose. A further development followed in 1865, when it was agreed to permit the BA examination papers as well as those for Matriculation to be sat in Mauritius. Arrangements were made with the Colonial Office for the scripts to be sent out to the custody of the Governor, and the Chaplain to the Bishop of Mauritius was appointed as sub-examiner. The same arrangement was sought by Gibraltar in 1866, and extended to Canada in 1867, while in the case of Australia it was felt that 'the length of the voyage and the comparative infrequency of postal communication will interpose a very prolonged interval between the examination and the publication of its result in the colony'. In 1869 the Secretary of State for the Colonies nevertheless wanted the scheme extended to the West Indies and Tasmania. The University of London was beginning to act upon its imperial aspirations. The growth in the number of candidates presenting themselves and in the 'output' of the University is charted in table 3.2.

Table 3.2   *Numbers of Examination Candidates and of Bachelor's Degrees Awarded, 1838–70*[14]

	Matriculation		BA		LLB		MB		BSc		Total in all examinations	
	No. of cands.	No. passed	No. of cands.	No. passed	No. of cands.	No. passed	No. of cands.	No. passed	No. of cands.	No. passed	No. of cands.	No. passed
1838	23	22	–	–	–	–	–	–	–	–	23	22
1839	31	30	17	17	3	3	10	9	–	–	88	77
1840	77	69	32	30	3	2	20	19	–	–	186	162
1845	113	103	40	37	2	2	17	16	–	–	216	194
1850	206	190	70	58	3	3	18	12	–	–	355	310
1855	209	172	75	63	5	5	18	14	–	–	358	299
1860	428	291	101	63	9	9	31	24	8	2	788	532
1865	616	397	104	50	18	18	24	23	15	9	1137	712
1870	845	429	121	61	8	4	24	24	21	11	1459	750

128 The Royal College in Mauritius as it appeared in 1865 when University of London examination papers were sent out through the Colonial Office to be sat there. This development, the first time London exams were taken overseas, marks the beginning of a world-wide role for the University.

From the outset, scientific subjects had been given considerable stress in the University's examinations. There was a third dimension of change following the 1858 Charter, a major development permitting the University to award scientific degrees. The case for greater attention to experimental science in the examinations of the University was put in a letter addressed to the Senate in July 1857, signed by twenty-four of the leading lights in the world of science, such as A.W. Hofmann of the Royal College of Chemistry, John Tyndall of the Royal Institution, Lyon Playfair of the Department of Science and Art, T.H. Huxley of the Government School of Mines, as well as William Sharpey and A.W. Williamson of University College, and Sir Charles Wheatstone of King's and Sir Charles Lyell formerly of that College.

With further modifications to the proposed new Charter in mind, the matter was referred to an important committee consisting, besides the Chancellor, the Vice-Chancellor, and the Registrar, of Neil Arnott, W.D. Brande, Sir James Clark, Michael Faraday, George Grote, and James Walker, all of them Fellows of the Royal

129 King's College, notwithstanding its Anglican origins, had an early commitment to scientific research. In 1843 Prince Albert visited the College to open George III's Scientific Museum which Queen Victoria presented to the College. He is shown here inspecting one of the earliest of Professor Charles Wheatstone's prototypes of the electromagnetic telegraph, with wires communicating from the College across Waterloo Bridge to the summit of the shot tower on the south bank.

130 The Birkbeck Laboratory at University College pictured soon after its opening in 1846. It was built to commemorate George Birkbeck's services to education, and it was the first university teaching laboratory for chemistry. Bench accommodation was provided for twenty-four students, each place with gas and water laid on. The *Illustrated London News* pronounced it 'the most perfect of its class in the kingdom'.

131 The Royal College of Chemistry, founded in 1845, was the earliest of the various institutions that were in 1907 to coalesce to form Imperial College. Prince Albert laid the foundation stone of its new laboratory premises in Oxford Street in 1846. The College was attended by 'gentlemen following chemistry as a profession or as an object of scientific taste, chemists and druggists, medical students and medical officers in the army, clergymen, agriculturalists, manufacturers in almost all branches of the chemical arts...'.

132 The second oldest of the ancestor institutions of Imperial College was the 'Government School of Mines and Science applied to the Arts', as it was originally called when it opened in 1851 in the newly-built Museum of Practical Geology in Jermyn Street. Its aim was 'to give a practical direction to the course of study, so as to enable the student to enter with advantage upon the actual practice of mining'.

Society. Soon after they began a series of meetings to collect evidence, a powerful memorial was addressed to the University by twenty leading scientists (including some who had signed the first letter). It is believed that this memorial was drafted by T.H. Huxley, and it merits quotation. It is a central document in the nineteenth-century reorganization of knowledge, a process in which the University of London played a crucial part.[15]

The branches of human knowledge at present academically recognised are those of Arts, Theology, Law, and Medicine. But this fourfold division, though possibly sufficient in the age in which Universities took their rise, has become utterly inadequate as a recognition of the great classes of knowledge which at the present day subserve the discipline of the individual mind or promote the good of mankind. In fact, a fifth branch of knowledge – Science – the result of the search after the laws by which natural phenomena are governed, apart from any direct application of such laws to art – has gradually grown up, and being unrecognised as a whole, has become dismembered; some fragments consisting of Mathematics and such branches of Physics as are capable of Mathematical treatment, attaching themselves to Arts; others, such as Comparative Anatomy, Physiology, and Botany, clinging to Medicine, amidst whose professors they took their rise.

No evil could result from this arrangement, to the undeveloped Science of a century ago, when Electricity, Heat, Magnetism, Organic Chemistry, Histology, Development, Morphology, Geology, Palaeontology, branches of knowledge which constitute the very essence of Science as distinguished from Arts and Medicine, were non-existent. Now, however, the attainment of proficiency in any one of these sciences is acknowledged to be the worthy object of a life's labour; and society, appreciating the value of their fruits in alleviating the wants of man, practically regards the pursuit of these sciences as Professions, and honours those who follow them.

The Academic bodies, on the other hand, continue to ignore Science as a separate Profession; and even the University of London, though especially

133 Michael Faraday, FRS (1797–1867): his research at the Royal Institution, particularly on magnetic force, marked him out as one of the leading scientists of the age. Eccentrically professing Sandemanianism, he lived modestly and refused all public honours, regarding his seat on the Senate of the University of London from the time of the foundation until 1863 as his greatest honour.

instituted to meet the wants of modern times, can confer no Degree upon the first Chemist and Physicist of his age, unless he possess at the same time a more than average acquaintance with classical literature ... We conceive such a state of things as this not only anomalous in itself, but in the highest degree injurious to the progress of Science; for those who have the direction of youth, finding Science unrecognised as a profession discourage it as a pursuit ...

The remedy for these evils appears to us to be, that the Academic bodies in this country should (like those of France and Germany) recognise 'Science' as a Discipline and as a Calling, and should place it on the same footing with regard to Arts, as Medicine and Law.

The points were equally powerfully made in oral evidence to the committee. 'I think', said Huxley, 'that any person who watches the progress of knowledge at the present day, must see that science is taking a constantly increasing share in the affairs of the world, and that the time is rapidly approaching when no person who is not moderately conversant with scientific matters will be able to take part in ordinary conversation or to consider himself an educated person.'[16]

Huxley was preaching to the converted. The committee proposed to institute 'such new Degrees as may operate (without prejudice to the existing Degrees in Arts) in multiplying scientific students, – in prescribing, for diligent but desultory students a better direction and a methodized sequence of subjects, – in opening new paths to academical eminence, corresponding to the large development of inductive research which characterises the modern European mind...' As a result, the University established a new fourth faculty, the Faculty of Science, and created the new degrees of Bachelor of Science and Doctor of Science. The regulations for the BSc required two sets of examinations to be passed, the second examination involving compulsory papers in five subjects: mechanical and natural philosophy; chemistry, inorganic and organic, theoretical and practical; animal physiology; geology and palaeontology; logic and moral philosophy. Additional examinations were required for the degree to be taken with honours in particular subjects. The Treasury approved the additional costs of examining the new degrees and in the autumn of 1860 the first BSc with honours emerged in the form of Alexander Crum Brown, a student of the University of Edinburgh, later to be a distinguished chemist. Two years later he passed the further examination for the new doctorate

134 This cartoon of unknown provenance among the Huxley papers at Imperial College, dating from soon after the publication of Darwin's *Origin of Species* (1859), shows the University of London firmly behind scientific progress in the battle with religious reaction. Besides Darwin, Tyndall and Huxley, science is shown as being led by Carpenter, the Registrar of the University.

and became the first DSc. Whatever dispute there might be about other changes introduced in the 1858 Charter, the encouragement given to scientific education must count as one of the University's great contributions to progress.

Science was one thing; women were another. When the University was established in 1836 the position of women was not yet on any valid progressive agenda, and for some thirty years afterwards the expansive reference in the Charter to 'all classes and denominations... without any distinction whatsoever' was held legally not to apply to persons of the female sex. Not until the 1850s and 1860s did it come to be realized that women were not only the largest of all minority groups, but that women were the only minority group who were in fact a majority of the population. The middle of the nineteenth century witnessed the beginnings of an enormous shift in attitudes towards the position of women in society. A great campaign began in various ways. A key part related to education, as it became evident that the provision of schools for girls comparable to those for boys was lamentable, and the provision of higher education for women was non-existent.

The lead was taken in London in 1848, the year of revolutions in Europe, by the foundation of Queen's College in Harley Street, the first college in the country to be established specifically for the education of women. The moving spirit was F.D. Maurice, the profoundly serious Christian Socialist clergyman who was a professor at King's College, and he and other professors from King's began the teaching of young women at Queen's College when it commenced as a branch of the Governesses' Benevolent Institution. A similiar college with different roots was inaugurated in 1849 as the 'Ladies' College in Bedford Square', established through the efforts of Mrs Elisabeth Reid, herself strongly Unitarian, drawing upon the support of other nonconformists, in contrast to Queen's College, which was firmly Anglican. The first professors at what became known as Bedford College were drawn from University College, and included W.B. Carpenter, later the Registrar of the University. The differences between the two women's colleges replicated closely, though twenty years on less antagonistically, those between King's College and University College at the time of their foundation in the 1820s.[17]

The teenage girls and the few more mature ladies who attended the lectures in the early days of these two colleges were beginning to open a path that was to have a major impact on higher education, but they did not yet begin to aspire to come within the compass of the University of London. The first shot in the battle to extend the

135 The Rev. F.D. Maurice (1805–72), Chaplain of Guy's Hospital and Professor first of English and History and then of Divinity at King's College from 1840 until his dismissal in 1853 for theological unorthodoxy. Intensely serious, though unable to keep order in his classes, he became the founder of Queen's College in Harley Street in 1848 and of the Working Men's College in 1854.

136 Mrs Elisabeth Jesser Reid (1789–1866), the wealthy Unitarian widow who founded Bedford College in 1849. 'She was one of the present age', said Henry Crabb Robinson, 'and made both friends and foes by her zeal which sadly outran her discretion.'

137 The original home (until 1874) of the 'Ladies' College in Bedford Square' (no. 48, originally numbered 47). 'Bedford Square has been chosen as a suitable situation, from its being in the centre of a populous and wealthy neighbourhood, where such advantages as this College affords will be particularly valued.'

University's degrees to women was fired from a different direction in May 1856. During the brief interregnum between the death of the first Registrar and the appointment of Carpenter as his successor, the following innocently worded letter was received by the University:

Sir – Can a woman become a candidate for a Diploma in Medicine, if, on presenting herself for examination she shall produce all the requisite certificates of character, capacity and study from one of the Institutions recognised by the London University?
An answer will oblige
Yours respectfully,
Jessie Meriton White

The request came at a sensitive time in medical education. The 1854 Act had recognized London degrees for the purposes of medical practice, and discussions were under way concerning registration with the General Medical Council which was to be instituted in 1858. The University ducked its opportunity of striking an early blow in women's campaign for professional recognition. The Senate took legal advice and consequently returned the reply that it did not consider itself empowered to admit females as candidates for degrees. It was premature for Miss White to take a place in the history of the University. She took her place elsewhere, marrying an Italian count, and becoming 'famous as Madame Mario during the Italian Revolution, as the leader of a band of ladies who took charge of the nursing in the hospitals of Naples'.[18]

The matter came before the University again in 1862 when an even more famous aspirant to the medical profession, Elizabeth Garrett, sought to become a candidate for the Matriculation examination. By a single vote the Senate resolved to stand by the earlier decision. Elizabeth Garrett's father pressed her case, with the support of others who desired to raise the standard of female education: 'as the University requires no residence', he argued, 'and the Examinations involve nothing which could in the slightest degree infringe upon feminine reserve, we believe that by acceding to our wishes you would be conferring an unmixed benefit'. In May 1862 the Senate addressed itself to a motion seeking a modification of the Charter to enable women to become candidates for degrees on the same terms as men. The nature of the debate is unfortunately not recorded, but the vote that followed resulted in a tie, with George Grote as Vice-Chancellor leading the ayes. The casting vote of the Chancellor, however, by convention given to the status quo, meant that the University again lost the opportunity of giving a great boost to the women's cause.

When the issue came before the University a third time in 1866,

Convocation was successful in getting its more modest proposal accepted. The aim now was not the granting of fully fledged degrees to female candidates, but the instituting of special examinations for women. From the start, the University had been empowered to award 'Certificates of Proficiency' as well as degrees, a power that had been toyed with but not taken up, but which it was decided to activate in the case of 'such Female Candidates as shall satisfactorily pass an Examination, special in its nature but not on the whole less difficult than the existing Matriculation Examination'. The new examination, for females over the age of 16, required a pass in no fewer than six papers – Latin (with grammar, history and geography); English language, English history and geography (physical and topographical); mathematics; natural philosophy; two of a choice of Greek, French, German and Italian; and either chemistry or botany. A Certificate of Higher Proficiency was also to be offered in one or more of fourteen subjects. The regulations were framed to take account of the worries expressed by the Home Office about 'the possible ill effects that might occur to those qualities of the female character which it is always desirable to foster and promote' and the need 'to prevent the excitement and inconvenience which might arise from bringing these young persons up to London for examinations'. A 'suitable Female Attendant' was to be provided 'within call' at Burlington Gardens to 'wait at once upon any candidate who may require her services'. The necessary supplemental Charter was obtained for this purpose in 1867, and in 1869 nine pioneering girls were duly subjected to examination by no fewer than seventeen male examiners. Six of them were deemed

138 A Certificate of Proficiency as awarded in the 'General Examination for Women', instituted by the University in 1869 and continued for ten years up to the time when the Matriculation and degree examinations were thrown open to women on the same terms as men. Few candidates were attracted for this short-lived innovation. The numbers increased from nine in 1869 (of whom six passed) to only forty-two in 1878 (of whom twenty-four passed).

University of London.

This is to Certify, That *Alice Mary Marsh* Passed the *General Examination for Women* in the University of London in the year 18*78*, And that she was placed in the

FIRST DIVISION.

June 19, 1878.

William B. Carpenter

Registrar.

to pass: they represented a modest but hard-fought contribution to progress.

Soon after the University had moved into its new accommodation in Burlington House, it began to agitate for more space and for 'an appropriate Edifice belonging exclusively to itself'. There were frequent niggling disputes with the Royal Society about shared rooms, as there had been with the School of Design at Somerset House, especially at examination times, when the University's needs for examination accommodation were increasing substantially. The changes in location, the Senate plausibly declared in 1859, 'give the University itself a temporary and provisional character and lower it in the estimation of the Candidates, the Graduates and the Public'. Permission to erect a laboratory at Burlington House for purposes of the new practical examinations in chemistry was refused by the Office of Works in 1860. Outside accommodation had to be hired. For the examinations in 1863 a rifle shed in a nearby garden belonging to the Royal Irish Volunteers was rented. Pressure on the government was increased, the University insisting that 'its present buildings are quite inadequate to accommodate the large number of candidates presenting themselves at the Literary Examinations', as well as being 'altogether incapable of supplying the requisite facilities for those Practical Examinations for Degrees in Science and in Medicine'. In July 1864 the Chancellor and Vice-Chancellor led a deputation to the Prime Minister, Lord Palmerston, on the subject. The University, they informed him, was 'fast rising to a position as the Head of all the Higher Education of the Empire not embraced by the older Universities', responding to 'the general requirements of the times' particularly in medical and scientific education, but hampered by 'the want of an Edifice' and the consequent 'recourse to temporary expedients of an almost humiliating character'. Early the next year a further urgent appeal was made to W.E. Gladstone as Chancellor of the Exchequer, and later in 1865 the new Prime Minister, Lord Russell, was addressed on the subject. Progress was 'cramped', Russell was informed, by the University's 'want of due prominence as a visible feature of the Metropolis'. 'To not a few even instructed people', Grote wrote as Vice-Chancellor, 'in London, as well as many in the provinces, its very existence is unknown; while many who possess some knowledge of it and interest in it identify it with University College.'

Soon afterwards, the government accepted the University's case and decided to provide it with the 'Edifice' that it needed for reasons both of space and image. The extent to which Earl Russell personally was responsible for this decision is unsure. That he was an

139 Robert Lowe (1811–92), the first MP for the University of London from 1868 until 1880 when he was raised to the peerage as Viscount Sherbrooke. He was Chancellor of the Exchequer from 1868 to 1873 and Home Secretary from 1873 to 1874. 'The University of London', he said in 1870, 'is a great intellectual mint, to which gold may be brought from every quarter, and from which, when stamped, it may go current all over the world.'

enthusiastic supporter of the University is clear. He had, after all, as Lord John Russell, been one of the founders of the University of London Mark I in 1826, and a major influence behind the establishment of the University of London Mark II in 1836. What is certain is that it was his second ministry in 1865–6 which decided to find the money to provide the University of London with its first proper home. While the impressive new building in Burlington Gardens was being constructed between 1867 and 1870, the University operated from its fourth and most ignominious address: 17 Savile Row.

During its temporary encampment there, the University received a notable indication that it had begun to arrive in the public mind. The Reform Act of 1867 permitted it to elect a Member of Parliament as the Universities of Oxford and Cambridge had long been entitled to do, as the University of Dublin had since 1800, and as the Scottish universities were enabled to do at the same time. The graduates of the University had long campaigned for this privilege, accepted in principle by Disraeli as Chancellor of the Exchequer in 1852 but withheld on account of what in the House of Commons he then called the 'University's immature constitution and imperfect development'. Though the University of London was by no means mature or perfect by 1867, Mr Gladstone pronounced it 'ripe for representation'. The members of Convocation, now nearing two thousand in strength, were proud to be able to elect Robert Lowe – a member of the Senate since 1860 – as their MP in 1868, especially since he became Chancellor of the Exchequer in Gladstone's first government then formed.[19] In 1836 the Chancellor of the Exchequer had contrived to provide a university in London; in 1868, the University of London was able to provide a Chancellor of the Exchequer.

Examining versus Teaching, 1870–1900

Voltaire said once that he had only two objections to the title of the Holy Roman Empire, one that it was not Holy, and the other that it was not Roman. I am disposed to suggest two similar objections in practice to the title of the University of London; one, that it is not a University, and the other that it is not of London.

REV. HENRY WACE, DD, Principal of King's College, in his evidence in 1888 before the *Royal Commission on Whether Any and What Kind of New University or Powers is or are Required for the Advancement of Higher Education in London* (1889), p.182.

London University, with its hard examinations to all-comers, has been difficult, but a possible and encouraging way from down under below there, to a position as teacher, as journalist, or what not, to a breathing space wherein a young man of this type may find his possibilities. So long as *his* way keep open, open beyond any risk of tampering, the 'reformers' may, for all I care, tinker as they like with the rest of the University structure, organise boards of fellows and high professors, re-construct the charter to give one another honorary degrees, put an easy medical degree upon the market, and enrich this great Metropolis with a University worthy of its County Council.

H.G. WELLS in the *Saturday Review*, 14 December 1895, p.804.

The University of London moved confidently into its new building in Burlington Gardens in 1870. It had slipped virtually unobserved into its apartments at Somerset House in 1836, but now the purpose-built accommodation was opened with appropriate pomp and ceremony by Queen Victoria. The opening of the 'beautiful and spacious building', she declared on 11 May 1870, marked the beginning of a 'new era in the history of the University'. The 'growing usefulness of the University', she noted, had coincided with the years of her reign.

The much desired edifice had a complicated building history. It was provided by the 'liberality of Parliament', and the plans for it had to be approved by the House of Commons, the Office of Works, and the Treasury, with a strictly limited amount of consultation with the University itself. The architect was Sir James Pennethorne, the heir of Nash, at the end of his career as the designer of a number of government buildings. His first design was classical in character, acceptable to the Russell ministry. The new Conservative

140 The University's new building in Burlington Gardens in 1870. Pennethorne's ostentatious design had a façade ornamented by twenty-two statues: Newton, Bentham, Milton and Harvey, above the portico, representing the University's four Faculties of Science, Law, Arts and Medicine; Galen, Cicero, Aristotle, Plato, Archimedes and Justinian on the central balustrade representing 'ancient culture'; on the east wing (to the left) six 'illustrious foreigners' – Galileo, Goethe and Laplace on the balustrade, and Leibnitz, Cuvier and Linnaeus in niches; on the west wing (to the right) six 'English worthies' – Hunter, Hume and Davy on the balustrade, and Smith, Locke and Bacon in niches. The building now houses the Museum of Mankind, and attentive visitors may observe outbreaks of the University's coat of arms and 'UL' monograms amidst the ethnographical exhibits.

government in 1866 wanted something 'more Medieval or Renaissance' and so he produced an 'Italian Gothic' design. After the building was begun in 1867, the work was suspended by the Office of Works while a third design was produced. It was distinguished by a façade, based on the front of Burlington House, prominently adorned with no fewer than twenty-two statues. The result was a building of ostentatious external appearance, with an interior that was described as 'ostentatiously plain'.

The Commissioner of Works challenged the selection of Jeremy Bentham to represent English law among the statues, but the Senate firmly resolved unanimously that 'no name can be selected so suitable as that of Bentham to represent the Faculty of Law in the University of London'. The Senate got their way with Bentham, but gave in with Shakespeare, who was replaced by Hume among the representatives of English knowledge on the façade. On the grounds that 'the genius of Shakespeare was independent of academic influence', his statue was placed on the staircase inside the building. The University's exchanges with the Office of Works on the matter of the statues were bizarre, but wholly revealing of the

141 Queen Victoria passing through the lobby of the Burlington Gardens building on the occasion of the opening in May 1870. On her right is the Chancellor, Lord Granville, and on her left George Grote, the Vice-Chancellor. The statue of Shakespeare can be seen on the stairs.

142 Lord Granville moving his address before Queen Victoria in the theatre of the new building. Her speech declaring the building open was followed by the conferring of degrees on new graduates. Apart from five 'privileged ladies', females sat in the gallery.

dependent position in which the University was placed in regard to the government.[1]

This point cannot be better illustrated than by quoting a letter, written by the Office of Works to the Registrar after the official opening, reporting on an inspection of the building personally undertaken by the Commissioner of Works in Mr Gladstone's government.[2]

He desires me to point out, with reference to the Note on the Requisition for a Carpet for the Reading Room (that 'the Room will be used for the Meetings of the Committee of Convocation'), that a Committee Room has already been appropriately furnished, and that the requirements of this Room would, he thinks, be best met by the supply of some cheaper material, such as Kamptulicon.

In regard to the Requisition for 50 additional Chairs, similar to those supplied to the Refreshment Room, I am to state that the First Commissioner is of opinion that it is not desirable to supply Chairs of an expensive character for the use of Students, and desires me to suggest that, should it be found necessary to provide increased accommodation on special occasions for large numbers of Candidates for Examination, it would be more reasonable to follow the example of College Halls, the Halls of Lincoln's Inn &c., and furnish benches for the purpose.

Upon the subject of the Clocks demanded for the Senate Room, the Registrar's Room, and the Committee Room, I am to inform you that the First Commissioner has given directions for the supply of a Clock of an appropriate design to the Senate Room, and for the transfer of the Clock which is now in the Senate Room to the Committee Room, by which arrangement a Clock will be provided for each of the Rooms mentioned.

With reference to the request for Curtains for the Registrar's Room, I am to request you to inform the Senate that it is contrary to the practice of this Department to supply Curtains to Official Rooms, and that Curtains were provided for the Senate Room and the Committee Room because it appeared to the Board that in rooms so appropriated they were necessary; I am, however, to say that if the Senate are of opinion that a bad effect is produced by there being curtains in these rooms, with which your own room is *en suite*, the First Commissioner will give directions for those curtains being removed.

With regard to the demands for a Mahogany Book-wagon, Writing Table, Cases of Pigeon-holes, and Arm Chair for your own room and that

143 Another view of the same occasion. The Prince and Princess of Wales flank the Queen; the Vice-Chancellor, the Registrar, the Chairman of Convocation (Dr John Storrar) and the MP for the University back up the Chancellor; and both Gladstone and Disraeli can be seen in the front row of the fashionable audience of eight hundred.

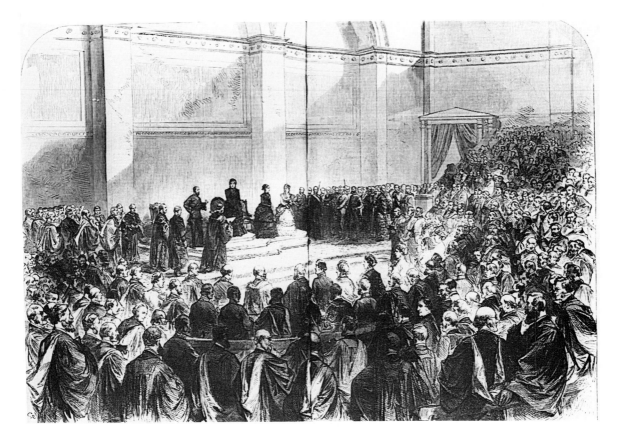

144 Balancing the theatre at the eastern end of the building was the University Library at the western end, though it must have been pretty bare of books at the time of the opening. It had to double up as an examination hall, shown here in a photograph taken in the 1890s laid out for a practical examination in botany or zoology.

of the Assistant Registrar, I am to state that directions have been given for the supply of one Case of Pigeon-holes fitted according to your own plan, and that the consideration of the other items has been postponed for further proof of their necessity; the First Commissioner is, however, of opinion that, when the above articles shall have been supplied, there will be an ample supply of furniture in these two rooms.

The extraordinary concern of a minister of the Crown with the *minutiae* of carpets and chairs and clocks and curtains and pigeon-holes is strikingly evident. The University of London, for all the splendours of its new building, remained under a peculiarly direct system of government control.

Once installed in a building for itself, the University of London began to acquire some – not many – of the characteristics that might be expected of a university. In 1871 it was proposed that, having acquired a building as well as parliamentary representation, the University should aim at acquiring a library. The sum of £1000 was provided for the purpose by Sir Julian Goldsmid (1838–96), later a member of the Senate and briefly Vice-Chancellor in 1895–6. Soon afterwards, Lord Overstone – a member of the Senate from 1850 to 1877 – acquired the two thousand volumes of the 'remarkable collection of mathematical works' that had belonged to Augustus De Morgan and presented them to the University in the hope that they 'may prove the first fruits of a library which shall ere long become such in all respects as the London University ought to possess'. In 1871 George Grote's death also brought the bequest of over 5 000 of his books on classics and ancient history. The Assistant Registrar, a new office established in 1870, was made responsible for the library. In 1871 a committee was appointed to draw up regulations for its use, and six years later in 1877 regulations were eventually produced and the library was at last opened.

While it was acquiring a library, the University also acquired the first lecturing and research institution to come under its own direct control. The Brown Animal Sanatory Institution owed its origin to Thomas Brown, who died in 1852 leaving money to the University for founding 'an Institution for investigating, studying, and . . . endeavouring to cure maladies, distempers, and injuries, any Quadrupeds or Birds useful to man may be found subject to'. It was believed that Brown had really intended his benefaction to go to University College, and that it only came to the University owing to the confusion between the two bodies. Brown's will was challenged on other grounds, first by his family and then by the University of Dublin, the conditional legatee, and the case was taken to the Court of Appeal, which declared that the University of Dublin's case against the University of London was 'so thoroughly without

145 The bust of Augustus De Morgan (1806–71), presented to the University by those who held him in veneration. He was a fascinatingly profound Professor of Mathematics at University College in 1828–31 and again in 1836–66, both periods being terminated by resignation on grounds of deeply-felt principle. He refused to permit a likeness of himself in the College to which he had brought great distinction; consequently this bust is to be seen still among the catalogues in the University Library.

146 The Brown Animal Sanatory Institution established by the University in 1871 in Wandsworth Road, Battersea, where it remained until it was destroyed in an air-raid in 1944. 'By those owners whose living depends wholly or in part upon their horses or donkeys the Institution is very highly appreciated.'

147 No picture of the first four female graduates of 1880 can be traced; here three of the twenty-one who graduated in 1882 are shown. The press was much given to quoting Tennyson's lines about 'sweet girl graduates in their golden hair', though these appear to be resolutely brunette. The picture appeared in the *Girl's Own Paper*, which also contained an article on 'University Hoods and How to Make Them'.

foundation that it must be dismissed with costs'. The Senate allowed the funds to accumulate for nineteen years, and in 1871 with the total of £33,800 built the Brown Institution in Battersea. John Burdon Sanderson, FRS, Professor of Physiology at University College, was appointed as the first of a distinguished series of Professor-Superintendants. A good deal of research was undertaken into the diseases of animals in the laboratory and a great many animals were provided with treatment at the hospital, both as in-patients and as out-patients. By the end of the century, over 100,000 animals had been treated, mainly horses, dogs and cats. The Brown Institution was a useful and worthwhile establishment, but it was an odd excrescence on a University whose only other function was to provide a system of examinations.[3]

The most important development of the University in the years after it moved into its new building was the full admission of women to its examinations on equal terms with men. In 1874 twenty-nine of the women who had passed the special examinations for women instituted in 1869 petitioned the University 'earnestly desiring that women be admitted to the degree examinations ... both on account of the great practical benefit such degrees would be to those who obtained them, and because it is believed a stimulus would be thus given to the higher education of women'. Petitions were also received from the National Union for Improving the Education of Women and several of the Ladies' Educational Associations in various parts of the country. In 1875 the Senate narrowly carried a motion declaring that there was 'no sufficient reason for perpetuating the slight differences which at present exist between the curricula of the Women's General Examination and the Matriculation Examination'. A fillip to the women's cause was given by an Act of Parliament in 1876 permitting – though not requiring – medical examining boards to admit women. The Royal College of Physicians and the Royal College of Surgeons did not act upon this enabling power until 1908 and 1909 respectively, though the Royal College of Physicians of Ireland from 1877 provided an entrée for women to the medical profession.

Earlier in 1877, the Senate bravely voted to seek a supplemental Charter to enable it to confer medical degrees on women, despite a petition from 230 medical graduates (including three members of the Senate) claiming that such a step would be 'detrimental to the interests of the University'. One member of the Senate, Sir William Jenner, a leading doctor, attempted to articulate the view of inarticulate reaction: he would, he declared, 'rather follow his dear daughter to the grave than see her subjected to such questions as could not be omitted from a proper examination for a surgical degree'.[4]

148 By 1891 there were eighty-seven women among the graduates; two are shown here at Presentation Day in Burlington Gardens receiving their degree certificates from the Vice-Chancellor, Sir James Paget.

Later in 1877 the Senate, nevertheless, finally voted in favour of admitting women to degrees in all faculties, a decision which logically followed. The necessary supplemental Charter was obtained for this purpose in 1878. The University received an address signed by no fewer than 1960 women expressing their 'heartfelt gratitude for the noble part it has taken in coming forward first among the universities of Great Britain to propose to open all its degrees to women, and thereby to place them in the position, so long coveted, of free intellectual activity, alike unhindered by mistaken protection and unfettered by ancient prejudice'.

The revolution, desired for over twenty years by some, and feared by others, passed off without difficulty. Sixty-eight women presented themselves for the first non-sexist examination for Matriculation in 1879, and fifty-one passed; twelve women also presented themselves for the Intermediate Examination in Arts and nine passed. The first women graduates were produced in 1880 when four passed the final examination for the BA. It was widely regarded as the 'special glory' of the University of London that it permitted women to graduate. The testimony of one of the first women graduates, Elizabeth Hills, is worth quoting for what it reveals about the practical difficulties they had to overcome.[5]

The wife of a professional man of limited income and the mother of children, the elder of whom with others I was engaged in teaching during part of the day, I had neither time nor money for attendance at college classes, but I gladly availed myself of the first opportunity for graduation offered by the new Charter, and felt justified in devoting what leisure I had, which was chiefly after 10 p.m., when the children were asleep, to the work of preparing for graduation.

Mrs Hills obtained her degree as the result of purely private study.

GIRL GRADUATES.

[At the half-yearly meeting of the Convocation of the University of London, which has just been held, Lady Graduates for the first time took part in the proceedings.]

GIRL Graduates! Old Dons, declare
    You think the innovation pleasant,
To sit in Convocation there,
    And find, strange sight, the Ladies present.
Full surely you must all confess,
    'Mid high debate in Greek or Latin,
You love the rustle of a dress,
    And academic silks and satin.

With brow serene and earnest looks,
    Those learned Ladies took their places;
A Poet said that all his books
    Consisted of fair women's faces;
So London Dons, methinks, will steal
    Full many a glance of admiration,
And, after this gay meeting, feel
    There's pleasure e'en in Convocation.

With such an audience, I opine,
    The men will feel themselves quite heroes;
'Twill mend their manners, and the line
    Goes on " *Nec sinit esse feros.*"
If *Place aux dames!* should make the fair
    Preside, a curious question this is—
How should a man address the Chair,
    If Mr. Chairman is a "Missis"?

Thus Woman wins. Haul down your flag,
    Oh, stern misogynist, before her.
However much a man may brag
    Of independence, he'll adore her.
Traditions of the bygone days
    Are cast aside, old rules are undone;
In Convocation Woman sways
    The University of London.

149 In 1882 female graduates were admitted as members of Convocation. Soon afterwards this piece of poetry appeared in *Punch*.

150 Sophie Bryant (1850–1922): one of the first women to take a BSc in 1881, she was the first woman to attain a doctorate when she took a DSc in 1884. Mrs Bryant was an inspiring schoolteacher, successor to Miss Buss as Headmistress of the North London Collegiate School, 1895–1918, and also one of the first women to be a member of the Senate in 1900–7.

Two women obtained the BSc in 1881, and two more the MB in 1882. The first woman to attain a doctorate followed in 1884, when Sophie Bryant became a DSc.[6] The numbers of women obtaining degrees increased steadily. By 1885 over 10 per cent of the graduates were women, by 1895 women formed over 20 per cent of the graduates, and in 1900 for the first time they constituted over 30 per cent of the graduates, when of the 536 graduating in that year, 169 were women. It was so complete a revolution that it soon appeared to have been inevitable.

The first teaching institution specifically intended to train women for degrees was the London School of Medicine for Women, which opened in 1874. It was unusual in having its founder, Sophia Jex-Blake, as one of the first fourteen students. She had been one of the 'seven against Edinburgh' who had heroically struggled to become medical students at that university in 1869–73, before turning to London to seek what Edinburgh denied. The London School grew under its first male Dean, establishing links with the Royal Free Hospital, and in 1883 Mrs Elizabeth Garrett Anderson became Dean. Following her rejection by the University in 1862, she had qualified as a medical practitioner through the Society of Apothecaries, becoming the second woman after Elizabeth Blackwell (who had qualified in the United States) to be recognized by the Medical Register. She had also become the first woman to take an MD in Paris. 'She is independent in fortune,' wrote W.B. Carpenter, the Registrar of the University, in 1868, 'but has taken up the object for the love of it, and has wisely made the diseases of children her speciality. Her sister is wife to Mr Fawcett (MP), and I occasionally meet her in society. She is *now* a very quiet lady-like person, quite different from the bumptious self-asserting girl she seemed to me when she came to me six years ago. I suspect that the educational discipline she has gone through has toned her down favourably.'[7] By 1882 the London School of Medicine for Women produced the first two in the growing stream of medical graduates that it was to contribute to the profession.

Two other women's colleges, both also in due course to become 'schools' of the University, were opened in the 1880s. Westfield College was born in 1882, when it was established with an endowment of £10,000 provided by Miss Ann Dudin Brown for 'founding and perpetuating a college for the higher education of women on Christian principles'. The guiding spirit was Constance Maynard, a former student of Girton College while it was still in its nursery at Hitchin, and also of the Slade School of Fine Art, established at University College in 1871 with a benefaction from Felix Slade. She was devoutly evangelical, and the founding Council shared her

151 A group of teachers at the London School of Medicine for Women photographed in the 1890s. Sitting second from the left is Dame Mary Scharlieb (1845–1930), in 1882 one of the first two women to graduate in medicine, and in 1888 the first woman MD (and also the first woman JP).

missionary concerns. Miss Maynard explained the curiously off-hand way in which the College was christened.[8]

Then there was the name; I consulted two or three members of the Council and we settled on 'St Hilda's'. I had just time to have the gate-posts painted and to have a good lot of writing paper headed thus, when down on me came a wretched little school in the neighbourhood which bore the same name, fiercely threatening to go to law if the gate-posts were not obliterated. I shewed the letter to Miss Metcalfe and she said the legal right was on their side, and we must change. Looking out of the window she said, 'The aspect is west. We must have a name, you see – *Westleigh* sounds a little too like John Wesley, so let us say *Westfield*. It is only provisional and before the students are ready for the first University examinations, we can change it.' So *Westfield* College it was to be, the name that was to represent the work of my life.

Westfield College grew up, according to its first historian, 'almost like a child in the desert', while the other new residential college for women grew up in Egham.

The Royal Holloway College was established with the largest single benefaction to any part of the University of London. Thomas

152 Graduates at the London School of Medicine for Women (later the Royal Free Hospital School of Medicine) photographed *c*.1894, with Elizabeth Garrett Anderson as Dean in the centre. For long after its foundation in 1874 it was the only medical school which admitted women, and rightly is regarded as 'the mother school of all British medical women'.

Holloway (1800–83) made a fortune out of patent medicines. Starting with pots of ointment in the 1830s, and soon developing Holloway's Famous Pills, he was one of the pioneers of modern advertising techniques. By the 1850s he was spending tens of thousands of pounds a year on advertising. The ingredients of the pills were a closely guarded secret, but recent analysis has shown them to consist largely of aloes, powdered ginger, powdered jalap, cambogia and hard soap, with a coating of sugar. They were harmless, but they sold like wildfire. Holloway never wished to enter 'society', but he sought to make a splash. 'I desire in some way or other', he wrote in 1871, 'to devote for public and useful purposes a sum equivalent to that given by the late Mr Peabody – but I find much difficulty in discovering the best means and purposes to which such a sum could be devoted, so as to do the greatest public good.' Eventually, by 1874, he settled upon the idea of founding a

153 Elizabeth Garrett Anderson (1836–1917), photographed in the 1870s: the second woman to become a recognized medical practitioner in 1865 through the Society of Apothecaries before that door was slammed, she was a leading campaigner to open new doors for women in medicine (and also the first woman to be a Mayor). As Dean of the London School of Medicine for Women from 1883 to 1903, she insisted that the students dress like ladies and behave like gentlemen.

college 'to afford the best education suitable for Women of the Middle and Upper Middle Classes'. A ninety-three acre site on Egham Hill was purchased, and the chosen architect, W.H. Crossland, was despatched to make plans of the Château de Chambord in the Loire valley as a model for the building on which Holloway was to spend over half a million pounds. A further £200,000 was provided as an endowment. To add two noughts to the sum of nearly £800,000 which Holloway lavished on his college in the 1880s would not greatly exaggerate the value in terms current a century later.

The extravagance of the Royal Holloway College made the other women's colleges in London look modest indeed. The opportunities offered by the University's full recognition of women in 1878 were not taken by Queen's College, which became what it remains, a public school for girls. Bedford College, followed by Westfield College, in their different ways, increasingly concentrated on providing facilities for women to study for the newly-available degrees. The results at Royal Holloway College were not commen-

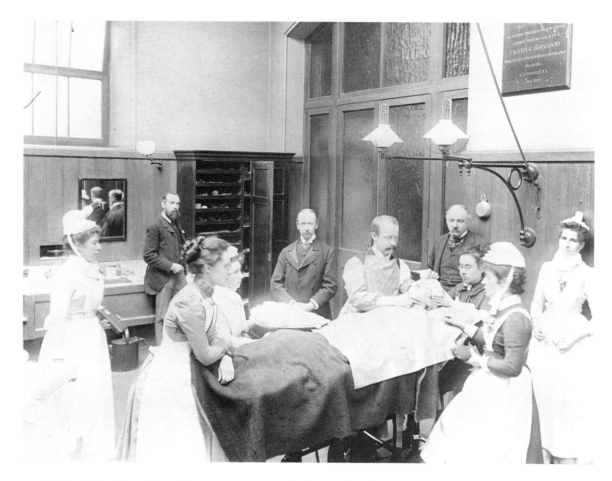

154 The Royal Free Hospital, founded in 1828, distinguished itself by being the first hospital to provide facilities for the clinical instruction of women in 1877. Here some of the pioneering women students of the London School of Medicine for Women can be seen in the operating theatre.

155 The students of Westfield College photographed outside the original premises in Maresfield Gardens, with Constance Maynard, the first Mistress of the College from its foundation in 1882 until 1913, sitting in the centre. 'We were all photographed,' she wrote in her diary on 22 July 1885, '21 in all, by Elliott & Fry. It was windy and rainy and we "felt ugly".'

surate with the scale of the investment, and the greatest contributions to the cause of women's education were made without architectural statement by King's College and especially at University College.

In 1878 University College became the country's first co-educational institution. When the University opened its examinations to women on equal terms with men, University College was ready to admit the first women undergraduates in its Faculties of Arts and Laws and of Science (though not Medicine). The ground for this development had been carefully laid over the previous ten years. In 1868–9 lectures organized by the London Ladies' Educational Association were given outside the college premises; in 1869–70 some of the courses for ladies were taught within the college at times deliberately chosen to avoid the possibility of meetings with male students; then from 1871–2 gradual moves were made towards mixed classes, first in art and political economy. By 1874–5 more than 300 ladies were enrolled. The process of assimilation was master-minded by Henry Morley, the energetic Professor

156 In 1891 Westfield College moved to Kidderpore Hall, the nucleus of its present site at the top of Finchley Road in Hampstead, shown here in a photograph taken in the 1920s.

157 One of the more modest of the newspaper advertisements for 'Holloway's pills' on which was based the vast fortune of the founder of Royal Holloway College.

of English. In 1878–9 no fewer than 288 women were registered as undergraduates, and they rapidly came to constitute a good third of the student body. It was a notable achievement.[9]

At King's College, by contrast, separate development was favoured. The Principal of King's in 1871 claimed that 'the inconveniences of access through the bustle of the Strand would prejudice any attempt to open its teaching to ladies', and after a trial at a firm distance in Richmond, lectures for ladies were instituted from 1878 in Kensington, a locality where young ladies seeking accomplishments were in good supply. In 1885 the 'Ladies' Department' was opened in a house in Kensington Square, the origin of what was later to become – after a period as the 'Women's Department' (1902) – first King's College for Women (1908), then King's College of Household and Social Science (1928), and ultimately Queen Elizabeth College (1953–85).[10]

The developing opportunities for women's education in London thus took different institutional forms, some originating before 1878, some created after the University's important innovation in that year: together, they undoubtedly marked the beginning of a new epoch. The wider significance of what the University of London did for women in 1878 cannot be over-estimated. Miss Buss, one of the pioneering headmistresses, said: 'the opening of the London University degrees to women has probably produced more effect in a short time on the education of girls than any other event in the history of education for some time past. It has done this by raising the standards, and still more by liberalising the curriculum of many girls' schools, so as to bring about an important development of studies more especially on the science side.'[11]

In the 1870s and 1880s other developments came under the expanding umbrella of the University of London. In 1877 regulations were adopted for degrees in music – 'a higher distinction than the certificate of any purely professional body', requiring 'evidence of general culture as well as of special proficiency' – a development which required the creation of a fifth faculty, the Faculty of Music. The 'distinctive educational degree' recommended to the University soon afterwards was not accepted, but the need was recognized for an examination in the theory and practice of education for the purpose of distinguishing qualified teachers. In 1881 regulations were adopted for what was called the 'Teacher's Diploma', a postgraduate qualification for an occupation that was beginning to regard itself as the largest profession (with over 158,000 teachers recorded in the 1871 census). A further educational development came in 1877 with the adoption of a scheme for the 'inspection and examination' of schools 'other than primary' by the University. Inspectors were to be appointed to report on the work of each class in the 'Grammar and other Secondary and High Schools' which asked to take part in the scheme, on the proficiency of their teaching and on the 'methods, discipline and general condition of the School'. A list of schools so inspected was to be published each year in the *Calendar*. This was an important extension of the work of the University, one intended to give it even more central a role in the whole educational system of the country.

Much time was spent by the Senate in appointing all its examiners, chosen from among applicants in response to public advertisement. After 1858 it was no longer possible for members of the Senate themselves to serve as examiners, and examiners could not serve for longer than five years at a stretch. There were modifications and developments in the scheme of examinations at intervals, if rather lengthy ones. In 1863 degrees in surgery were introduced (by special clause in a new Charter), and in 1867 the LLB was opened to candidates who had not previously graduated in Arts. In 1875 the regulations for the BA were revised, as were those for the BSc in 1877.

In 1880, after discussion of 'the expediency of recognising Original Research as a qualification for the higher degrees of the University', it was agreed to permit a thesis embodying 'properly-authenticated Independent Research' to be submitted for the DSc, previously awarded only on the basis of written and practical examinations. From 1886 the higher examinations were done away with and submission of a thesis became the only path to a doctorate in science. DLit candidates, who had to have passed the MA exams as well as the stringent higher examination introduced in 1865,

158 Henry Morley (1822–94), the Professor of English at University College from 1865 to 1889 who masterminded the gradual process by which the College became co-educational between 1869 and 1878. Perhaps the most prolific lecturer ever known in British academic life, he also created the nineteenth-century equivalent of paperbacks with his famous cheap editions of the classics in 'Morley's Universal Library' in the 1880s. His *Punch* sobriquet of 'Professor More-and-Morley' was energetically earned.

159 Holloway College on Egham Hill being opened on 30 June 1886 by Queen Victoria, who bestowed on it the prefix 'Royal'. The building, begun in 1879, was designed in a grand and opulent French Renaissance style by W.H. Crossland. It was far from filled by the first twenty-eight female students when they moved into residence in October 1887.

160 One of the features of Royal Holloway College was – and still is – the Picture Gallery containing the remarkable collection of paintings acquired by Thomas Holloway in 1881–3, displayed 'for the edification of the students and the public'. In the foreground of this early photograph can be seen the portraits of the founder and his wife: Jane Holloway died in 1875 before the building was begun, and Thomas Holloway died in 1883 before it was completed. They had no children.

161 The 'Ladies' Department' of King's College ('Women's Department' from 1902) was opened at 13 Kensington Square in 1885, where it was housed until 1915. Women were then admitted to King's College itself, after which the Kensington offshoot moved and went through a complexity of changes, becoming Queen Elizabeth College from 1953 until 1985, when it was re-amalgamated with King's.

were at the same time required to submit what was called 'an original printed essay or thesis' – 'not less in length than 32 closely-printed octavo pages, such as those for the *Quarterly* or *Edinburgh Review*'.[12] In 1893 the regulations requiring the thesis to be printed were modified to permit typewritten theses to be submitted. The quiet revolution which was to make research a major part of the work of universities was beginning to affect the University of London even before it was contaminated by contact with the traditional concern of universities: teaching.

The University of London was accused of making a fetish of exams. It certainly insisted on the complete separation of the functions of teaching and examining. The University stood aloof from teaching. A suggestion in 1864 that Convocation might organize some lectures produced an irritable declaration from the Senate that 'it would not be desirable that lectures should be established in connection with the university'. The University's theatre in Burlington Gardens was used after 1870 by such bodies as the Royal Geographical Society for lectures, but the University itself neither taught nor sought close links with the institutions that did. The University of London Mark II only asked questions.

In this respect, it was an object of emulation overseas. In 1850 the Queen's University was created in Ireland on the model of the University of London to provide degrees for students from the colleges established at Belfast, Cork and Galway. In 1853 the University of Toronto was founded, taking the University of London as its explicit model, with a university to examine and a college to teach. When the first three universities were established in India in 1857 at Madras, Calcutta and Bombay, they too were provided with constitutions modelled on that of London. The Indian universities were set up to test education obtained elsewhere, rather than as places of instruction themselves. Exactly the same model was adopted by the University of New Zealand, which became another of London's children in 1874.[13]

The growth in the numbers of candidates presenting themselves for the London examinations is shown in tables 4.1, 4.2, and 4.3, together with the numbers of those successful in obtaining matriculation, bachelor's degrees and higher degrees. The last quarter of the century saw considerable growth in the quantities of people availing themselves of the qualifications provided by the University at these different levels. For the University itself, and for higher education in London in general, the last quarter of the nineteenth century was a period of almost continual controversy. For over twenty years the structure of higher education in London was intensely debated and fought over, and even two Royal Commissions devoted to the subject were not able to reconcile all the issues involved.

The great debate began soon after the University was proudly installed in its new premises at Burlington Gardens. The University of London was, after all, as Sir William Allchin put it, 'an Examining Board, *urbi et orbi*, financially controlled by the State, and divorced both in principle and practice from teaching and from teachers'. 'It may be urged', Allchin wrote in 1900, 'that the most thorough-going admirers of the University are inclined to shut their eyes to other influences which have been at work and have assisted in promoting a higher level of general education during the past quarter of a century, and to attribute too great a share in the result to the mere examination paper'. 'It would not be difficult to show', he concluded, 'that in many respects the University has not kept abreast with the times, even in its own province of examination, and that the syllabuses are in some cases antiquated and effete. Nor could it well be otherwise when teachers as such have no voice in the arrangements, and the control is vested in a Senate, many of

Table 4.1 *Numbers of Candidates for Matriculation and for all Examinations, 1870–1900*[14]

	Matriculation		Grand Totals	
	No. of cands.	No. passed	No. of cands.	No. passed
1870*	845	429	1459	750
1875*	1056	542	1893	1020
1880	1400	680	2572	1321
1885	1900	1094	3477	2037
1890	2762	1278	4984	2502
1895	3420	1710	6219	2987
1900	4341	1917	7130	3316

*Includes those passing the 'General Examination for Women' retrospectively deemed in 1878 to have passed Matriculation.

Table 4.2 *Numbers of Bachelor's Degrees Awarded, 1870–1900*[15]

	BA		BSc		LLB		MB		BS		BMus		Totals	
	No. of cands.	No. passed	No. of cands.	No. passed	No. of cands.	No. passed	No. of cands.	No. passed	No. of cands.	No. passed	No. of cands.	No. passed	No. of cands.	No. passed
1870	121	61	21	11	8	4	24	24	3	3	–	–	177	103
1875	106	61	31	20	25	13	28	19	7	7	–	–	197	120
1880	170	94	58	27	30	19	60	39	9	8	3	2	330	189
1885	339	183	68	38	32	12	73	51	18	17	1	0	531	301
1890	401	219	145	71	37	23	99	80	33	24	5	1	720	418
1895	498	219	196	96	38	26	149	97	48	41	4	0	933	479
1900	361	202	258	135	30	21	192	92	46	20	3	2	890	472

Table 4.3 *Numbers of Higher Degrees Awarded, 1870–1900*[16]

	MA		DLit		DSc		LLD		MD		MS		DMus		Totals	
	No. of cands.	No. passed	No. of cands.	No. passed	No. of cands.	No. passed	No. of cands.	No. passed	No. of cands.	No. passed	No. of cands.	No. passed	No. of cands.	No. passed	No. of cands.	No. passed
1870	15	9	1	0	7	6	2	2	16	11	0	0	–	–	41	28
1875	15	7	0	0	2	0	6	2	10	6	0	0	–	–	33	15
1880	21	14	2	0	11	1	3	1	22	18	1	1	–	–	60	35
1885	24	16	3	1	11	6	1	0	39	27	2	1	2	2	82	53
1890	38	26	2	2	6	0	7	3	41	33	4	4	0	0	98	68
1895	46	20	0	0	12	6	8	5	61	48	7	3	2	0	136	82
1900	37	22	3	1	8	7	13	2	50	29	3	2	3	1	117	64

whom have never been teachers and others have long since ceased to instruct.'[17]

Criticism along these lines grew louder and louder. Public voice was first given in 1873 by Sir Lyon Playfair, the distinguished chemist, formerly a student at University College, then MP for the Universities of Edinburgh and St Andrews. 'A University which combines the teaching and examining functions', he stated, 'aims and succeeds at producing an *educated* man; an Examining Board can only be assured that it has produced a crammed man. . . . the Examining Board looks only to knowledge, however acquired, as the result; but the real University looks upon it less in that light and more as a manifestation of the student's successful attention to a prescribed course of study organised for and necessary to his mental discipline and development.' The same point was made equally publicly a few years later by Sir George Young, the charity commissioner and intrepid alpine climber who was President of the Senate of University College. 'I believe that the most valuable agency in education is the personal presence of a very able man working in an institution and influencing those with whom he comes into contact,' he declared in 1877; '. . . it is expedient, nay, it is almost necessary, that he should be supported by having some voice, some control in the conduct of the examinations which are to test the qualities of those students who come under his influence.'

Considerations such as these led to a resolution of Convocation later in 1877 inviting the Senate 'to consider by what measures the connection of the affiliated colleges with the University may be strengthened'. Convocation began to argue for 'some stronger and mutually advantageous influence of the University upon its colleges and schools, and of these educational bodies upon the University', maintaining that 'few of the members of Convocation who take an active interest in University affairs have ever acquiesced in the exclusive character so often assigned it of a government examining board'.[18]

The Senate of the University noted these arguments with a conspicuous lack of enthusiasm. When the case for establishing boards of the examiners or a representative board elected by the colleges furnishing candidates was pressed by Sir Joshua Fitch, a leading inspector of schools and member of the Senate, in 1882, the Senate was inclined to resolve that such moves were 'not practicable or expedient'. Indeed, when Fitch drew attention to the anomaly of the continued printing of the lists of 'institutions in connection with the University' in the *Calendar*, despite this having been an admitted dead letter since 1858, the Senate resolved to omit the listing from 1884. The Senate attempted to ignore what was becoming a mounting campaign for reform.

The campaign was given a new urgency after 1880 following the Charter creating the Victoria University. Owens College, Manchester, became the first constituent part of a federal university in the north of England, later joined by Yorkshire College, Leeds (founded in 1870) and University College, Liverpool (founded in 1882). The Victoria University was later (in 1903) to break up, the constituent parts becoming separate universities, but not before the first of the late nineteenth-century new provincial universities had a significant impact on the controversies in London. In the 1880s it came to be strongly felt by University College and by King's College that Manchester had achieved what they lacked: degree-giving powers

162 George Grote (1794–1871) painted by Millais in the last year of his life: he was a member of the Senate from 1850, and Vice-Chancellor from 1862 until he died in 1871. He had been the youngest member of the founding Council of the University of London Mark I in 1826, and succeeded Lord Brougham as President of University College in 1868. He was equally renowned as a banker, an MP, and historian of Greece.

SIR JOHN LUBBOCK, M.P., F.R.S.

How doth the Banking Busy Bee
Improve his shining Hours
By studying on Bank Holidays
Strange Insects and Wild Flowers!

163 Sir John Lubbock, FRS (1834–1913),
Vice-Chancellor from 1872 to 1880,
subsequently succeeding Lowe as MP for the
University from 1880 until 1900, when he
was raised to the peerage as Lord Avebury.
Like his father (see **96**), he was both banker
and scientist. His researches on ants were
especially important, and he was widely
known as the instigator of the Bank Holidays
Act of 1871.

164 The 2nd Earl Granville (1815–91), the
second (and longest-serving) Chancellor of
the University for thirty-five years from
1856 to 1891. A leading Liberal, related to a
good many other members of the peerage,
he was three times Foreign Secretary and
twice Colonial Secretary. 'He combined
sanity and tact in counsel with a suave
firmness in public.'

for the benefit of their own students. Both colleges were larger than Owens College, Manchester, and both were convinced that the division of academic labour settled upon in 1836, and vitally compromised in 1858, increasingly operated to their disadvantage as London teaching institutions, universities themselves in all but name.

In May 1884 the 'Association for Promoting a Teaching University for London' was founded, with members drawn from University College and King's College, together with representatives of various of the London medical schools. The Association sought 'the conferring of a substantive voice in the government of the University upon those engaged in the work of University Teaching and Examination', and recognition of the 'existing institutions in London of university rank' as 'the bases or component parts of the University'. Plans were drawn up for the forming of faculties and boards of studies controlling a 'Teaching University' to be grafted on to the existing University of London, reconstituted into a 'dual organisation'. 'London does not possess any university at all,' wrote Karl Pearson, the battling Professor of Applied Mathematics at University College, soon afterwards. 'The nearest approaches to such an institution are University and King's Colleges, together with the medical schools. To term the body which examines at Burlington House a University is a perversion of language, to which no charter or Act of Parliament can give a real sanction. The promoters of the new scheme have by their adoption of the word "teaching" given additional currency to the fallacy that a university can be anything else than a teaching body.' The battle lines were drawn.

Under Sir James Paget as Vice-Chancellor from 1883, the University was somewhat more receptive to proposals for adaptation than it had been when the movement began. 'The members of the Senate', Sir Joshua Fitch noted, 'could not fail to be struck with the contrast between the decisive and masterly chairmanship of Sir George Jessel, whose reputation as one of the strongest judges on the Equity Bench has never been questioned, and the gentle and considerate supervision of the affairs of the University by his successor.' Jessel in 1882 had firmly ruled that the proposals for boards of studies were inconsistent with the University's Charter. Paget was disposed to treat the proposals more sympathetically, but the opportunity of a peaceful reform was missed.[19]

Soon afterwards, the apparent unity between the teachers and the graduates broke down. In 1885 Convocation found that it could not support the proposals put forward by the Association for Promoting a Teaching University for London. Convocation, which

165 Sir George Jessel (1824–83), Master of the Rolls 1873–83, 'the most practical of lawyers'. He was Vice-Chancellor from 1881 to 1883, the first graduate of the University to serve in this office (BA 1843, MA and gold medal 1844). In 1840 the dates of the examinations had been changed to avoid a clash with the Jewish Day of Atonement in order to enable him and his brother to take matriculation.

166 Sir James Paget, FRS (1814–99), lecturing on anatomy at St Bartholomew's Hospital Medical College in 1874, soon before becoming President of the Royal College of Surgeons. A member of the Senate from 1860, he was the first teacher to become Vice-Chancellor, serving in that capacity in the difficult years from 1883 to 1895. 'On the Senate, his modesty and patience led him sometimes to be a little too tolerant of irrelevant speech, and to listen with scrupulous deference to the opinions of others, especially younger men.'

hitherto had undeniably been a force for the improvement of the University, began to move into a period of unpredictable confusion in which the merits of reform were swamped by a reactionary cry of 'Our degrees are in danger! No lowering of the standard!' In particular, the graduates assembled in Convocation began to dread that their privileges would be threatened by the proposals to give more influence to the colleges and to the teachers. There were many meetings of Convocation in 1885–6, and the way forward became increasingly clouded. Majority opinion clutched at the principle of the separation of the powers of teaching and examining and held that this principle would be endangered by any of the schemes of reform being proposed. While the Senate looked as if it might become more flexible, Convocation became agitatedly inflexible.

University College's response was first to toy with the idea of applying to become a constituent college of the Victoria University, and then to join with King's College in petitioning for the creation of a new university, a university *for* London as distinct from the 'University of London'. For this proposed new university, the name of the 'Albert University of London' was suggested, no doubt with an eye to encouraging support in high quarters. A draft charter was

167 A pioneering development at King's College was the introduction of 'evening classes' in 1855, aimed at 'extending the boundaries of useful knowledge to the commercial youth of the metropolis'. To celebrate their success, a fashionable *soirée* was held in January 1859. 'The whole of the rooms of the college were thrown open for the occasion; but the spacious lecture-hall, the long corridors and galleries, the libraries and museum of the establishment, were barely sufficient to accommodate the visitors.'

168 The teachers involved in the 'Evening Class Department' at King's College in 1872. In the 1860s over 600 young men, mainly clerks in government offices and banks, were attracted to what Charles Dickens identified as 'the college by gaslight in the Strand'. They were diligent and serious, in contrast to what the historian of King's called 'the riotous hobbledehoys who, under parental compulsion, constituted the day classes'.

drawn up in 1887, proposing that University College and King's College should be the first constituent colleges, with provision for the admission of medical schools and other colleges, linked together by arrangements for assemblies of faculties and boards of studies. The petition to the Privy Council argued that 'except by the situation of its headquarters, the University of London does not belong more to London, or to the London District, than to any other part of England, or of the Empire; and that valuable as has been the influence which it has exercised over many educational Institutions, and great as have been the services thus rendered to the cause of Education, its existence and present work do not supply the place, or furnish an argument against the establishment of a University ... in and for London'. The severance of the work of examination for degrees and the work of higher teaching had, it was strongly argued, 'an injurious effect upon University Education', tending to 'deprive instruction and study of that power of transforming the mind of the learner which is their most valuable function'. What was proposed was 'a complete metropolitan university' much as envisaged in 1836, but unfulfilled in subsequent developments.

The decision to petition in this way dramatically split the Council of University College. A third of the members resigned, including Lord Kimberley, the President, and Sir Julian Goldsmid, the Vice-President and Treasurer. They saw the petition as amounting to a proposal that 'the professors and teachers should confer degrees upon their own students', a proposal later to be compared to auditing one's own accounts, or, more enigmatically, as 'branding your own herrings'. In the crisis of 1887, the majority of the University College Council supported the general view of the professors that a university was needed in London which was not disadvantaged in comparison with those developing on a much smaller scale in vari-

PROF. PISTRUCCI.
PROF. BENTLEY. F.L.S.
Dr. J. B. YEO. M.A.
J. W. LAMB.
J. W. CUNNINGHAM.
S. McCAUL. B.C.L.
REVd PROFr DREW. M.A.
PROF. BUCHHEIM. PhD.
PROF. RYMER JONES. F.R.S.
C. J. PLUMPTRE.
DON B. B. AGUIRRE. B.A.
REV. E. H. PLUMPTRE. M.A.
REVd A. BARRY. D.D. PRINCIPAL.
CANON OF WORCESTER.
LEONE LEVI. F.S.A. F.S.S.
REVd T. A. COCK. M.A.
REV. O. ADOLPHUS. M.A.
PROF. CUTLER.
PROFr. A. MARRIETTE. B.A.
PROF. THOROLD ROGERS.
PROF. GLENNY.
PROF. HUGHES. F.R.G.S.
RICHARD MORRIS. L.L.D.
L. STIEVENARD.
W. A. THOMAS.
PROF. J. TENNANT.
W. R. HARTLEY.

PROFESSORS & STAFF OF KINGS COLLEGE (EVENING CLASSES) 1872.

SAWYER & BIRD, 87 REGENT ST.

145

169 An evening lecture at the Birkbeck Literary and Scientific Institution in 1877. 'Here the student may, if he feel inclined, busy himself with abstract subjects like Hebrew, Philosophy and Differential Calculus, or he may revel in the lighter paths of Music and Elocution.' There were 950 students in the music classes, and 29 in the class preparing for the University's matriculation exam. The presence of women will be observed.

ous provincial centres, not only in Manchester, Liverpool and Leeds, but also in Birmingham, Bristol, Nottingham, Sheffield and Cardiff. At the same time, the Privy Council received another petition from the Royal College of Physicians and the Royal College of Surgeons seeking degree-giving powers in medicine and surgery under a joint Senate of their own. The Senate of the University, bogged down in an attempt to produce a compromise plan, in January 1888 first voted narrowly against the proposal that there be a Royal Commission into the whole matter, and then in February voted in support of the suggestion. For the government, confronted by such conflict, a Royal Commission appeared to be the only way out.

In May 1888 a Royal Commission was duly appointed 'to inquire whether any and what kind of new university or powers is or are required for the advancement of higher education in London'. Lord Selborne, an able lawyer and former Lord Chancellor, was to be chairman, and the other members were three lawyers and three teachers, all unconnected with the University of London: J.T. Ball was a former Lord Chancellor of Ireland and Vice-Chancellor of the University of Dublin; Sir James Hannen was a judge; G.C. Brodrick was Warden of Merton College, Oxford; Sir William Thomson, later Lord Kelvin, was Professor of Natural Philosophy at Glasgow;

Sir George Stokes was Lucasian Professor of Mathematics at Cambridge and President of the Royal Society; and the Rev. J.E.C. Welldon was Headmaster of Harrow, and later Bishop of Calcutta. Brodrick dropped out after one meeting, but the others spent several intensive days hearing a great quantity of evidence from forty-five witnesses in the summer of 1888. They presented their report in just under a year.

The Royal Commission rejected the claims for separate medical degrees awarded by a non-university body, and concluded that the case for a teaching university was 'made out'. They were unclear, however, on how this should be brought about. Three of the members wanted the University to be 're-modelled' to bring about a closer connection with the teaching institutions – 'concentrating and utilising all the strength and experience of the existing university, and of the existing teaching agencies, as far as possible, in one great institution'. Three others (Thomson, Stokes and Welldon) produced a note of dissent, doubting 'the possibility of effectually

170 Roundell Palmer, 1st Earl of Selborne (1812–95), Chairman of the first Royal Commission of Inquiry into the University of London in 1888–9. He brought to the practice of law 'a mind as keen and subtle as that of one of the great medieval schoolmen'. He was Lord Chancellor in 1872–4 and again in 1880–5, being created an earl when the new law courts in the Strand were opened in 1882.

combining the functions of an examining, and of teaching as well as examining, university into the University of London, and on this account we should have preferred the establishment of a new teaching university for London, leaving it to the London University to continue to discharge its present functions'. They nevertheless concluded, somewhat confusingly, that 'we acquiesce in the recommendation that an attempt should be made to unite the teaching and examining functions in a single university'.[20]

The minutes of evidence and the appendices attached to the report present a large amount of interesting information about the University and the teaching institutions in London. Much of it is highly quotable. Arthur Milman, Carpenter's successor as Registrar from 1879 to 1896, for example, implied in his evidence that there were close relations between the University and the teaching institutions, while Henry Wace insisted he could not understand this. 'I have been Principal of King's College now for nearly five years', he said, 'and never during that time have I received one single communication, of any nature whatsoever, from any official connected with the University of London.'[21] Further quotation will be resisted, since the report – massive quarry of data concerning the battle though it is – had little practical effect. It cannot be said to have been received with enthusiasm in any quarter. 'The Report is a disappointment,' said *Nature* frankly. 'The spectacle of three eminent lawyers taking an eminently legal view of a question, and three teachers an educational view, is instructive and amusing, but it is not business.'[22] It nevertheless gave rise to much resulting business. The evident division of opinion among the members of the Royal Commission fuelled rather than quelled the flames. The Senate busied itself earnestly with attempts to produce a revised scheme of reconstruction, and over the next two years there was much toing and froing between all the interested parties. Agreement was eventually reached with the powerful medical interests, but in May 1891 the Senate's compromise was finally rejected by Convocation, which under the 1858 Charter had the power of veto.

The complexities of the developments following this *impasse* were chronicled in the blow-by-blow *Account of the Reconstruction of the University of London* on which many years were spent by Sir William Allchin, himself one of the protagonists, Dean of the Westminster Medical School, 1878–83 and 1891–3, Physician Extraordinary to Edward VII, and expert on indigestion. The whole of his third volume was devoted to the events 'from the rejection of the Senate's scheme by Convocation to the withdrawal of the Gresham Charter, 1891 to 1892'. Allchin died before he was able to carry his work beyond 1892. Only a brief summary of what eventuated can

171 The London Society for the Extension of University Teaching, founded in 1876, was an independent body with three representatives of the University on its council, including W.B. Carpenter, the Registrar. One of the first series of lectures was given on political economy by H.H. Asquith, the future Prime Minister. Ten years later sixty-one courses were being offered, with over 5000 attenders enrolled, and one of the lecturers was Carpenter's son.

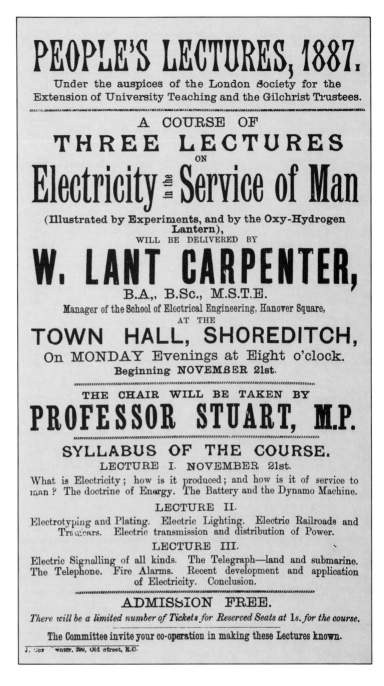

PEOPLE'S LECTURES, 1887.

Under the auspices of the London Society for the Extension of University Teaching and the Gilchrist Trustees.

A COURSE OF
THREE LECTURES
ON
Electricity in the Service of Man

(Illustrated by Experiments, and by the Oxy-Hydrogen Lantern),

WILL BE DELIVERED BY

W. LANT CARPENTER,

B.A., B.Sc., M.S.T.E.

Manager of the School of Electrical Engineering, Hanover Square,

AT THE

TOWN HALL, SHOREDITCH,

On MONDAY Evenings at Eight o'clock.
Beginning NOVEMBER 21st.

THE CHAIR WILL BE TAKEN BY
PROFESSOR STUART, M.P.

SYLLABUS OF THE COURSE.
LECTURE I. NOVEMBER 21st.

What is Electricity; how is it produced; and how is it of service to man ? The doctrine of Energy. The Battery and the Dynamo Machine.

LECTURE II.

Electrotyping and Plating. Electric Lighting. Electric Railroads and Tramcars. Electric transmission and distribution of Power.

LECTURE III.

Electric Signalling of all kinds. The Telegraph—land and submarine. The Telephone. Fire Alarms. Recent development and application of Electricity. Conclusion.

ADMISSION FREE.

There will be a limited number of Tickets for Reserved Seats at 1s. for the course.

The Committee invite your co-operation in making these Lectures known.

J. Cox Printer, 299, Old Street, E.C.

be given here. The first result of the University's inability to reform itself was the re-activation of the 1887 petition of University College and King's College seeking to become the nucleus of an entirely new university. In the summer of 1891 Privy Council hearings considered the issue, resulting in a recommendation that a charter be approved for the 'Albert University' (omitting 'of London'). An amended draft charter was drawn up, constituting University College and King's College as 'Colleges of all Faculties in the University' and the ten metropolitan medical schools as 'Colleges of Medicine in the University'. The university was to be, as Sir John Lubbock put it, 'a teachers' university as well as a teaching one, just sufficiently under the control of dignified outsiders to provide a check upon professorial cliques, or professorial prophet-worship, but practically worked and guided by teachers'.

The proposed university met with a deluge of opposition. The budding provincial university colleges objected strongly and the Victoria University petitioned against it. Convocation was predictably entirely against it. ('Convocation', wrote Karl Pearson in the *Pall Mall Gazette* in 1892, 'is *not* the University of London; it is not really the whole body of graduates of that University, it is rather the group of prehistoric meddlers and muddlers who believe that a University can thrive if it be governed, not by its teaching and examining executive, but by those whom the executive has stamped as taught. Such a group has practically been relegated to the election of members of Parliament at Cambridge, and the sooner it is reduced to a like harmless function in London the better.') Even some of the professors at University College did not support it, and in February 1892 one of them wrote to *The Times* to criticize the 'objectionable charter': 'The great failure', Professor Ray Lankester pointed out, 'of that scandalous attempt to force an ill-considered organisation upon London in the name of a University consists in the fact that Sir George Young's "Teaching University" has no professors or other teachers.' Two professors wrote to *The Times* to say that Lankester did not speak for all teachers at University College; four others then wrote to say that he did. The whole question became increasingly convoluted, and parliamentary objections to the Privy Council recommendation resulted in the withholding of consent to the Albert University charter in March 1892.

Faced with such deep divisions of opinion, the government felt that it must take some action, and in April 1892 it acted decisively: it appointed another Royal Commission. 'Meanwhile', concluded Allchin, 'the University of London kept on its same old course, making no real endeavour to meet the needs of the situation; the Senate contenting itself with passing futile resolutions which came

172 Railway development in Southwark obliged St Thomas's Hospital to move to Lambeth where new buildings were provided on a grand scale between 1868 and 1871 facing the Houses of Parliament across the Thames. 'London's most modern hospital' was constructed on principles approved by Florence Nightingale. The Medical School is the building on the left.

173 When Sir James Paget entered St Bartholomew's Hospital as a student in 1834 he was shocked to find that 'many of the lecturers told utterly indecent and dirty stories'. The teachers were no doubt reformed, but medical students maintained a certain hearty reputation. One of the earliest surviving pictures of students on other than formal occasions shows medics larking outside St Barts in a fracas with the police in the winter of 1876.

174 From the origin of the science degrees in 1860 there had been practical examinations in chemistry; this photograph shows the apparatus provided in Burlington Gardens in the 1890s.

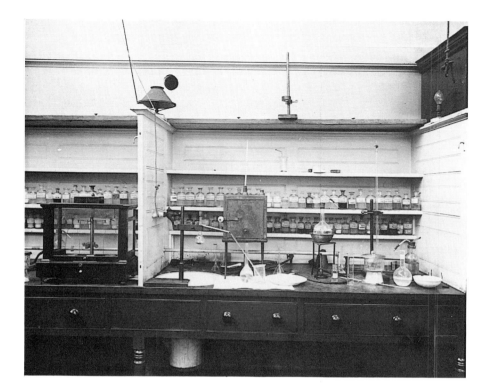

175 The BSc examinations in the late nineteenth century became increasingly both more practical and more specialized; for the honours degree, biology was separated from chemistry in 1863, and divided into botany and zoology in 1866. This photograph shows the apparatus and specimens provided for the examination in zoology at the end of the century.

176 Apparatus and specimens provided for the BSc examination in botany in the 1890s. An examination script lies ready to be completed on the table in front of a notice enjoining 'strict silence'.

177 Physiology emerged as a separate honours subject after the reform of the BSc degree in 1876; this photograph – also dating from the 1890s – shows the apparatus provided for the examination.

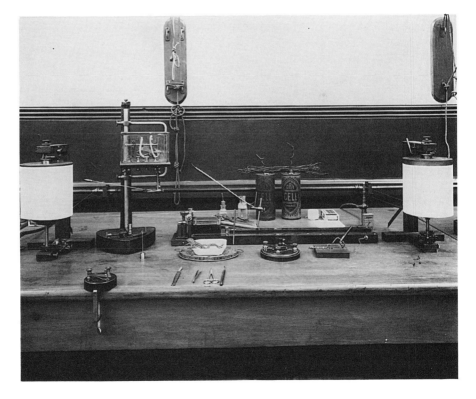

to nothing, and Convocation adopting motions which sounded important, but of which nothing more was heard.'[23] The new Royal Commission was more authoritatively composed than the first. The chairman, Lord Cowper, one of nature's aristocrats, had no previous connection with the University, but of the twelve other members, seven were fully familiar with the problems of higher education in London. Lord Reay, formerly Governor of Bombay, in whose house the Association for Promoting a Teaching University for London had been founded, was Vice-Chairman of the Council of University College (and Chairman from 1897 to 1921); Alfred Barry, formerly Archbishop of Sydney, had been Principal of King's College from 1868 to 1883; Sir Lyon Playfair had been a student and teacher at University College and a professor at the Royal School of Mines before becoming a professor at Edinburgh and an MP; Sir William Savory had been a student at St Barts before becoming a teacher and surgeon there; Sir George Humphrey, a medical professor at Cambridge from 1866 had also been a student at St Barts; John Burdon Sanderson had been Professor of Physiology at University College from 1870 to 1883, before going to Oxford; and James Anstie, a QC, had been the seconder of the Convocation motion in 1877 (see above p.140) which had been one of the starting-points of the whole issue. Besides them, the Commission included Henry Sidgwick, the very influential Professor of Moral Philosophy at Cambridge, another Cambridge professor, one from Glasgow, the Principal of Liverpool University College (and Vice-Chancellor of the Victoria University), and a Visitor in Lunacy, on whose appropriateness no comment will be passed.

The Royal Commission devoted sixty-eight days between May 1892 and March 1893 to the hearing of evidence, asking no fewer than 25,594 questions. It got fewer answers, but it produced a massive Parliamentary Paper some 1500 pages long. No other university in the world, it was said, was subjected to so voluminous a collection of documentation on its constitution. The Commission was known as the Gresham Commission, rather than the Cowper Commission, since by 1892 the 'Albert University' proposals had been re-named following the suggested incorporation of the Gresham College foundation in an effort to form a link with the City of London. An old tradition was harnessed to new proposals with what was hoped would prove a remunerative connection.

The report that was produced in January 1894 was much clearer and more specific than that of the Selborne Commission, but it was in essence the same. Again there was no unanimity, but the majority concluded that 'there should be one University only in London, and not two'. The existing University should be reconstructed to es-

178 The 7th Earl Cowper (1834–1905): one of the last 'great English noblemen of high lineage and broad possessions, of chivalrous manners and noble mien ... who played, without effort and with instinctive humility, an eminent part in things great and small'. Two of the greatest of the problems he grappled with were Ireland, where he was Lord Lieutenant in 1880–2, and the University of London, where he chaired the second Royal Commission in 1892–4.

tablish a teaching university 'on such a basis as will enable it, while retaining its existing powers and privileges, to carry out thoroughly and efficiently the work which may be properly required of a teaching University for London, without interfering with the discharge of those important duties which it has hitherto performed as an examining body for students presenting themselves from all parts of the British Empire'. There were to be internal students and external students, 'the only difference between the two classes of students being that the one class would pursue courses of instruction within the University leading up to the examinations, while the other class would receive their instruction elsewhere and, as at present, enter for the examination only'. Various of the teaching institutions in London were to become 'schools' of the University, retaining their separate identity, with their teachers either appointed or recognized by the University as a whole. The University was to promote research as well as teaching, especially in 'those branches of scientific research which are either neglected or so inadequately represented in England that advanced students cross the Channel in order to find elsewhere what a teaching University in London certainly ought to provide'. The need for greater funding was firmly recommended to the Treasury. Specific proposals were made for the constitution of the Senate, an Academic Council, and a system of Faculties and Boards of Studies.

Five notes of dissent were added by members of the Commission, two of them fundamental. Bishop Barry considered that the internal and external sides were incompatible, a view held even more strongly by Professor Sidgwick: 'Although I have signed this Report,' Sidgwick stated, 'I am decidedly opposed to the fundamental principle on which it is framed; namely, the principle of combining the ordinary work of a University with the function – now performed by the (so-called) University of London – of impartially examining students from all parts of the United Kingdom.'[24] Despite these ominous dissentient voices, the report of the Gresham Commissioners was received with more general approbation than the Selborne Report. Lord Herschell had said that he doubted whether a commission of archangels could frame a scheme which would meet with the approval of those who rejected the 1891 proposals, but Convocation, surprisingly, at once expressed its support. Convocation however did not give up what one writer called the 'truly Gilbertian idea that the graduates of a State-created, State-maintained Examining Board should be put in a position to veto the action of the State itself'.[25] The Commission had wisely recommended that the University should be reformed by legislation rather than by charter, but various spokes were put into the parliamentary

179 Suggestions for a motto for the University were drawn up in 1887, following a recommendation by Convocation that one should be adopted. The idea was approved by the Senate, but the question was dropped without a decision. It was raised again in 1921, when the University came close to adopting 'Pateat Omnibus Porta', but the issue was once more left undecided. One of the few occasions on which laughter was recorded at a meeting of the Senate was when a member of the administrative staff suggested 'To Teach the Senators Wisdom'.

UNIVERSITY OF LONDON.

PROPOSED MOTTOS.

Spiritus intus alit.
Sit felix prole virum. (Virgil.)
Amica veritas. (Cic.)
Hold truth evermore. (Browning.)
Prava ambitione procul. (Hor.)
Fontibus exit ab isdem. (Ovid.)
Undique conveniunt. (Virg.)
Let knowledge grow from more to more. (Tennyson.)
Gradatim vincimus. (Prov.)
Quis est sapiens ? (Pythagoras.)
Hic patet ingeniis campus.
Certusque merenti stat favor. (Claudius.)
Merenti favor.
Sola virtute distinguimur. (Prov.)
Thorough.
Post prœlia præmia.
Nihil humani alienum.
Ut sementem feceris ita et metes.
Vita sine literis mors est.
Animi cultus humanitatis cibus.
Uno avulso non deficit alter.
Sapiens qui assiduus. (Prov.)
Vim promovet insitam. (Hor.)
Per aspera et ardua.
Φως ξυρη αριστη ψυχη. (Heraclitus.)
Lumen siccum optima anima.
Religion, morality, knowledge. (Charter.)
Science, freedom, truth.
Forti nihil difficile. (Lord Beaconsfield.)
Virtute et labore.
Coronat virtus cultores suos.
Vitai lampada tradunt. (Lucretius.)
Sapere aude. (Hor.)
Sapere aude: incipe. (Hor.)
In omne volubilis ævum. (Hor.)
Consilio et prudentia. (Clancarty.)
In veritate victoria. (Huntingdon.)
Vincit omnia veritas. (Kinsale.)
Beatus qui invenit sapientiam. (Prov.)
Attendite ut sciatis prudentiam. (Prov.)
Sapientis conquerit doctrinam. (Prov.)
Fons vitæ eruditio. (Prov.)
       or
Fons vitæ scientia. (Prov.)

April, 1887.

U 51127. 75.—4/87. G. S. Wt. 1353. E. & S.

wheels attempting to give legislative effect to the 1894 proposals over the next four years.

The archangel responsible for the eventual achievement of the 1898 Act of Parliament took the canny form of R.B. Haldane, one of the succession of Scotsmen whose influence on education in London has been so powerful – and no one individual's influence on the University of London was ever so great or so manifold as that of Haldane. Haldane took it upon himself as an MP to force the reform of the University of London through the House of Commons. He formed a plotting alliance with Sidney Webb, and in her diary Beatrice Webb provides a glimpse into the frantic activity which ensued.

July 26th, 1897. Sidney and Haldane rushing about London trying to get all parties to agree to a Bill for London University. If it goes through, it will be due to Haldane's insistence and his friendship with Balfour – but the form of the Bill – the alterations grafted on the Cowper Commission Report are largely Sidney's. He thinks he has got all he wants as regards the Technical Education Board and the London School of Economics.

In his autobiography, Haldane provided an account rather more from his own point of view.

I saw that, as a first step at all events, the only way was to pass an act enlarging the existing University of London by giving it a powerful teaching side. This might be relied on in the end to absorb the other side by reason of its quality. Of this opinion also was my friend Sidney Webb, who

180 The 15th Earl of Derby (1826–93), Chancellor of the University for barely two years from 1891 until his death, though he had been a member of the Senate from 1856. Serving both under Disraeli as Foreign Secretary and under Gladstone as Colonial Secretary, he had a gift 'of making speeches with which everyone must agree, which at the same time was never commonplace'. Lord Derby's bequest to the University was applied to an award – the Derby Prize – still presented to the student most distinguishing himself in the honours examination in history, first introduced in the year of his death.

181 The many long meetings and fraught discussions about the future shape of the University of London that took place between 1884 and 1898 are difficult to illustrate. This drawing, the only one known of any of the meetings, captures something of the atmosphere of the period. It shows Lord Kelvin introducing a distinguished deputation to the Duke of Devonshire as Lord President of the Council in November 1895. Though he was the son of the first Chancellor of the University, he did not prove sympathetic to the efforts to reconstitute the University.

as the successful Chief of the Technical Education Board of the London County Council had great opportunities of studying the practical problem.

But the professors thought otherwise and they insisted on their plan. My difference with them was so serious that I had to resign my position as a member of the Governing Body of the University College of London. They wanted a second and professorial University in addition to or in substitution for the then existing University, and I knew that their ambition must fail.

Sidney Webb and I took counsel together. He was a very practical as well as a very energetic man. We laid siege to the citadel. He went round to person after person who was prominent in the administration of the existing University. Some listened, but others would not do so and even refused to see us. In the end we worked out what was in substance the scheme of the London University Act of 1898. The scheme was far from being an ideal one. It provided by way of compromise for a senate which was too large to be a really efficient supreme governing body for the new composite University, and it had other shortcomings of which we were well aware. But it did set up a teaching University, although Convocation, with its control of the external side, would remain unduly powerful. We saw that the scheme thus fashioned was the utmost we could hope for the time to carry, in the existing state of public opinion about higher education in London.

Bills in 1895, 1896 and 1897 failed, but Haldane — according to his own account — was inspired to get that of 1898 through, despite the opposition voiced by Sir John Lubbock as MP for the University.

For some time in the course of the discussion not a speech was made in its favour, and the prospects of the Bill seemed hopeless. I sprang to my feet when an opportunity at last offered, and I spoke for once like one inspired. I told the House of Commons of the scandal that the metropolis of the Empire should not have a teaching University to which students from distant regions might come as to the centre for them of that Empire. I showed how far we were behind Continental nations, and what a menace this was to our scientific and industrial prospects in days to come. I knew every inch of the ground, and displayed its unsound condition. We were far away from the days in which a step forward had been made by calling into being the Examining Body named London University, a creation which had given degrees by examination to those whom the Church had in the old days shut out from University status. That reform was in its time a most valuable service to the State, but it was a service which had become superseded in the light of new standards in University education which demanded much more.

'It is the best thing of the kind I have ever heard in the H. of Commons', wrote Asquith in a note of congratulation to Haldane, 'and in my experience I have never known a case in which a single speech converted hostile and impressed indifferent opinion in the House. The result must be some compensation to you for months and years of unthankful work.'[26]

The resulting Act established a commission to frame the necessary statutes for the University under Lord Davey, the lawyer

182 Lord Herschell (1837–99): a former student at University College, he was the first – and only – London graduate (BA 1857) to become Chancellor of the University, in which capacity he served from 1893 to 1899. The son of a dissenting minister of Polish Jewish descent, Farrer Herschell was a lawyer and a Gladstonian, and Lord Chancellor at the time of his appointment.

183 Richard Burdon Haldane, later Viscount Haldane (1856–1928), Secretary for War, 1905–12, Lord Chancellor, 1912–15, and again in the first Labour government of 1924. 'I have lived', he said, 'in the cause of education perhaps more than any other.' He had 'a sort of academic Midas touch in negotiation', and was largely responsible – among much else – for the 'patch-up' which brought about the University of London Mark III when it was eventually reconstituted by Act of Parliament in 1898. Later, in 1909–13, he dominated as chairman the third great Royal Commission into its organization.

184 One of the greatest of all surgeons was Joseph Lister, FRS (1827–1912), from 1897 Lord Lister, photographed here in 1890 in one of the wards of King's College Hospital, as rebuilt in 1861. From 1877 to 1892 he was Professor of Clinical Surgery at King's, where a memorial tablet prominently records: 'His name will be handed down to posterity as the founder of Antiseptic Surgery, one of the greatest discoveries in history and a source of inestimable benefit to mankind.' He had been a student at University College, where there is also a tablet to his memory: he is the only person to be so commemorated at both colleges.

Haldane most admired and under whom he had begun his career at the bar. The statutes duly produced in February 1900 provided the reconstituted University with its constitution of arranged complexity. The University of London Mark III of 1900, like the University of London Mark II in 1836, was born in compromise, and its birthmarks were there for the world to see.

Despite all the surrounding controversy, the numbers of examinees presenting themselves to the University grew from fewer than 2000 a year in the early 1870s to over 6000 a year in the late 1890s (see table 4.1). The pressure on space in Burlington Gardens mounted. In 1889 the Treasury refused to countenance any expenditure on the provision of additional accommodation. 'My lords are confident', said a Treasury letter, 'that the Senate will agree that the self-supporting capacities of the University should be encouraged in every possible way; and that any avoidable increase of its already heavy obligation to the State would be much to be deprecated.' The attempt in 1890 to have an extra storey added to the building got nowhere. To help with the necessary laboratory provision, the University was directed to investigate the possibilities of sharing the Royal College of Science's new premises in South Kensington. For a time in 1895 there was some hope of erecting University laboratories on a Millbank site, or on another site in South Kensington. But the government would not provide the money, and no solution to the accommodation crisis appeared to be forthcoming until the matter got into Haldane's hands in 1898.

185 Sidney Webb, later Lord Passfield (1859–1947) and Beatrice Webb (1858–1943), as painted at Passfield Corner by Sir William Nicholson for their 'joint seventieth birthday' in 1928. They founded the London School of Economics in 1895, the favourite child among the many enterprises they undertook together, such as their *History of Trade Unionism* (1894), their nine volumes on *English Local Government* (1906–29) and the founding of the *New Statesman* (1913). Socialism was once defined as a great spider with a little Webb at its centre. Sidney Webb was later to be defeated in elections for the University's MP (1918) and for the Chairmanship of Convocation (1922), but in the late 1890s he was at the centre of the efforts to reform the University.

Fresh from his parliamentary triumph, Haldane grasped the opportunity of being the intermediary between the government, the University and the Imperial Institute in negotiations to explore whether 'an adequate and dignified home for the University of London could be provided in the Imperial Institute buildings'. The Imperial Institute in South Kensington was something of a white elephant. To commemorate Queen Victoria's Jubilee in 1887 it had been decided to mount a permanent exhibition of the idea of the British Empire which would also be a source of information for, as T.H. Huxley put it, 'the man of business who wants to know anything about the prospects of trade with say, Borrioboola-Gha'. A remarkable building was erected to the design of T.E. Colcutt, ornately eclectic in style, with an amplitude of gables, towers, domes, arabesque embellishments, and a great campanile. Sir John Summerson called it '*the* representative public monument of the late Victorian London'. Queen Victoria herself found it 'very grand and

186 Three abortive attempts were made between 1895 and 1897 to give legislative effect to the recommendations of the Gresham Commission Report of 1894. 'The whole affair', wrote T.H. Huxley, 'is a perfect muddle of competing crude projects and vested interests ... anything but a patch-up is, I believe, outside practical politics.' A pamphlet stating the 'Plain Facts about the London University Bill' at the time of the fourth attempt in 1898 indicated the line-up in a not unbiased way, highlighting the equivocal position of the University's MP.

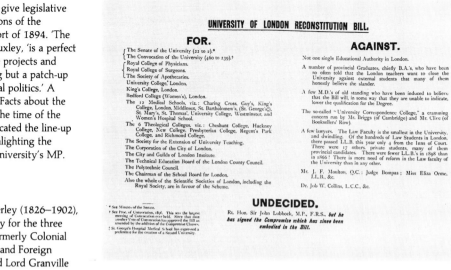

UNIVERSITY OF LONDON RECONSTITUTION BILL.

FOR.

{ The Senate of the University (22 to 2).*
{ The Convocation of the University (460 to 239).†
{ Royal College of Physicians.
{ Royal College of Surgeons.
{ The Society of Apothecaries.
University College,¹ London.
King's College, London.
Bedford College (Women's), London.
The 12 Medical Schools, viz.: Charing Cross, Guy's, King's College, London, Middlesex, St. Bartholomew's, (St. George's‡), St. Mary's, St. Thomas', University College, Westminster, and Women's Hospital School.
The 6 Theological Colleges, viz.: Cheshunt College, Hackney College, New College, Presbyterian College, Regent's Park College, and Richmond College.
The Society for the Extension of University Teaching.
The Corporation of the City of London.
The City and Guilds of London Institute.
The Technical Education Board of the London County Council.
The Polytechnic Council.
The Chairman of the School Board for London.
Also the whole of the Scientific Societies of London, including the Royal Society, are in favour of the Scheme.

* See Minutes of the Senate.
† See Proc. of Convocation, 1878. This was the largest meeting of Convocation ever held. Since that date another Vote of Convocation has approved the Bill as amended by the addition of the Compromise Clauses.
‡ St. George's Hospital Medical School has expressed a preference for the creation of a Second University.

AGAINST.

Not one single Educational Authority in London.

A number of provincial Graduates, chiefly B.A.'s, who have been so often told that the London teachers want to close the University against external students that many of them honestly believe the slander.

A few M.D.'s of old standing who have been induced to believe that the Bill will, in some way that they are unable to indicate, lower the qualification for the Degree.

The so-called "University Correspondence College," a cramming concern run by Mr. Briggs (of Cambridge) and Mr. Clive (of Booksellers' Row).

A few lawyers. The Law Faculty is the smallest in the University, and dwindling. Of the hundreds of Law Students in London, there passed LL.B. this year only 4 from the Inns of Court. There were 17 others, private students, many of them provincial candidates. There were fewer LL.B.'s in 1898 than in 1866! There is more need of reform in the Law faculty of the University than in any other.

Mr. J. F. Moulton, Q.C.; Judge Bompas; Miss Eliza Orme, LL.B., &c.

Dr. Job W. Collins, L.C.C., &c.

UNDECIDED.

Rt. Hon. Sir John Lubbock, M.P., F.R.S., *but he has signed the Compromise which has since been embodied in the Bill.*

187 The 1st Earl of Kimberley (1826–1902), Chancellor of the University for the three years prior to his death. Formerly Colonial Secretary, Indian Secretary and Foreign Secretary, he had succeeded Lord Granville as leader of the Liberal peers in 1891. 'He is', wrote Lord Dufferin, 'one of the ablest of our public men, but being utterly destitute of vanity, he has never cared to captivate public attention, and consequently has never been duly appreciated.'

imposing' when she opened it in 1893.[27] It was architecturally impressive, not to say overpowering; but it was not clear what it was for. No one realized this better than Lord Herschell, who was both Chairman of the Institute and Chancellor of the University. The Imperial Institute spent all its money on its grand building and rapidly got into financial difficulties. In 1898 the government had to come to its rescue, and proposed to solve the University's accommodation problem at the same time by offering a large part of the building.

It was calculated that, while Burlington Gardens provided floor space of only 20,400 square feet, the Imperial Institute offered a total of 94, 793 square feet, plus proximity to 14,000 square feet of examination space in the nearby laboratories of the Royal College of Science. Repeated visits were made to the building during 1899, on the first of which the Prince of Wales himself enthusiastically escorted the Senate round what was a pet project of his own. The new Registrar of the University (after 1896), F.V. Dickins, recommended acceptance of the proposal, arguing that 'Kensington offers a healthier and much quieter location for the University than Burlington Gardens, and fully furnished as are the Kensington buildings ... with electric and heating installations, as well as by reasons of their space and adjacent areas, they afford ample facilities for the present and future work of the University'. The University was tempted, and it fell. In 1899 the move to the Imperial Institute was agreed, a flit that was to prove disastrous for the University over the next thirty years.

188 One of the rooms in the University's building in Burlington Gardens arranged for a practical examination in physics in the 1890s. It has a depressingly ramshackle appearance, characteristic of the University on the eve of its move to the Imperial Institute building in South Kensington.

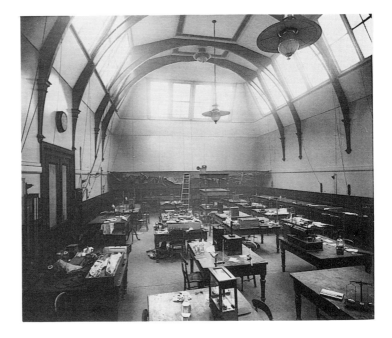

The Reconstituted University, 1900–1929

189 The staff of the central offices of the University photographed in South Kensington in 1908. Sir Arthur Rücker as Principal sits in the centre, with Sir Philip Hartog, Academic Registrar, 1904–20 (later Vice-Chancellor of Dacca) on his right, and Alfred Milnes, the External Registrar, 1901–15, on his left. Next to Hartog is R.D. Roberts, the Extension Registrar, 1902–11, formerly the Secretary of the London Society for the Extension of University Teaching and of the Cambridge Syndicate for University Extension. At the left end of the front row sits R.A. Rye, the first Goldsmiths' Librarian from 1906 to 1944, and at the right end sits T.L. Humberstone, later a doughty campaigner in various University and anti-University causes. *Previous page.*

190 A plan of the area around the Imperial Institute in the 1890s. In the half-century after the Great Exhibition of 1851, South Kensington became dominated by several national museums and by the institutions which coalesced to form Imperial College in 1907, existing in awkward proximity to the headquarters of the University.

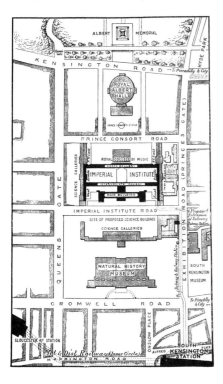

We have the most wonderful aggregation of institutions making up this University to be found anywhere in the world.

<small>SIR GREGORY FOSTER, *The University of London: History, Present Resources, and Future Possibilities,* 1922, p.8; the phrase used as the subtitle to S. Gordon Wilson, *The University of London and its Colleges,* 1923</small>

If a university is, whatever its type or form, a highly vitalised organism, vitalised, not by administrative means, but by ideas and ideals, with a corporate life, I confess myself unable to understand in what sense the University of London is a university at all. While avoiding the excesses and absurdities of Columbia and Chicago, it possesses even less organic unity than its nearest American relatives. It is not really a university, though it does possess central offices and an inclusive Court and Senate: it is a line drawn about an enormous number of different institutions of heterogeneous quality and purpose.

<small>ABRAHAM FLEXNER, *Universities: American, English, German,* 1930, p.231.</small>

What moved from Burlington Gardens to the Imperial Institute in 1900 was no longer 'the University', but 'the central offices' of the reconstituted University. The University of London was now a much more complex entity. The University of London Mark III had two distinct sides. There were the various colleges denominated as 'schools' of the University with their 'internal' students in the London area, and there continued to be the 'external' students who could be studying anywhere or nowhere. Degrees of comparable standing were to be provided for both categories; 'separate examinations (both intermediate and final)' shall be held for Internal and External Students respectively,' said the 1900 statutes, 'but the Senate shall provide that the degrees conferred upon both classes of Students shall represent as far as possible the same standard of knowledge and attainments'.[1]

The achievements of the old University were maintained: 'No religious test shall be adopted or imposed', for example, and 'No disability shall be imposed on the grounds of sex'. The proclaimed aims of the University were extended beyond those laid down in the seven Charters issued between 1836 and 1878:

The purposes of the said University of London are to hold forth to all classes and denominations both in the United Kingdom and elsewhere without any distinction whatsoever an encouragement for pursuing a regular and liberal course of education; to promote research and the advancement of science and learning; and to organise, improve and extend higher education within the appointed radius.

191 The jubilant building of the Imperial Institute in South Kensington erected between 1887 and 1893 which housed the central offices of the University from 1900 to 1936. To Betjeman the tower was 'along with St Paul's and the Houses of Parliament, one of the three great additions to the London skyline'. To the University the building, overwhelmingly splendid in appearance, proved increasingly unsatisfactory.

The appointed radius meant thirty miles from the central offices. The promotion of research and the improvement of teaching were the important additions to the University's functions after 1900.

The changes in the composition of the Senate were intended to reflect these developments. The Senate was expanded to consist of fifty-six members, including the Chancellor – seventeen elected by Convocation, sixteen by the teachers assembled in the revised Faculties of the University, two each by University College and King's College, two each by the Royal Colleges of Physicians and of Surgeons, one each by the four Inns of Court and two by the Incorporated Law Society, as well as one by the Corporation of London, two by the London County Council, one by the Council of the City and Guilds of London Institute, and four by the Crown. The number of faculties was expanded to eight by the addition of Engineering and 'Economics and Political Science (including Commerce and Industry)' as well – more controversially – as 'Theology'. Consequent new degrees were created. The BSc was expanded for Engineering and Economics into the BSc(Eng) and the

BSc(Econ), and the BD was instituted for Theology, with their attendant higher versions. Drawn into the eight faculties were the 'schools' of the University, originally twenty-four in number.

University College and King's College were both admitted as schools in all faculties of the University. The other schools were admitted in particular faculties. Royal Holloway College and Bedford College were admitted to the Faculties of Arts and Science, the Royal College of Science to the Faculty of Science, the Central Technical College to the new Faculty of Engineering, and the London School of Economics to the new Faculty of Economics. The ten metropolitan medical schools formed parts of the Faculty of Medicine – the eight which in origin antedated the University of London Mark II (the Medical School of St Bartholomew's Hospital, the Medical College of the London Hospital, and the Medical Schools of Guy's Hospital, St Thomas's Hospital, St George's Hospital, the Middlesex Hospital, the Charing Cross Hospital and the Westminster Hospital), and the two later foundations, the Medical School of St Mary's Hospital (founded in 1854) and the London (Royal Free Hospital) School of Medicine for Women (founded in 1874). There were six small long-established schools in the new Faculty of Theology, surprisingly given formal precedence over the other faculties. Hackney College and New College, both in Hampstead, trained candidates for the Congregational ministry, Regent's Park College for the Baptists, Wesleyan College, Richmond, for the Methodists, Cheshunt College for another brand of nonconformists, and St John's Hall, Highbury, for the Anglicans. By special arrangement, the South Eastern Agricultural College at Wye was

192 The imperial entrance hall of the Imperial Institute leading to the University's offices, which soon proved inadequate to house the growing central bureaucracy.

193 The University's house-warming in its new premises took place in May 1900 in the 'temporary' wooden structure at the back of the Imperial Institute built for the royal opening in 1893 which had to serve as the University's Great Hall. Lord Kimberley as Chancellor presented degrees and the Prince of Wales (soon to be Edward VII, in his robes as Chancellor of the new University of Wales) insisted on shaking hands with the flustered graduates. Sir Michael Foster (1836–1907), the great physiologist and MP for the University, 1900–6, congratulated the graduates on the luxury in which they were now examined, a comment which provoked much laughter.

SIR MICHAEL FOSTER COUNSELS THE GRADUATES

also included as a school in the Faculty of Science, even though it was outside the prescribed thirty-mile radius.

A pretty varied array of institutions was thus brought together in the reconstituted University. The important additions, beside University and King's Colleges, the medical schools and the women's colleges, which have already been discussed, were the institutions for the natural sciences and technology in South Kensington and the institution for the social sciences in the form of the London School of Economics. They were major innovations adding to the stock of knowledge in London.

The origins of what was to become Imperial College can be found in the Royal Commission on Scientific Instruction and the Advancement of Science chaired between 1870 and 1875 by the Duke of Devonshire, the University's first Chancellor. It had recommended that the Royal College of Chemistry should be consolidated with parts of the Royal School of Mines (as the Government School of Mines had become in 1863) and moved to the South Kensington site belonging to the Commissioners of the 1851 Exhibition. In 1881 the composite institution was entitled the 'Normal School of Science and Royal School of Mines', with T.H. Huxley as its first Dean. Its name was awkward and Huxley's choice of 'Normal School' on a French model proved unsusceptible to anglicization. In 1890 it became regularized as the Royal College of Science. At first the University was kept at a distance. 'We had

194 A map showing the 'schools' and the 'institutions having recognized teachers' of the University of London Mark III contained in the first pamphlet of *General Information for Internal Students* published in 1906 – the first map the University produced of itself since 1842, presenting a very different picture (cf. **124**).

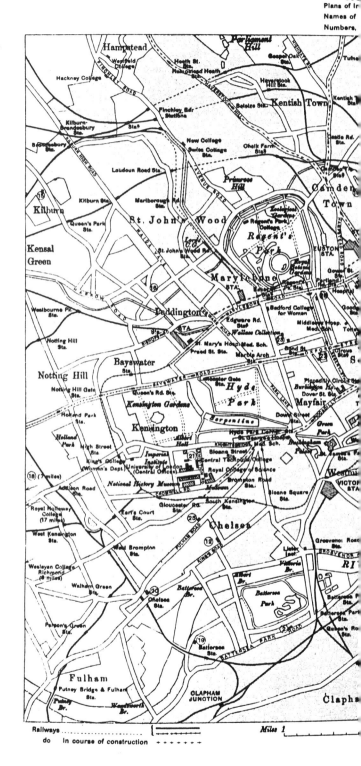

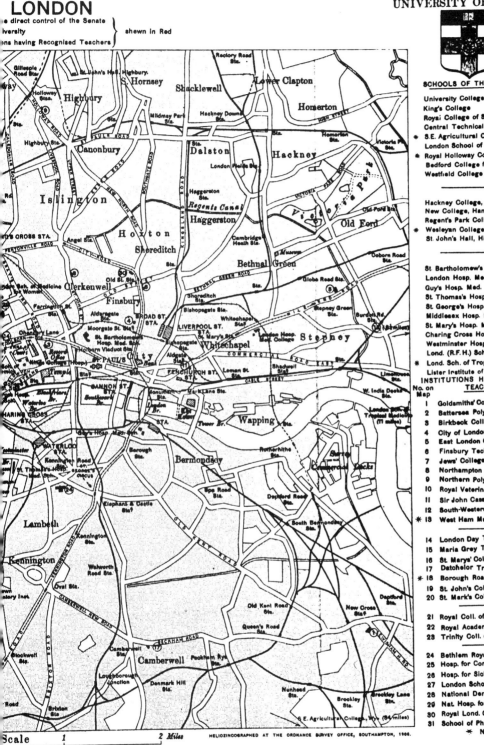

LONDON

...e direct control of the Senate
...iversity
...ns having Recognised Teachers ⎬ shewn in Red

UNIVERSITY OF LONDON

SCHOOLS OF THE UNIVERSITY

University College
King's College
Royai College of Science
Central Technical College
✱ S.E. Agricultural College, Wye
London School of Economics
✱ Royal Holloway College
Bedford College for Women
Westfield College

Hackney College, Hampstead
New College, Hampstead
Regent's Park College
✱ Wesleyan College, Richmond
St. John's Hall, Highbury

St. Bartholomew's Hosp. Med. Sch.
London Hosp. Med. College
Guy's Hosp. Med. Sch.
St. Thomas's Hosp. Med. Sch.
St. George's Hosp. Med. Sch.
Middlesex Hosp. Med. Sch.
St. Mary's Hosp. Med. Sch.
Charing Cross Hosp. Med. Sch.
Westminster Hosp. Med. Sch.
Lond. (R.F.H.) Sch. of Med. for Women
✱ Lond. Sch. of Tropical Medicine
Lister Institute of Preventive Medicine

INSTITUTIONS HAVING RECOGNISED TEACHERS

No. on Map	
1	Goldsmiths' College
2	Battersea Polytechnic
3	Birkbeck College
4	City of London College
5	East London College
6	Finsbury Technical Coll.
7	Jews' College
8	Northampton Institute
9	Northern Polytechnic Inst.
10	Royal Veterinary College
11	Sir John Cass Tech. Inst.
12	South-Western Polytechnic
✱ 13	West Ham Municipal Tech. Inst.
14	London Day Training College
15	Maria Grey Training College
16	St. Marys' Coll. Paddington
17	Datchelor Training College
✱ 18	Borough Road Coll. Isleworth
19	St. John's College, Battersea
20	St. Mark's Coll. Chelsea
21	Royal Coll. of Music
22	Royal Academy of Music
23	Trinity Coll. of Music
24	Bethlem Royal Hospital
25	Hosp. for Consumption
26	Hosp. for Sick Children
27	London School of Dental Surgery
28	National Dental Coll.
29	Nat. Hosp. for Paralysed & Epileptic
30	Royal Lond. Ophthalmic Hospital
31	School of Pharmacy

✱ Not shewn on the Map

Scale 1 · · · 2 Miles

HELIOZINCOGRAPHED AT THE ORDNANCE SURVEY OFFICE, SOUTHAMPTON, 1906.

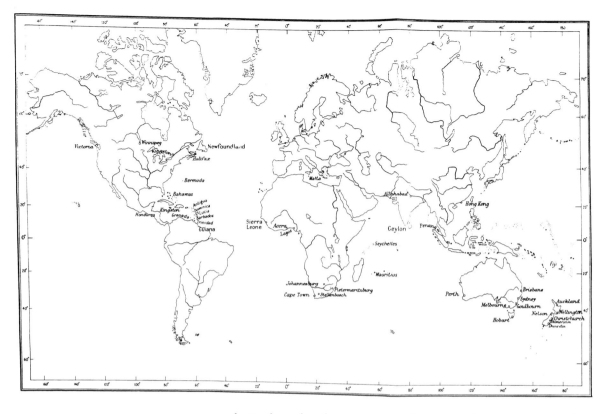

195 Besides the 'internal' side of the University of London, there remained the wider 'external' side. This map of the world identifies the various colonial centres overseas where London examinations could be taken between 1901 and 1910.

better keep free from any entanglement with universities', Huxley said, preferring to 'have everything in our system of instruction quite free from any syllabus laid down from the outside'. An entirely new body was created in 1878 as the City and Guilds of London Institute for the Advancement of Technical Education, a concerted effort of the City livery companies to do something for the trades from which they had become detached. In the forefront of its programme was the establishment of a Central Technical College for teaching more advanced than that provided by the lower-level technical colleges. It was decided to build the new College in South Kensington. Designed for 200 students, it opened in 1884. By the end of the century the two South Kensington colleges (three if the Royal School of Mines is counted separately) provided for a considerable range of sciences both pure and applied.

What South Kensington was beginning to do for the natural sciences and technology, the London School of Economics and Political Science was intended to do for the even more neglected social sciences. In 1895 Sidney Webb founded an entirely new institution without any British model, though on the lines of the *Ecole Libre des Sciences Politiques* in Paris. The first funds enabling him to begin the School came from a chance bequest from an eccentric Derby solicitor who left £10,000 to be used at Webb's discretion for advancing socialism and the objects of the Fabian Society. Webb used his discretion to ensure that the bequest was not frittered away on mere propaganda, but devoted to objective and impartial investigation and research, with 'educational lecturing' as a secondary intention. The first *Prospectus* (1895–6) of the School announced: 'While much attention will be given to the study of economic and political theory, the special aim of the School will be, from the first, the study and investigation of the concrete facts of industrial life and the actual working of economic and political institutions as they exist or have existed, in the United Kingdom or in foreign countries.' Webb was careful to appoint a non-socialist, W.A.S. Hewins, as the first Director, and he worked hard to ensure that the School, with its largely part-time students numbering over 400 by 1900, was accepted as the newest of the constituent parts of the reconstituted University.

Beside the constituent schools, the University's umbrella was extended over more than as many again 'institutions having recognized teachers'. The new statutes provided that there would be two categories of teachers in the University, those 'appointed' directly by the Senate, and a second category of those 'members of the teaching staffs of public educational institutions within the appointed radius whether Schools of the University or not as ...

196 In 1894 the old buildings of the decayed fifteenth-century college and grammar school at Wye were bought by the Kent and Surrey County Councils and re-opened as the South Eastern Agricultural College, which became one of the schools of the University in 1900. The hall – now a common room – was re-equipped as the refectory in 1894.

197 One of the new institutions provided by the drive to improve technical education, characteristic of the last quarter of the nineteenth century, was the South West Polytechnic Institute opened in 1895. Its objects were to 'offer to artisans and others engaged in technical and commercial industries a means of instruction in applied science and art, and similarly to women opportunities of training in cookery, dressmaking, and household management'. An 'institution having recognized teachers' of the University in 1900, it became 'Chelsea Poly' in 1922 and a school of the University in 1966 as Chelsea College.

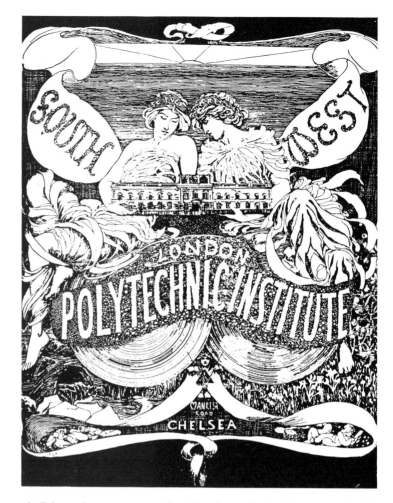

shall have been recognised as Teachers of the University by the Commissioners or shall thereafter be so recognised by the Senate'. Under this arrangement, a link was formed with a variety of other teaching institutions all over London – the various technical colleges and polytechnics that had grown up in the late nineteenth century, the several teachers' training colleges, and the music colleges. All the institutions at which individual teachers were 're-cognized' are listed alongside the map of the University in 1906 reproduced at **194**. It was a device of which Sidney Webb was particularly proud. All teachers, both 'appointed' and 'recognized', were members of the 'boards of studies' created for the thirty-two different subject-areas in which the reconstituted University was deemed to teach. The new boards were each to advise upon 'any matter relating to courses of study, provision for teaching or research, examinations and the appointment of Examiners, or the granting of degrees'.[2]

Efforts were made to include the Inns of Court in the reconstituted University either as separate schools or as a joint school. 'The Commissioners need scarcely point out', they wrote in 1899 to each of the four Inns, 'the great incentive and assistance which the Inns of Court have it in their power to offer the formation in London of a School of Law such as exists in the Universities of Continental countries and the United States, the want of which is not infrequently made a subject of reproach to this country.' The Inns of Court rejected this approach and their blunt letters of refusal were subsequently reprinted in the *Historical Record* and in the *Calendar* as a continued reproach.[3] 'We the more regret the conclusion', reported the Commissioners, 'because the University of London is honourably distinguished by being the first University in this country which conferred degrees in Laws after and as a result of adequate examinations ... We cannot but feel that the reconstitution of the University will be incomplete unless and until an adequate and effective Faculty of Laws has been established.'

Despite the inadequate gathering of the legal teaching arrangements, the grouping of the constituent bodies of the reconstituted University was almost as eclectic as the architecture of the building chosen for the new central offices. Additional schools were soon affiliated. Westfield College was admitted in the Faculty of Arts in 1902, the London School of Tropical Medicine and the Lister Institute of Preventative Medicine in 1905 into the Faculty of Medicine, the East London College into the Faculties of Arts, Science and Engineering in 1907, and the London Day Training College in the Faculty of Arts (Pedagogy only) in 1910. The reconstituted Senate – and its three standing committees, the Academic Council for the 'internal' side, the Council for External

198 The leading members of the staff of the London Day Training College photographed *c.*1913. The central figure is Sir John Adams (1857–1934), first Principal of the College and the first Professor of Education in the University. On the left is T.P. (later Sir Percy) Nunn (1870–1944), first appointed Lecturer in the Methods of Teaching Mathematics and Science in 1904, Vice-Principal from 1905, and Adams's successor as Principal in 1922. He exerted a profound influence on a generation of teachers through his *Education: Its Data and First Principles* (1920), and was responsible for transforming the College into the Institute of Education. On the right is Margaret Punnett, indispensable deputy to both Adams and Nunn.

199 The 'People's Palace' erected, as Queen Victoria said at the time of the opening in 1887, 'for the benefit of the people of East London, whose lives of unceasing toil will be cheered by the various opportunities of rational and instructive entertainment and of artistic enjoyment here afforded to them'. The attached technical schools grew into the East London Technical College (1896) and the East London College (1905), becoming in 1907 a school of the University, renamed in 1934 as Queen Mary College.

200 The London Day Training College was founded by the London County Council in 1902 just before the London Education Act of 1903 empowered it to become the local education authority and large numbers of secondary school teachers were needed. The College acquired a building of its own in Southampton Row, opened by Lord Rosebery in 1907. In 1932 it became the Institute of Education, moving to the northern wing of the Senate House in 1938; the Southampton Row premises became the Central School of Art and Design.

Students for the 'external' side, and the Board to Promote the Extension of University Teaching, taking over from the London Society for the Extension of University Teaching – set to work in earnest in the first decade of the twentieth century to fulfil its new obligations for organizing teaching and research throughout London.

The distinguished chemist Sir Henry Roscoe was re-elected Vice-Chancellor in 1901 and he suggested that the office, 'instead of being tenable during life, or the pleasure of the holder, as it practically has been in the past, should be tenable for a maximum of two years'. The new statutes required that members of the Senate (no longer entitled Fellows of the University) should elect one of their number annually to be Vice-Chancellor (as under the old Charters), but it now came to be accepted that the Vice-Chancellor should be re-elected only once to serve normally for a two-year period. The Vice-Chancellor remained unsalaried. The statutes permitted the Senate to appoint a 'Principal Officer', and they soon decided that it was necessary to act upon this power. After considering the titles of master, president, principal, provost, rector and warden, they voted for 'principal' and gave the post wide responsibilities to 'supervise the administration of the University, and advise the Senate and its committees on all matters relating to the internal and external organisation and development of the University'. The appointment committee recommended William Garnett, the secretary of the Technical Education Board of the LCC, but the Senate chose to appoint the physicist, Sir Arthur Rücker. He shouldered an enormous task.

At the first meeting of the Senate which Rücker attended as Principal in July 1901, it was pointed out that the expansion of the work of the central offices required the purchase of a third typewriter. A few months later a fourth 'and possibly fifth' typewriter was said to be urgently required: 'Owing to the great pressure of committee work it sometimes happens that two, or even three, officers simultaneously require the use of a typewriter for the preparation of minutes, reports, etc.' From March 1901 the officers of the University ceased to be civil servants, as they formally had been hitherto, and from May 1902 women typists were employed. The drive towards a central bureaucracy got off to a good start.

A change of major importance in the financial basis of the University was also made in 1901. Since 1884 the University had been seeking to alter the arrangement whereby the Treasury provided its building and equipment, even its stationery, and paid the salary of the officers and the other administrative expenses, collecting the examination fees in return, with the deficiency made up by annual

201 Sir Henry Roscoe, FRS (1833–1915), between 1896 and 1902 the last Vice-Chancellor of the old University and the first of the new. An outstanding chemist, he had been a student at University College in the early days of the Birkbeck Laboratory and had taken a PhD under Bunsen in Heidelberg before becoming Professor of Chemistry at Owens College Manchester from 1857 to 1885. He sat on the Royal Commission leading to the Technical Instruction Act of 1889 which channelled 'whisky money' into technical education.

202 The University presented its first honorary degrees in June 1903 to the Prince of Wales (LLD) and the Princess of Wales (DMus), later King George V and Queen Mary. The occasion was the first Presentation Day presided over by the 5th Earl of Rosebery (1847–1929), the former Prime Minister and Derby winner, as Chancellor of the University from 1902 to 1929. Honorary degrees were also presented to Lord Lister (DSc) and Lord Kelvin (DSc), two 'princes of science' as Rosebery called them.

203 Presentation Day in 1903 was the first to be held in the Albert Hall, filled to capacity with representatives of all the different institutions and groups of persons connected with the University, assembled together for the first time. Rücker read the Principal's annual report outlining the initial efforts of the reconstituted University to co-ordinate higher education in London.

204 Sir Arthur Rücker, FRS (1848–1915) was chosen to be the first Principal of the University between 1901 and 1908. He had been one of the founding professors at Yorkshire College, Leeds, in 1874, and Professor of Physics at the Royal College of Science from 1886. He insisted on a salary of £2000 a year and a guaranteed three-month vacation.

parliamentary vote. It was a complex financial arrangement, and one unparalleled in other universities. It became increasingly anomalous as the modest trickle of finance provided by the government to the new provincial universities from the 1880s took the form of outright grants with fewer strings attached. In 1901 the Chancellor of the Exchequer recognized that 'the existing financial arrangements are incompatible with the altered position of the University, and somewhat derogatory to its independence'. A fixed grant-in-aid was substituted. It was calculated at £8000, exclusive of rent, rates and external maintenance of the headquarters building, intended to cover 'the cost of internal maintenance and repairs, fuel, light and water, stationery and printing, estimated for the future at £4800, leaving a sum of £3200 towards the cost of the salary of a Principal Officer, additional examining, clerical and other officers, and incidental expenses'. The new arrangement was, in principle, a great advance but the sum proposed was hardly princely. The Senate accepted the proposal, but promptly resolved that 'the grant-in-aid proposed by the Treasury is wholly inadequate to enable the University to fulfil the work thrown upon it by the University of London Act, 1898'. The Treasury was not moved.

One of the grounds for objecting to the old arrangement was that the direct system of government financing discouraged gifts and endowments and 'diminishes the interest which the inhabitants of London ought to take in their chief academic institutions'. The University of London Mark II indeed had received virtually nothing by way of private or civic benevolence. In proposing the new arrangement, the Treasury expressed the hope that the University would 'appeal with success to the City of London or to local or private munificence for the means required fully to carry out the objects for which it is now constituted'.[4] It was only the grant of £10,000 a year newly provided by the LCC which enabled the University of London Mark III to begin to pretend to embark on its large aims.

Two notable gifts soon came from the Goldsmiths' Company, first a library and then a whole college. The library was the great collection (over 50,000 items) on economics and economic thought formed by H.S. Foxwell, who was Professor of Political Economy at University College from 1881 to 1927, as well as a teacher at the LSE and in Cambridge. Foxwell devoted much of his life to acquiring books, letting it be known that he believed a library was better than a wife. Eventually he got married and the library had to go. The Goldsmiths' Company bought it and presented it to the University in 1903. (Foxwell later built up a second library, almost as comprehensive as the first; that in turn was sold in 1929 to Harvard.) What

205 The Goldsmiths' Company presented their 'Technical and Recreative Institute' at New Cross to the University and it was re-opened as Goldsmiths' College in 1905, with a complex constitutional basis. To the premises originally built for the Royal Naval School in 1843, new buildings designed by Sir Reginald Blomfield were added in 1908, seen here on sports day in that year.

206 Professor A.D. Waller, FRS (1856–1922), pictured with his beloved pet dog 'Jimmie' which featured in his successful experiments to develop the electro-cardiograph (and in 1909 in questions in Parliament). From 1902 Waller directed the University Physiological Laboratory which anomalously remained in the Imperial Institute after the failure to establish a central Institute of Medical Sciences.

became the Goldsmiths' Library of Economic Literature was added to the University Library, re-opened in the Imperial Institute after some years of chaos in 1906. A year after they had made this present to the University, the Goldsmiths' decided to offer the whole of the New Cross premises of the Goldsmiths' Company's Technical and Recreative Institute, a sort of polytechnic for south London founded in 1891. It was re-opened as Goldsmiths' College in 1905. From the start it was a hybrid institution, part teachers' training college, part school of art, part adult education centre. To confound description further, Goldsmiths' College was owned by the University, but was not a school of the University. It belonged to the University, but it did not belong to the University. It was not an easily classifiable entity, but it was an evident addition to the already complex pattern of the new University of London.

The first piece of major reorganization the reconstituted University attempted ended in disaster. The University plunged into the deep end of academic politics – the reorganization of medical teaching. It nearly drowned. Plans were formulated to centralize the pre-clinical teaching of medicine in a new Institute of Medical Sciences to be built in South Kensington and in 1903 the University's first public appeal for funds was launched for this purpose. Four years later, with £70,000 raised towards the total of £375,000, the proposals had to be dropped, not for lack of finance, but for lack of agreement among the Faculty of Medicine. The various medical schools simply refused to accept any scheme of centralized co-operation. In 1907 the funds raised had to be publicly and damagingly returned to the donors. 'The ignoble petty competition between the schools,' commented one observer, 'the undercutting of fees, the jealousy by the small of the great, by the unendowed of the endowed, is once more in full swing.' Some less general measure of co-operation was subsequently achieved, with the medical schools

207 The elegant letter-heading used by Goldsmiths' College in the 1910s.

UNIVERSITY OF LONDON
GOLDSMITHS' COLLEGE
NEW CROSS. S.E. ⊛⊛⊛

of St George's, Westminster and Charing Cross giving up their pre-clinical teaching to the much larger establishments at University and King's Colleges. A relic of the scheme remained in the form of the Physiological Laboratory established in the Imperial Institute in 1902, an island of academic research amidst a sea of administrators. As a department of the University, not connected to a school, it was a constitutional curiosity, surviving with financial support obtained by the Director, A.D. Waller, from his wife's family, the rich biscuit-making Palmers. For twenty years Waller enjoyed taking part in most of the University's controversies and the Physiological Laboratory did useful work, but it did not outlive him. It was to be closed in 1923, and the space greedily taken over by the growth of administration.

The other major piece of reorganization the University embarked upon was less disastrous than the abortive Institute of Medical Sciences, but little less controversial. As an impressive gesture of confidence intended to make the idea of the teaching University a reality, University College offered to 'incorporate' itself into the University. The College proposed to vest its freehold and all its buildings in the University, agreeing to cease to exist as a separate legal entity, with the Senate becoming its governing body. A successful appeal was launched in 1902 to fund this change, inaugurated by the Drapers' Company agreeing to pay off the College's accumulated deficit of £30,000. It was necessary for University College School and the Medical School to be constituted as separate bodies. In 1907 University College School's new buildings were opened in Hampstead and the new University College Hospital Medical School was opened on the other side of Gower Street. Much space was released for development on the University College site at the same time as the legal ramifications of the University College London (Transfer) Act of 1905 came into effect. King's College followed suit. King's College School had already migrated from the Strand to Wimbledon in 1897 and though the King's appeal was less successful than that of University College, enough money was raised to enable the King's College London (Transfer) Act of 1908 to take effect in 1910. King's College School and King's College Hospital Medical School became separate

208 Sir Edward Busk (1844–1926), painted by Sargent: a City solicitor who was the longest-serving Chairman of Convocation from 1892 to 1922, uniquely combining this office with the Vice-Chancellorship between 1905 and 1907.

209 The souvenir menu cover of a reception held by the municipality of Paris in 1907 for the University of London delegation visiting the French capital to celebrate the intellectual *entente cordiale* and the University's arrival in the international academic world.

bodies, as did the College's Theological Department. The two main London colleges were no longer to be competing little universities by themselves – so it was argued – but were now to work together as incorporated parts of one great University governed by committees of its Senate, the University College Committee and the King's College Delegacy.[5] The Principal of the University proudly announced that it would be difficult to exaggerate either the importance of the union thus accomplished or the significance of the opportunities created for the improved organization of teaching. What Rücker found difficult, others were to find easy. The incorporation of the two colleges did not, in the event, produce the unity that was hoped for.

By the end of the first decade of its reconstituted existence, the University of London, especially its doubly reconstituted 'internal' side, became conscious that with a total of over 4000 registered students it exceeded both Oxford and Cambridge in size, and that it had become easily the biggest university in the country. In 1908 Sidney Webb said it was still difficult to persuade people that there was a University of London, yet it was the fourth or fifth largest in the world. The University moved in various ways to polish its self-image. Rücker began to edit the *London University Gazette* as an official organ to inform the University about itself. In 1902 Roscoe presented a handsome mace designed by Omar Ramsden to be the symbol of the Vice-Chancellor's authority for ceremonial purposes. In June 1906 a great 'French Academic Visit' was arranged, with 'many French men of letters and of science' coming to London 'to draw closer the bonds between the two countries'. An 'intellectual *entente cordiale*' was celebrated, with receptions at the Foreign Office and at Windsor, marking the 'bringing together of the University of Paris and one of the more recent of her offspring'. In May 1907 delegates from the University went to Paris for a return official visit. After Presentation Day in 1907 the first University service at Westminster Abbey was held, somewhat controversially given the non-sectarian basis of the University; it was not regarded as an official occasion, though the officers of the University attended in their robes. In 1909, as part of the over-enthusiastic drive for the reconstituted University to take on all the trappings of the traditional universities, an agreement was reached to establish the 'University of London Press' with a gentleman, ignorant of publishing, who had astutely registered the title earlier. For many years books were published under its imprint, but it became a department of Hodder & Stoughton, without any control by the University.[6] In 1910 the office of Public Orator was created, with the duty of 'writing Latin and English addresses', elegantly carried out by Professor E.A. Gardner (until 1932, with an interruption in the First World War).

In various ways the University, hitherto a *mater* not so much *alma* as *dura*, began to attempt to acquire a human face. As well as teachers, the University found that it had acquired students for the first time after 1900. It took some time to adjust to this discovery. In 1905 a Students' Representative Council was formed 'to represent student interests, to afford a recognised means of communication between students and the University authorities, and to promote intercourse between the Schools'. A University of London Musical Society was also founded in 1905, holding its first concert in the Jehanghir Hall at the Imperial Institute under the guidance of Sir Frederick Bridge, the first King Edward Professor of Music in the University. The Athletic Union followed in 1906, beginning a great tradition of intercollegiate sporting activities. The first University Union Society was also founded in 1906, though it never succeeded in acquiring premises of its own and its activities were limited to the holding of peripatetic debates around the various colleges. Other societies were begun, the Inter-Collegiate Law Students' Society in 1909, the Chess Club in 1910, the Women's Swimming Club in 1911. A movement to promote hostels or halls of residence for students started. In 1909 an Appointments Board was established 'to assist graduates and students of the University in obtaining appointments, and to co-ordinate and to supplement the work done by the Schools and Institutions of the University with this aim'. In these years, the presence of 'undergrads' began to make itself felt at Presentation Day, the University's only formal public occasion. A 'good deal of noisy demonstration by the undergraduates in the gallery' came to be a feature of the proceedings. In 1909 the Vice-Chancellor made reference to their 'ebullitions' – 'those facetious felicities', he called them, 'which so immensely enliven the monotony of our proceedings'. In the first decade of the twentieth century the University thus became aware of having a student body, however divided the students were in their loyalties. The life of the University as a community was further advanced by the establishment of a 'University Club' for graduates and officers of the University, opened in 1914 in premises in Gower Street, pointedly chosen as more topographically central than South Kensington.

Public evidence of the developing University spirit among the students of the various colleges was provided by the 'brown dog affair' of 1907–8. A famous libel action in 1903 had completely cleared physiologists at University College of any cruelty to the dog used humanely for experimental purposes, but anti-vivisectionists had a statue of the 'brown dog' erected on a recreation

210 In 1907 designs were registered for ribbons in the University colours around a jacket with the University arms as a badge, and also for a hat ribbon, a silk scarf and a tie: part of the Edwardian effort to bring the Varsity touch to the London undergrad.

ground in Battersea in 1906. Student demonstrations against it hit the headlines in 1907. There were many lively meetings and marches and several students were fined for riotous behaviour. The issue escalated and became tangled, as such issues do, when a suffragette meeting was disrupted by 'brown doggers' smashing tables, chairs and water jugs, 'and one steward had his ear badly torn'. Eventually, the offensive statue was removed, but not before it had resulted in 'drawing together the undergraduates from all Schools of the University ... teaching them to work together unitedly in a way that no previous incident had done'.[7] The organization which more than any other brought together students from the different colleges was the University contingent of the Officers' Training Corps created in 1909 by Haldane as part of the army reforms he effected as Secretary of State for War. No fewer than 783 students enrolled as cadets in the first year of the OTC, and by the end of 1910 there was a strength of over 950. Besides the military training it provided, the OTC became a centre for much energetic (male) student activity. It met a need no other student body could yet rise to.

By then, Haldane had had a greater and more direct impact on the structure of the University of London. He was, more than anyone else, responsible for the creation of the Imperial College of Science and Technology in 1907. The three constituent parts – the Royal School of Mines, the Royal College of Science and the Central Technical College (re-named in 1907 the City and Guilds College) – had existed for a generation in close proximity in South Kensington, but with little co-operation between them. Haldane was not alone in seeing them as a potential nucleus of an English version of the famous German *Technische Hochschule* at Charlottenburg. As chairman of a departmental committee appointed by the Board of Education in 1904–6, he was responsible for the proposal that they should be joined together to form a concentration of resources 'to give the highest specialised instruction and to provide the fullest equipment for the most advanced training and research in various branches of science, especially in its application to industry'. Without losing their separate identity, the three institutions were rapidly brought together to form the new Imperial College by charter in 1907. Imperial College became a school of the University in 1908, but with a recommendation that a Royal Commission should examine the way in which it should form part of the University. There was strong pressure that it should 'incorporate' itself fully as University College and King's College had done. There was even stronger pressure that it should constitute a separate university in its own right. The Senate of the University was ill-constituted to address itself sensibly to so critical an issue, quite apart from all the

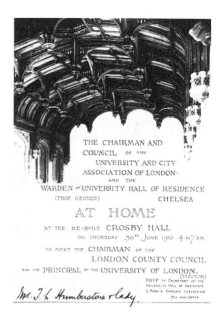

211 The first hall of residence recognized by the University was opened in Chelsea in 1908, under the control of Professor Patrick Geddes, the famous educationalist, sociologist and town-planner, who somehow combined the post with the chair of botany at Dundee. Soon afterwards Crosby Hall, a fine fifteenth-century City residence, was rebuilt nearby and developed into an independent women's hostel.

212 In 1906 anti-vivisectionists erected a statue in Battersea of the famous 'brown dog' supposedly 'done to death' in the laboratories of University College in 1903. The provocative inscription duly provoked the students of University College and the other colleges and medical schools, leading to a 'crescendo of disorder' in 1907 when students took direct action against the statue amidst a series of protest meetings and marches. The issue united London students as they had never been united before. The statue was eventually removed in 1910.

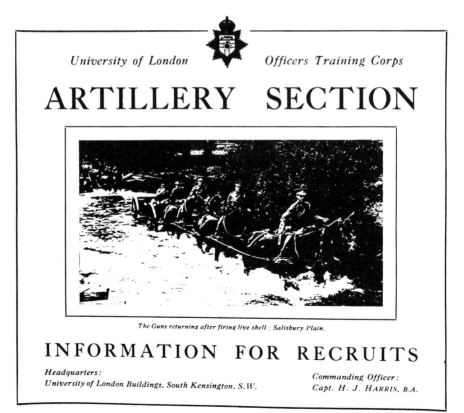

University of London — Officers Training Corps

ARTILLERY SECTION

The Guns returning after firing live shell : Salisbury Plain.

INFORMATION FOR RECRUITS

Headquarters:
University of London Buildings, South Kensington, S.W.

Commanding Officer:
Capt. H. J. HARRIS, B.A.

213 The first general parade of the University's OTC was held on the occasion of Presentation Day in May 1909. The Director of the Territorial Force spoke from the balcony of the Imperial Institute to the men, over 400 of them drawn up for inspection.

214 By the eve of the First World War the strength of the OTC consisted of over 950 students who had all volunteered to join as cadets. The establishment consisted of a battalion of infantry, an artillery section, a company of engineers and a medical unit. Training camps were held on Salisbury Plain.

215 Besides providing military training and guards of honour at University ceremonies, the OTC was a centre of much social activity, with dinners, theatricals and 'smoking concerts'. Lord Rosebery, as Chancellor, presided at the first annual dinner in 1911.

other besetting problems on which it could not agree. The Senate favoured the appointment of a new Royal Commission, but it was shocked in 1909 to find that one was set up without further consultation, and that Haldane was to be the chairman in addition to his responsibilities as a member of the Cabinet.

The terms of reference of the Royal Commission were sweeping:

to inquire into the working of the present organisation of the University of London, and into other facilities for advanced education (general, professional, and technical) existing in London for persons of either sex above secondary school age; to consider what provision should exist in the Metropolis for University teaching and research; to make recommendations as to the relations which should in consequence subsist between the University of London, its incorporated Colleges, the Imperial College of Science and Technology, the other Schools of the University, and the various public institutions and bodies concerned; and further to recommend as to any changes of constitution and organisation which appear desirable.

216 Sir Philip Magnus (1842–1933), the gravely energetic Jewish minister who was the first Organising Director of the City and Guilds of London Institute, 1880–1913. He was elected Unionist MP for the University in 1906, sitting until 1922. 'The Commons is, I am sorry to say', he wrote after ten years' experience, 'the last place in which any speaker urging educational reform receives a sympathetic hearing'.

Apart from Haldane, the seven other members were all unconnected with the University of London. Lord Milner had been much concerned with the Empire; Sir Robert Romer had been a Lord Justice of Appeal; Laurence Currie was a banker; Sir William M'Cormick was the secretary of the Carnegie Trust for Scottish Universities (and later the first chairman of the re-founded UGC in 1919); E.G. Sargant was the educationalist in Milner's circle; and Mrs Creighton, widow of the historian Bishop of London, was the statutory woman. That there was no medical member was immediately found deeply sinister. During the four years until it reported in 1913, Haldane's Royal Commission hung like an ominous cloud over the University, legitimizing procrastination of all major decisions.

In 1900 the University of London attempted to turn over a new leaf, but the blots of the old disputes continued to show through. The University was, Sir Ray Lankester plausibly claimed in 1912, 'the largest body of committees and sub-committees in the world — elected chiefly by the managing committees of a number of struggling schools and underpaid colleges in London, and so organised as to defeat each other's purposes'.[8] While it was becoming the largest university in Britain and in the British Empire, the University was controlled by a Senate that represented only some of the heterogeneous elements it brought together, as well as other interests that were divergent on almost every possible issue. The absence of any power to delegate business, it was admitted in 1908, 'paralyses the activities of the Senate by choking its agenda with the minutiae and petty details of administration'. The various colleges continued to consider themselves before the University as a whole. Above all, the transition to the new order was bedevilled by the great divide between the 'internal' and the 'external' interests. The old duality of teaching university versus examining university became a new dualism of college versus university. Moreover, after University College and King's College were incorporated into the University, it was felt, as A.D. Waller put it in 1912, that they 'have steadily drawn the clothes over to their side of the bed, and steadily complained of the intolerable pretensions of the External bedfellow'.[9] The resulting acrimony was most evident in the long battle which took place concerning the site of the University headquarters.

By 1907, the expansion of its activities meant that the University found its accommodation at the Imperial Institute 'wholly inadequate'. As early as 1902, despite the use of 'ice-pails' to keep the temperature down, the conditions for examinations in the so-called Great Hall — the 'temporary' structure of wood and cor-

217 The first of the scientific teaching institutions in South Kensington out of which Imperial College was to grow, pictured soon after its opening in the 1870s as part of the Royal School of Mines. In 1881 it became the Normal School of Science and in 1890 the Royal College of Science. Later known as the Huxley Building, it is now the Henry Cole wing of the Victoria and Albert Museum. The atmosphere of the 1880s when H.G. Wells was a student is captured in his novel *Love and Mr Lewisham* (1900).

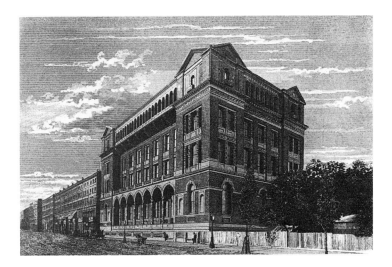

218 The Central Technical College (later known as the City and Guilds College) in Exhibition Road, South Kensington, as drawn when building began in 1881 by the architect, Alfred Waterhouse, who knew how to hide a practical interior behind an imposing façade. It was demolished in 1962 and replaced by buildings designed by architects with different ideals.

rugated iron erected for the royal opening in 1893 – proved to be appalling. The Principal informed the Treasury that 'several candidates generally faint or have to be removed from the Hall'. The Fire Brigade recommended that large ceremonial occasions should not be held there, though for many years they had to be. Lord Rosebery admitted that it was 'far more suitable for the rearing of tropical tree ferns . . . than any purpose of public utility'. Examinees elsewhere in the building were no better off. 'In the dimly-lighted and mouldy basement', a 1910 press report stated, 'examinations were being conducted in rooms whose approaches resembled the ancient catacombs.' Many of the 150 administrative and secretarial staff were by then housed in wooden partitions constructed in the long corridors. There was much memorializing of the government on the subject, and much intense construing of the Treasury Minute of 1899 which apparently promised not only the Imperial Institute accommodation, but: 'and also such provision as may hereafter be needed for the full extension and development of the University'. Treasury Minutes are generally composed carefully to avoid rash statements, but many held that this was an open-ended promise of further government support. All agreed that some meaning had to be attached to the phrase.[10] The Treasury kept mum.

Much later, Sir Halford Mackinder, Director of the London School of Economics from 1903 to 1908, gave an account of an episode of scheming not revealed in the official records of the University.[11]

As the result of secret negotiation it became suddenly known in the autumn of 1905 to those whom it should concern that on certain conditions the University could have the whole of the building at South Kensington which was erected for the Imperial Institute, and a proposal was entertained for spending £100,000 economically on a great hall behind the existing façade. Eleven members of the Senate, including Principals Gregory Foster and Headlam, Sir William Ramsay, Professors Hill, Farmer, and Loney, Dr Russell Wells, and the late Vice-Chancellor Hatton, banded themselves together in opposition. We met first in my room at the School of Economics, and through that winter 'the Eleven' dined together frequently and took counsel. A majority of the Senate were for accepting the bird in the hand, but our group was united in the view that the centre of the University must be in the centre of London, in a building erected for the purpose, which every cabman would know as the University, and that it should be near the British Museum and within the belt of great colleges aligned from Bedford College to King's College. Aldwych at that time still largely unoccupied by buildings, and we had our eyes on a site there and around Lincoln's Inn Fields, but we had not even a prospect of money.

Feeling ran high between the practical men and the idealists. The critical meeting of the Senate took place on March 7, 1906. The Chancellor, Lord Rosebery, was brought down to preside and keep the naughty boys in order. He spoke up for South Kensington, as did Lords Justices Cozens Hardy and Fletcher Moulton, and Sir Francis Mowatt, ex-Permanent Secretary to the Treasury. Their policy in the debate had been settled at a dinner on the 5th given by Sir Henry Roscoe. The proceedings were complicated by vexed questions concerning the Faculty of Engineering, by the still acute rivalry between the externals and the teachers, and by the desire of some to help incidentally in solving the financial difficulties of the Imperial Institute, but we kept our front unbroken, the other side did not venture to challenge a direct vote involving the main issue, and the negative therefore prevailed.

What began in 1905 was to be the major political issue for the University over the next twenty-two years. Much debilitating and self-destructive energy was devoted to it. The question of the location of the central offices became a symbol for the differences between the interests so hopefully but inadequately brought together by the reconstitution of 1900.

Frantic discussion of the issue was unleashed by an interim report of the Haldane Commission published at the end of 1911. 'We think', said the Commissioners, 'that, whatever its future constitution may be, it is a matter of national importance that the University of London should be recognised and accepted as a great public institution.' They therefore recommended 'that such an institution should have for its headquarters permanent buildings appropriate in design to its dignity and importance, adequate in extent and specially constructed for its purposes, situated conveniently for the work it has to do, bearing its name and under its own control'. It was considered that the Imperial Institute building failed to satisfy this purpose and that it could not be made suitable. It was not sufficiently central.

219 A view produced for the *Graphic* of the site proposed by the Haldane commission in 1911 for the central building of the University. The 2½ acres belonged to the Bedford estate in Bloomsbury, immediately to the north of the new extension to the British Museum. The Senate House was eventually built on the site between 1933 and 1938.

THE ACADEMIC SIDE OF BLOOMSBURY
THE PROPOSED SITE FOR LONDON UNIVERSITY

It lies on the western side of the circumference of a circle which embraces most of the University Institutions of importance, and we have had evidence that its remoteness has occasioned much inconvenience and loss of time to those who are concerned with the working of the University, and has exercised a harmful effect on its development. The buildings are shared with the Imperial Institute and are known by that name, and they have never become associated with the University in the minds of the public. The care of the fabric is in the hands of Your Majesty's Office of Works, so that the University is not master in its own house.

The recommendation was that 'as large a site as possible should be obtained in a central position, and buildings erected for a reconstituted University which would be the visible sign of its recognition and acceptance as a great public institution'.

When this recommendation was hurriedly published, Haldane had already identified the area of the present Senate House as the most appropriate site for the University's central building. He had obtained the personal approval of the Prime Minister and had secretly established a body of trustees (including the mysterious Sir Francis Trippel, as well as the Chancellor, Lord Rosebery) to acquire the money to buy the land from the Duke of Bedford, who was keen to sell. The Bedford estate had already begun to redevelop the area, widening the former Keppel Mews North in 1907 to create a fine new thoroughfare named Malet Street after the Duke's brother-in-law Sir Edward Malet, the diplomat who, as the *DNB* points out, had in the 1880s 'helped to restore financial stability and soothe native unrest in Egypt'. The Drapers' Company generously offered £60,000 and other promises were confidentially received towards the cost, not openly revealed but reported to be £375,000. The Senate of the University was not consulted at all, and the Senate was furious. At its meeting in March 1912, the Vice-Chancellor, Sir William Collins, hopping mad at not being consulted himself, offered his resignation. The offer was not accepted at the time, but a few weeks later by one vote the Senate did not re-elect him as Vice-Chancellor. The standing committee of Convocation censured the Chancellor for agreeing to become one of the trustees, though Rosebery confessed that he could not believe it 'entered anyone's head that the University would object to money being collected for it'.

The extraordinary controversy over the site issue spilled out into the press and the resulting consternation was reported with glee. 'During the last few days', one newspaper noted in April 1912, 'the average Londoner has probably heard more about the University of the metropolis than at any period of its existence.' The Senate refused to countenance the possibility of the Bloomsbury site, the

220 Another view of the same site in 1914. The other empty site, shown in black between Gower Street and Malet Street, was then being proposed for the projected Shakespeare Memorial Theatre. It later became the site of the London School of Hygiene and Tropical Medicine.

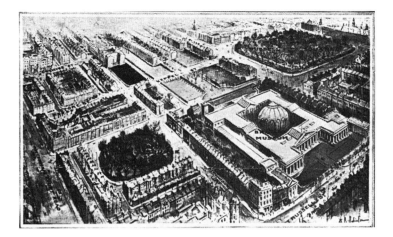

221 In 1912–14 the first stage of a convoluted debate was actively pursued concerning the merits of the original proposed site in Bloomsbury compared with various other sites, four of which are shown here: the Foundling Hospital site also in Bloomsbury, Somerset House, and two south bank sites, one next to the new County Hall and one the future site of the National Theatre.

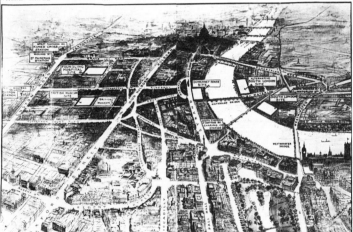

222 Soon after the Bloomsbury site was first proposed, this design for the new building was suggested in 1912; classical re-revival buildings – a sort of cross between University College and County Hall – were to face the new British Museum extension across ornamental gardens.

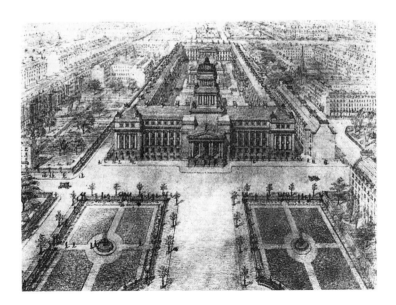

offers of money were spurned, and the merits of as many as twelve alternative sites were agitatedly canvassed. In July 1913, the Senate voted in favour of the Foundling Hospital site, despite the absence of any offers of financial support for it, but later swung to support staying in South Kensington. The whole episode was a fiasco. It reflected no credit on the University at all. Haldane's plot was a conspicuous failure. 'Haldane', as Campbell-Bannerman said, 'always prefers the backstairs to the frontstairs; but it does not matter; for the clatter can be heard all over the house.'[12] The clatter was heard all over London in 1912.

The controversy was not settled when the final report of the Haldane Commission was published in March 1913. The flames were fanned. Sweeping changes were proposed for the constitution of the University. The central recommendation was that 'the teaching of the University in its several faculties should be concentrated as far as possible in one place'. 'We think the aim should be to bring the Constituent Colleges and University Departments together . . .

223 A cartoon satirizing some of the reaction to the Haldane Report, appearing in the first (and only) issue of *The Undergraduate*, the magazine of the Students' Representative Council, in 1913.

and group them round the central buildings of the University . . .' A 'University quarter' needed to be created in which all London's teaching resources should be re-grouped by faculty and subject in a new centralized system replacing the various existing institutions which had grown up separately. 'So strongly indeed do we hold the view that . . . it would be better not to interfere at all with the existing constitution than to attempt anything less fundamental.' In essence, it was strongly argued that the faculties should replace the colleges. The Senate was to become a much smaller body, an executive committee of fifteen members, under a 'Court', a large representative governing body of some 200 members, with a permanent salaried Vice-Chancellor at the head. Completely revised constitutional arrangements were spelt out in detail in the Haldane Report. The University of London was to be reconstituted on the lines of the unitary English provincial universities, with strong influences from the Scottish universities and from the German universities so much admired by Haldane, an alumnus of Edinburgh and Göttingen.

The proposal that the external degrees should be phased out provoked a predictable outcry from many members of the Senate and of Convocation. The radical changes proposed for medical education especially produced a horrified reaction from the medical establishment. The medical schools were prepared to use the University of London for purposes which suited them, but were totally opposed to being in any way directed, or co-ordinated by the University. In the history of one of them there is a revealing erratum slip: 'It should be noted that when the University of London was reconstituted in 1900 the Middlesex Hospital Medical School became a School of the University.'[13] That this fact was not noted in the text is wholly revealing of the attitudes of the medical schools in general. They were not to be pushed around by the upstart University, much less by a Royal Commission unreceptive to received English medical wisdom, and which suggested anything so distressing as reform. Haldane's medical proposals were indeed drastic. He was influenced by the views of Abraham Flexner, an American who compared medical teaching in London unfavourably with that of other countries. 'Clinical teaching in London', Flexner argued,

remains an incident in the life of a busy consultant who comes to his post through promotion on the basis of seniority, and visits his too miscellaneous wards twice weekly in the afternoon between, perhaps, two and four, in company with his house physician and clinical clerks. There is no certain or direct interaction between the fundamental scientists and the clinicians . . . The first step in the direction of modernising education would appear to lie in the total conversion of an existing School or in the creation in London of a new School, the clinical Faculty selected upon precisely the same lines as the scientific Faculty, the entire body of teachers animated by one ideal and working as an organic unit towards a single end. The clinician's relation to the hospital must reproduce the chemist's relation to his laboratory.

Haldane proposed that it was 'necessary to appoint and pay professors of the various branches of clinical medicine and surgery who will devote the greater part of their time to teaching and research'. A new type of 'hospital unit' under the control of a new type of professor had to be created. Haldane's proposals were castigated as 'the attempted Germanization of London University', and gave rise to much bitter controversy.[14]

In August 1913 the Board of Education set up a powerful departmental committee under the chairmanship of Sir George Murray, a former Permanent Secretary of the Treasury, to determine the steps to be taken to enforce Haldane's proposals on the University of London. The committee was grappling with its task when fate intervened in the form of the First World War. The committee came to an abrupt end and the reform of the University was left in suspense. The Vice-Chancellor, Sir Wilmot Herringham, opened the new session in October 1914 wearing the uniform of a lieutenant-colonel commanding a military hospital instead of his vice-chancellorial robes. He soon left for the front in France, and was succeeded by another uniformed medical man, Sir Alfred Pearce Gould. In 1915, Rücker's successor as Principal, Sir Henry Miers, overwhelmed by his administrative burdens and the stress of the conflicts within the University, resigned. 'The work attached to the Principalship of the University of London', he was quoted as saying, 'is almost more than can be expected of any one man.' He took refuge in the quieter pastures of the Vice-Chancellorship of Manchester. As an economy measure, the office of Principal was left vacant for the rest of the war.

Much of the University's manpower was diverted to the war effort. Large numbers of students answered their country's call and within the first year, 226 had been killed. The loss of students brought about a disastrous fall in the fee income on which the University was heavily dependent. A special grant from the Treasury enabled the University to keep going, but the Senate resolved to suspend all new developments during the war. Nevertheless there were at least three noteworthy wartime developments. One of the Haldane recommendations relating to King's College was put into effect. What in 1908 had become King's College for Women was set to develop as a separate women's college in Kensington, but Haldane thought

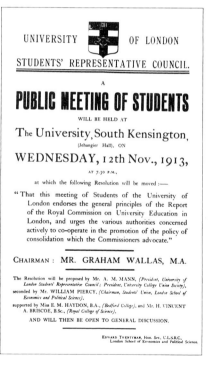

224 The first general meeting of students was called in November 1913 to discuss the Haldane Report. Over 1500 attended, and the debate was vigorous. The chair was taken by Graham Wallas, author of *Human Nature in Politics* (1908), and Professor of Political Science at LSE, 1914–23.

DR. SCOTT LIDGETT PLEADS FOR A GREAT LONDON UNIVERSITY.

225 Scott Lidgett (1854–1953) pleading for 'a great London University' at an LCC meeting in July 1914 while the post-Haldane departmental committee was discussing its future. A Methodist minister who founded the Bermondsey Settlement and edited the *Contemporary Review*, he was leader of the Progressive Party on the LCC, 1918–28, and later Vice-Chancellor of the University in 1930–2.

226 Sir Henry Miers, FRS (1858–1942), the second Principal of the University between 1908 and 1915. 'The ideal chairman of committees', with great Old Etonian charm, he had worked on mineralogy at the Natural History Museum and taught crystallography at the Central Technical College before becoming Waynflete Professor of Mineralogy at Oxford, 1895–1908. 'Always conciliatory and anxious to extract the best from the views of opposing parties, he held the University together at a time when it was threatening to fall apart.'

227 Sir Alfred Pearce Gould (1842–1922), the wise and kindly surgeon who was Dean of the Middlesex Hospital Medical School, 1886–92, Dean of the University Faculty of Medicine, 1912–16, and Vice-Chancellor, 1915–17, photographed wearing the vice-chancellorial robe over his Royal Army Medical Corps uniform.

it was unnecessary. He recommended instead that part of it should become what he called a University Department of Household and Social Science. The new buildings begun on Campden Hill therefore did not become King's College for Women in 1915, but housed a new institution of indeterminate status which became a separate school of the University in 1928 as King's College for Household and Social Science. In 1915 there was another development at King's that initiated what was also later to become a separate institution. Under the aegis of Ronald Burrows, Principal of the College from 1913 to 1920, King's became a 'powerhouse of academic propaganda in favour of national self-determinaton for the peoples of eastern Europe'.[15] Thomas Masaryk, in temporary exile from what he hoped would become Czechoslovakia, was given an unpaid post, along with other emigrés. A School of Slavonic Studies in embryo was established, years before it became independent of the College in 1932. Thirdly, after a long period of planning, the School of Oriental Studies was constituted as a separate school of the University in 1916 and opened in 1917. Teaching posts in various oriental subjects were transferred there from both King's College and University College.

The years after the end of the war were ones of considerable expansion, building rapidly on the trends established before 1914. The scale of the University increased conspicuously. Sir Cooper Perry, the former Vice-Chancellor who became Principal when that post was re-filled in 1920, could soon speak of the 'almost geometrical progress' of the University. At University College the number of students increased from just over 2000 on the eve of the war to over 3000 in the early 1920s. By 1923 King's College had

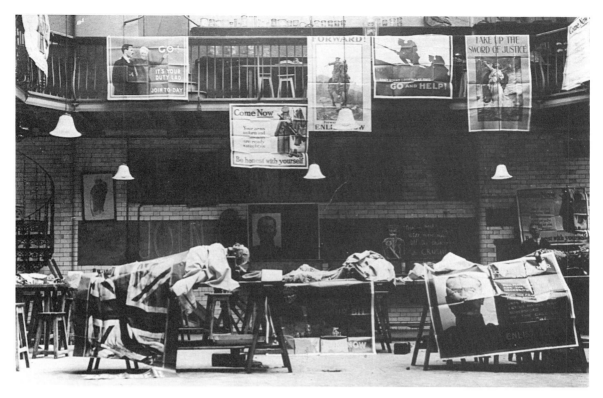

228 A gruesome but symbolic scene in the dissecting room at St Bartholomew's Hospital Medical College photographed in 1915, with First World War recruiting posters surrounding the cadavers.

229 Most colleges were depleted of students between 1914 and 1918; one that was not was the new Department of Household and Social Science, part of the King's College for Women which existed only in name. 'Cookery lessons in a trench dug-out' were a feature, 'as a training for nurses leaving for the front, where the cooking is often done out of doors'.

230 The new buildings in Campden Hill, Kensington, designed by Adams, Holden and Pearson for King's College for Women, but opened in 1915 for the Department of Household and Social Science when the bulk of King's College for Women was amalgamated with King's College itself in the complicated aftermath of the Haldane Report.

over 4000 students. Bedford College never had more than 300 students before it moved to Regent's Park in 1913; in the 1920s it had 600. A similar story was repeated throughout the various colleges whatever their size or type, and the overall results of the expansion are indicated in the statistics in table 5.1. The rapid growth is evident in the numbers of students, examinees and graduates in the periods immediately before and immediately after the war.

Table 5.1   Numbers of Students, Examination Candidates and Graduates, 1900–30[16]

	Internal Students	Total no. of candidates for all exams	Bachelors	Masters	Doctors	Total
				Degrees Awarded		
1900	–	7,130	472	24	40	536
1902–3	2,004	10,557	585	43	64	692
1905–6	2,987	10,826	754	15	69	829
1910–11	4,424	12,820	1,153	39	75	1,267
1915–16	3,621	11,920	673	56	43	772
1920–21	8,099	23,562	2,111	112	82	2,305
1925–26	9,400	32,353	3,118	147	216	3,481
1930–31	11,452	39,323	3,336	207	271	3,814

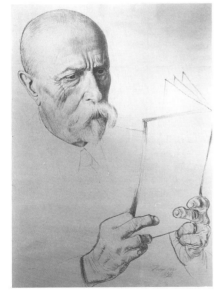

231 Thomas Masaryk (1850–1937), after the First World War to be the first President of Czechoslovakia, inaugurated while in exile in England in 1915 the School of Slavonic Studies at King's College with a much-publicized lecture on 'The Problem of Small Nations in the European Crisis'.

Expansion was evident too in various buildings. Sir William Beveridge, Director of the London School of Economics from 1919 to 1937, was given to claiming that he ruled over an empire on which the concrete never set. In 1922 the new main building for LSE was opened, and the School's premises increased two and a half times by 1937. A similar claim could have been made by the Provost of University College, where the Anatomy Building, opened in 1923 and funded by a large benefaction from the Rockefeller Foundation, was the largest development. Behind the expansion was a growing supply of finance. Income from tuition fees was still the biggest single source of finance, so the increase in student numbers led to a direct increase in income. After 1919 the niggardly flow of money from the government was substantially increased. In that year the University Grants Committee was established as an independent standing committee to allocate the grants provided by the

232 The School of Oriental Studies, proposed in a report in 1908, was opened as a school of the University in 1917 in the building of the former London Institution (founded 1807) in Finsbury Circus, bringing together teachers of oriental subjects from University and King's Colleges.

233 Sir Cooper Perry (1856–1938), the powerful Dean of Guy's Hospital Medical School, 1888–93, and Superintendent of Guy's Hospital, 1893–1920. Despite his Old Etonian shyness, he served as Vice-Chancellor of the University, 1917–19, and then as Principal, 1920–6. 'He published practically nothing; his life's work is embodied in minutes, memoranda, and charters. Those who worked behind the scenes knew his value, his massive intellect and constructive capacity.'

Treasury. Previously, from 1889, there had been a series of *ad hoc* committees advising on the distribution of the £15,000 per annum made available, a sum which had increased to £148,000 by 1911–15. In 1919–20 the total grant was increased to over a million pounds. The grants awarded by the UGC to the London colleges in 1920–1 are given in table 5.2, which also indicates their other sources of finance. There were in that year twenty-three London institutions receiving grants (apart from the central University) and twenty-three universities and university colleges in the rest of the country – fourteen in England, four in Wales and five in Scotland (Oxford and Cambridge were not included until 1923–4). Society was giving an enhanced role to higher education, and London was at last playing a leading part.

University teachers became increasingly full-time, and increasingly concerned with research as well as teaching; students became increasingly specialized, and the research student emerged. Before the war the University had begun to formulate a policy concerning the granting of the title of university professor, but the matter was fraught with difficulties, since such teachers were paid by the various schools, not by the University. (It was easy enough to agree to confer the first title of Professor Emeritus on Sir William Ramsay, the Nobel Prize-winning chemist, when he retired from the chair of chemistry at University College in 1913.) A university professoriate was gradually created, with the subordinate ranks of reader, senior lecturer, lecturer and assistant lecturer, all with increasingly regularized and standardized rates of pay, replacing the old erratic system based on payment of a proportion of the fees received. The

Table 5.2   Sources of Income, 1920–21[17]

	Endowments		Donations		Grants from Local Authorities		Parliamentary Grants		Tuition Fees		Other Income	
	£	%	£	%	£	%	£	%	£	%	£	%
University Central Funds	2.985	2.3	938	0.7	3,150	2.4	8,000	6.0	–	–	117,222	88.6
Bedford College	4,927	9.4	254	0.5	4,975	9.5	15,934	30.4	25,735	49.1	558	1.1
Charing Cross HMS	950	20.6	26	0.6	–	–	1,200	27.3	2,258	51.4	–	–
East London College	9,350	26.3	–	–	1,525	4.3	15,120	42.5	9,070	25.5	271	0.8
Imperial College	15,365	8.7	6,425	3.6	20,860	11.8	80,550	45.7	51.868	29.4	1,376	0.8
King's College	3,859	3.7	1,287	1.2	7,000	6.8	36,476	35.3	48,748	47.1	6,067	5.9
KCHMS	9	0.2	6	0.1	–	–	1,200	25.9	2,338	50.5	1,074	23.2
KC Dept. of H. & Soc.Sci.	1,863	10.8	275	1.6	1,500	8.7	6,645	38.7	6,666	38.8	231	1.3
London HMS	1,156	3.2	100	0.3	–	–	13,000	35.8	16,643	45.9	5,387	14.9
LS Med. for Women	1,369	4.5	551	1.8	–	–	6,500	21.3	21,442	70.2	688	2.3
Middlesex HMS	1,803	6.6	102	0.4	–	–	2,500	9.1	13,553	49.5	9,427	34.4
Royal Dental HS	293	1.7	–	–	–	–	1,000	5.8	11,763	68.6	4,096	23.9
Royal Holloway College	12,278	30.9	–	–	–	–	3,000	7.6	23,593	59.5	802	2.0
St Barts HMC	1,276	4.0	–	–	–	–	12,000	7.2	18,967	58.8	–	–
St George's HMS	591	21.2	75	2.7	–	–	700	25.1	455	16.3	973	34.9
St Mary's HMS	101	0.8	1,700	13.2	–	–	3,000	23.3	8,071	62.7	–	–
St Thomas's HMS	3	–	–	–	–	–	10,030	46.9	10,853	50.7	517	2.4
LSE	8,569	15.4	–	–	6,225	11.2	18,500	33.3	21,693	39.0	625	1.1
SOS	2,071	9.8	3,115	14.7	1,333	6.3	11,580	54.8	2,850	13.5	184	0.8
LS Trop.Med.	2,094	24.5	1,627	19.0	–	–	1,500	17.6	3,247	38.0	76	0.9
UC	14,754	10.4	4,401	3.1	6,748	4.7	42,000	29.5	65,920	46.3	8,652	6.1
UCHMS	4,608	20.2	–	–	–	–	10,500	46.0	7,592	33.3	122	0.5
Westfield College	728	8.8	–	–	1,000	11.2	3,000	33.6	3,752	42.0	390	4.4
Westminster HMS	10	1.0	15	1.5	–	–	300	29.7	686	67.9	–	–
London Total	91,027	9.0	20,897	2.1	54,316	5.4	304,235	30.2	377,763	37.5	158,967	15.7
National Total	337,844	11.2	81,214	2.7	280,900	9.3	1,013,970	33.6	972,987	32.2	333,584	11.1

NOTE: The Schools of the University listed are those receiving grants direct from the University Grants Committee.
The national total is for all English, Scottish and Welsh universities excluding Oxford and Cambridge.

emergence of the full-time university teacher was marked by the foundation of the Association of University Teachers as a national body in 1919, the same year as the UGC was established on a permanent footing. One of the most successful parts of the constitution of the University of London Mark III was the creation of boards of studies on which recognized teachers served. By 1923 there were forty-two such boards and 854 recognized teachers in the University.

In 1903 a new structure of 'honours degrees' was established in place of the old system whereby additional exam papers could be taken for 'honours' in particular fields after papers in a demanding range of subjects had been passed. Thereafter students increasingly took honours degrees in specialized subjects rather than general degrees. Two specific developments in 1921 indicated the full acceptance of specialized research as a central concern of the University. The first PhDs were awarded and the University established its first research institute of a new type.

A conference of all British universities was held at the Imperial Institute in 1917 at which it was recommended that the degree of doctor of philosophy should be introduced in Britain, to be awarded 'after a period of not less than two years whole-time work devoted to advanced study or research'. The aim was, at least in part, to realign the flow of foreign students who before the war had gone to Germany to work for such a degree. The dissension that had come to characterize the workings of the University of London meant that it took longer to agree to introduce the degree than other universities, but it was accepted in 1919 and first awarded in 1921 to sixteen individuals on the basis of the theses they produced. The PhD became rapidly naturalized. Within five years over a hundred were being awarded annually and over two hundred a year within twelve years.

The commitment to research in fields beside the natural sciences was marked too by the foundation of the Institute of Historical Research in 1921, which became the model for later 'institutes' directly under the Senate of the University rather than part of one of the schools. It was the creation of A.F. Pollard, Professor of Constitutional History at University College since 1903. He had previously worked on the *Dictionary of National Biography*, and that magnificent co-operative enterprise of the 1890s was the seed. 'The Dictionary Office', as Sir John Neale well put it,

with its team of workers mastering a technique that they handed on to new recruits, and with its well-equipped, specialised library, gave him the idea from which ultimately was to come his conception of a postgraduate

234 The PhD, a major innovation, was introduced in 1921. One of the first to receive the new degree was Lillian Penson, who later made her mark on the University in other ways: see **309**.

UNIVERSITY OF LONDON

WHEREAS *Lillian Margery Penson* OF *University College* HAS PURSUED A COURSE OF STUDY PRESCRIBED BY THIS UNIVERSITY AND HAS PASSED THE REQUISITE EXAMINATIONS BY THESIS AS AN INTERNAL STUDENT

NOW THEREFORE THIS IS TO CERTIFY THAT *she* HAS THIS DAY BEEN DULY ADMITTED BY THE SENATE TO THE DEGREE OF *Doctor of Philosophy in the Faculty of Arts* AS AN INTERNAL STUDENT IN THE UNIVERSITY OF LONDON.

Given under my hand this *twentieth* day of *July* one thousand nine hundred and *twenty one*

Principal Officer

Chancellor

Academic Registrar

235 The first occupier of the University site was the first of the Senate Institutes, the Institute of Historical Research, founded in 1921, originally housed in a temporary hut in Malet Street soon notorious among historians as 'Tudor Cottage'.

seminar as a group of scholars, young and old, meeting in a library, as scientists in a laboratory, to discuss their work and aid each other by the incidental dissemination of both method and knowledge.[18]

Teachers and undergraduates in the various colleges were linked together in the Haldanesque idea of the 'School of History' of the University; postgraduate students and teachers in their capacity as researchers were to be brought together at the Institute of Historical Research which took physical shape in 1921, albeit in the unprepossessing form of a hut. It rapidly established itself as a centre of national and international importance.

Developments such as these were partially obscured by years of wrangling about the Bloomsbury site. As President of the Board of Education in 1920, H.A.L. Fisher, the historian, former Vice-Chancellor of Sheffield and instigator of the 1918 Education Act, communicated a government offer intended to discharge its responsibility to the University enshrined in the 1899 Treasury Minute. The offer was to buy from the Duke of Bedford the site rejected by the University in 1912, together with further contiguous land to the north extending across Torrington Square up to the southern side of Gordon Square. Including roads and open spaces there were eleven prime acres to be presented for the formation of a 'University Quarter' to contain 'new Head Quarters for the University and for Colleges and Institutions connected with it, including King's College, whose premises in the Strand are now inadequate for its needs'. Fisher hoped that 'the existence of a striking block of academic buildings in such a central position might be expected to provide an appeal to the imagination of Londoners and

236 The Institute of Historical Research was still in its temporary hut in 1936, before moving into the new Senate House seen towering behind in this *Evening News* cartoon of that year.

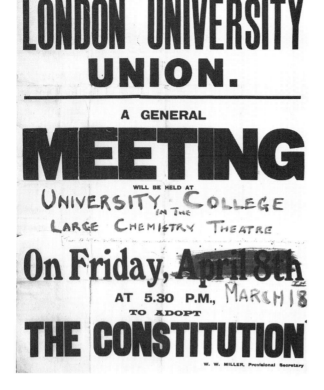

LONDON UNIVERSITY UNION.

A GENERAL

MEETING

WILL BE HELD AT

UNIVERSITY COLLEGE
IN THE
LARGE CHEMISTRY THEATRE

On Friday, April 8th

AT 5.30 P.M., MARCH 18

TO ADOPT

THE CONSTITUTION

W. W. MILLER, Provisional Secretary

The London University Union Society

A

MEETING

Will be Held on

WEDNESDAY, JULY 6th

at 7.45 p.m., at

ESSEX HALL, ESSEX ST., STRAND,

when

The Rt. Hon. LORD ROBERT CECIL, K.C., M.P.,
will Deliver an important Speech on

The Present Disposition of Political Parties

The Chair will be taken by
B. I. EVANS, B.A., *President of the London University Union Society*

Invitations will be sent to all Members of the Union in
due course.

A certain number of tickets are available for visitors. Applications
for these should be addressed to W. W. Miller, 1, Gamlen Rd., S.W.15

N.B.—Original Membership of the Union is now closed. Until the
end of term Students may join as Ordinary Members by payment
of £1.1.0 only.

Printed by WE. CLEMENTS PRESS LTD., PORTUGAL ST., W.C.2

WHAT THE UNIVERSITY UNION HAS TO OFFER.

[Taken for VINCULA by Photo News Agency.]

Left : The Common Room, open from 2.30 to 10.30, where teas are served. There is another room like this needing only the furniture.
Right : The Debating Hall which is available for all kinds of meetings.

237 The University of London Union constituted itself on 18 March 1921 in a meeting held at University College. The poster advertising the meeting gave a somewhat provisional impression, but there had been careful preparation and the Union was immediately vastly more successful than the Students' Representative Council and the old Union Society had been before the war.

238 The new Union grew out of the flourishing University Debating Society whose President, Ifor Evans, was elected as the first President of the Union in 1921, and well-organized meetings were soon attracting large attendances. Ifor Evans resigned in the course of the first year to take up a post elsewhere, but he was later to figure large in the University again as Principal of Queen Mary College and Provost of University College (see **323**).

239 Before the end of 1922 the YMCA Pickwick Hut in Malet Street was taken over for the Union and opened by Lord Haldane. It was a rather austere home for the Union for eight years, but one proudly used by the rapidly growing number of students.

visitors from overseas which is at present sadly lacking'. In 1921 the government bought the whole site from the Duke of Bedford for £425,000. The agreement contained an obligation to use the site before April 1926, failing which the Duke was to regain possession. In the following five years the University manoeuvred itself into an extraordinary position of indecision which ensured that when the time limit expired the site was in fact returned to the Duke of Bedford.

A number of factors contributed to this almost incredible situation. Finance, prejudice and King's College all played their part. King's College was placed in a particularly difficult position by the terms of Fisher's offer. The offer was conditional upon King's moving to Bloomsbury so that the new central buildings of the University could be flanked by those of the two incorporated colleges. But King's did not want to move and there was no money on offer to finance new buildings. Moreover, the King's College premises were in the hands legally not of the incorporated College controlled by the Senate and its Delegacy, but of the old unincorporated King's College Council which continued to govern the Theological Department under the system of dualism introduced by the King's College (Transfer) Act of 1908. The other side of the government offer of the Bloomsbury site was that it would acquire the buildings of King's College and of the Imperial Institute for civil service use. To King's this appeared as a threat of eviction from premises that it liked and homelessness on an empty site that it did not. After four years of argument the government in 1924 offered £370,000 in compensation for the King's premises, but this was estimated to cover only a third of the cost of rebuilding in Bloomsbury. King's dug its heels in and refused to move.[19]

The Senate had no power of compulsion. In any case, the 'external party' on the Senate were opposed to any move to Bloomsbury. To them South Kensington was a symbol of the University being something more than the internal side with its ambitious schools led by University College, and it was anathema to them to permit the University to move into physical proximity with that over-reaching College in Bloomsbury. Other sites were feverishly canvassed. Attention was drawn to the delights of Holland Park and Ken Wood, both on the market. There was no money for them, and they were not being offered by the government, but a large part of the Senate was prepared to clutch at anything to avoid surrendering to Bloomsbury. The University was unharmoniously divided into two camps, symbolized by the different colours of the bindings of the two sets of regulations. The *Regulations for Internal Students* were 'bound in cardinal red, said to indicate the hinge-like nature of the

VINCULA

AN ORGAN OF STUDENT LIFE IN THE UNIVERSITY OF LONDON.

No. 1.   LONDON, NOVEMBER 8, 1922.   THREEPENCE.

EMBARRAS DE RICHESSE.

THE FUTURE M.P. FOR LONDON UNIVERSITY—AND HIS RIVALS.

[Photo]   [Elliott & Fry.
Sir S. RUSSELL-WELLS, M.D., B.Sc., F.R.C.P.,
The late Vice-Chancellor,
CONSERVATIVE CANDIDATE.

[Photo]   [Blake Studios, 106, New Bond Street.
Professor A. F. POLLARD, M.A., Litt.D.
Professor of History in the University,
LIBERAL CANDIDATE.

[Photo]   [Caswall Smith.
H. G. WELLS, B.Sc.
Author and Journalist,
LABOUR CANDIDATE.

The candidates for the University are gentlemen of undoubted integrity and superior intellectual calibre. We doubt if any other constituency in the kingdom has three men of such ability and reputation appealing for its suffrages. Whatever happens we are sure of an M.P. who will be a worthy representative of the University and an adornment to the House of Commons. We wish all three could be elected. As that cannot be, may—whom did you say, dear readers—yes, may *he* win.

POINTS FROM THE ELECTION ADDRESSES.

I.—SIR SYDNEY RUSSELL-WELLS.

(*In the form of a letter to Sir Forrest Fulton, President of the University of London Unionist Association.*)

I have been a life-long Conservative and am equally opposed to reactionary and to revolutionary measures. I am a firm believer in steady evolutionary progress and profoundly distrust all violent breaks from the experience of the past. We are not in ourselves superior to our fathers and should learn from their wisdom and experiences, but we are infinitely inferior to them if we do not advance as much

(*Continued on p. 2, col. 2*).

II.—PROFESSOR A. F. POLLARD.

The University of London Liberal Society has done me the great honour of inviting me to contest, as a Liberal, the Parliamentary representation of the University; and it is my privilege to submit to your judgment the grounds upon which I am asking for your support at the poll. I can only hope that twenty years' teaching in the University of London, which has not been "of one's life a thing apart," and an absorption in its welfare which did not begin with the prospects of a Parliamentary contest nor limit itself to a

(*Continued on p. 2, col. 3*).

III.—MR. H. G. WELLS.

I am standing as the chosen representative of the Labour Party, which to-day stands for all the creative work in the State—from the work of the field labourer to the work of the doctor, journalist, teacher, minister, works manager, and scientific investigator; and its policy is a policy of steady, watchful, generous, comprehensive, scientific re-organization amid the strained, shattered, wasteful, and life-destroying confusion in which we live to-day. It is not necessarily antagonistic to the interests and claims of property, honestly

(*Continued on p. 3, col. 1*).

The Fortnight's Events—Page 5.   *Sport—Page 6.*   *Subscription Terms—Page 8.*

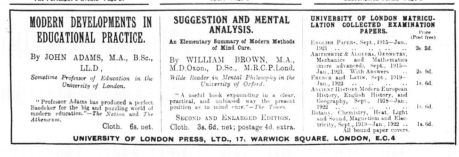

"Let us now praise famous men."

No. 1. Sir Gregory Foster, B.A.(Lond.),
Ph.D.(Strassburg).

Internal side as well as its cardinal arrogance', said the great Provost of University College, Sir Gregory Foster, in 1922, while the other set were bound in 'cerulean blue, indicating the sweet simplicity of the External side'.[20] The blues did not appreciate Foster's irony. They dug their heels in and in June 1925 the Senate found itself obliged to reject the offer of the Bloomsbury site. Without a further word to the University, the government in March 1926 returned the site to the Duke of Bedford and recovered the £425,000 they had paid for it.

This left the two University institutions which had been tentatively housed on the site in an impossible position. Wartime huts in Malet Street had been used to accommodate both the Institute of Historical Research and the University of London Union. Historians and students united in outcry. Pollard, as Director of the Institute of Historical Research, received notice to quit from the Bedford estate

240 *Vincula* was begun in 1922 as 'an organ of student life in London'. The first page of its first issue was devoted to the candidates for the University's parliamentary seat in the General Election of 1922.

241 Sir Gregory Foster (1866–1931), the virtual re-founder of University College as its highly-regarded first Provost from 1906 to 1929. He had been the second Principal of the College in 1904–6, when the title was changed as part of the preparation for incorporation into the University. He became Vice-Chancellor in 1928–30, having been an ardent campaigner for the Bloomsbury site.

242 The ballot paper issued to members of Convocation to vote for the University's MP in the 1922 election. There were 11,241 electors, 8623 men and 2618 women.

Place a **X** against the name of the Candidate for whom you vote, and write your name, and particulars required, in the **TWO** places indicated by 1 and 2 below.

UNIVERSITY OF LONDON.

Parliamentary Election, 1922.

Voting Paper.

(1) I
give my vote as indicated below :—

(Insert full Christian names and surname, with Degree and College, if any.)

Candidates.	Vote.
PROFESSOR ALBERT FREDERICK **POLLARD**, M.A. (Oxford), Litt.D. (Manchester), F.B.A.	
SIR SYDNEY **RUSSELL-WELLS**, M.D., B.Sc. (London)	
HERBERT GEORGE **WELLS**, B.Sc. (London)	

I declare that I have signed no other voting paper and have not voted in person at this election for the university constituency of London.

I also declare :—
(In the case of a man) that I have not voted at this general election in respect of any qualification other than a residence qualification.
(In the case of a woman) that I have not voted at this general election for any other university constituency.

(2)

Signature of Elector

Address

The   day of   1922.

I declare that this voting paper (the voting paper having been previously filled in), was signed in my presence by who is personally known to me, on the   day of   1922.

Signature of Witness

Address

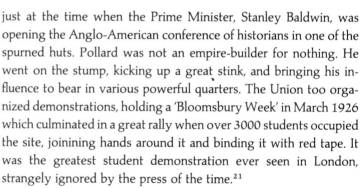

GRADUATION SONG

Poem by John Drinkwater.   *Music by John Ireland.*

TO BE SUNG IN UNISON BY ALL PRESENT

Pilgrims from many paths we came
To where the roads of Empire meet,
Our lives to kindle at the flame
Of schools wherein a million feet
Have trod the years, or with a fame
That yet along the years shall beat.

    O London maids and London men
    Bring in the golden age again.

In no seclusion pastur'd round
As where the Cam and Isis flow,
Our cloister'd learning have we found,
Where loud the tides of traffic go.
Our nightingales have been the sound
Of London bells from Fleet to Bow.

    O London maids and London men
    Bring in the golden age again.

Life calls us, and we bid farewell
To this the latest of our springs,
But on our travels we will tell
How fellowship of gentle things
Is kept for ever where they dwell
Who know the song that England sings.

    O London maids and London men
    Bring in the golden age again.

In field or market place or mill,
Beneath a dear or alien Sun,
We'll build a generation still
Of faith and honour here begun,
That sires of the old English will
Shall know their own and cry : Well done !

    O London maids and London men
    Bring in the golden age again.

243 The 'graduation song' written by John Drinkwater at the request of the University, first sung at Presentation Day in 1926. It now seems very much a period piece, but it proved no more popular than the 'University anthem' composed three years previously by Sir Frederick Bridge with words from *Ecclesiasticus* suggested by Rudyard Kipling. Both were soon dropped.

244 Sir William Beveridge, later Lord Beveridge (1879–1963), whose reports on social insurance (1942) and full employment (1944) were to lay the foundations of the welfare state. He was Director of the London School of Economics from 1919 to 1937 and Vice-Chancellor of the University in 1926–8, when he was largely responsible for the third and successful attempt to acquire the Bloomsbury site.

just at the time when the Prime Minister, Stanley Baldwin, was opening the Anglo-American conference of historians in one of the spurned huts. Pollard was not an empire-builder for nothing. He went on the stump, kicking up a great stink, and bringing his influence to bear in various powerful quarters. The Union too organized demonstrations, holding a 'Bloomsbury Week' in March 1926 which culminated in a great rally when over 3000 students occupied the site, joinining hands around it and binding it with red tape. It was the greatest student demonstration ever seen in London, strangely ignored by the press of the time.[21]

It was at the moment of this dramatic *impasse* that Sir William Beveridge entered the field. He had been Director of the London School of Economics since 1919 and, though a member of the Senate, he had played little part in University-wide affairs. Having received what he called 'an SOS' from Sir Cooper Perry as Principal, Beveridge attended the Senate meeting in March 1926 to move a resolution that there should be an attempt to recover for University purposes at least some of the £425,000 which the government had received back from the Duke of Bedford. 'As mover of the resolution', he wrote, 'I suggested names for the deputation – all the elder statesmen of the Senate. I could not decently suggest myself –

I was still a new boy – but I had the wit to name Graham Wallas, and he had the wit to say that he could not serve and to suggest me instead. No one had the quickness to say him nay. This was an object lesson to me of the importance, in public assemblies, of hunting in couples... thus, for the first time, I broke into the heart of University affairs.' Sir Douglas Logan later quoted this passage enunciating the principle of 'hunting in couples', noting that it 'equals in perspicacity anything which Cornford promulgated in *Microcosmographia Academica*'.[22]

Beveridge was therefore a member of the University's deputation in June 1926 which was confronted by Winston Churchill as Chancellor of the Exchequer. Churchill rubbed their noses in the situation the University had got itself into. 'You have so handled the matter', he growled, 'that it has all fallen to the ground, and the site has been resumed by the Duke of Bedford, the institutions that you have built up in temporary structures there are all under notice to move; the government are free from their offer which you have rejected... and at the end of it all, here we are without any plans for concentrating the University, with a great deal of time lost, and with a great deal of the work done now in jeopardy.' Churchill thought it was a 'most lamentable position of affairs'; he could not comprehend 'the fatuity, the hiatus of thought which led to the loss of this tremendous offer'. Soothed by Beveridge, Churchill subsequently agreed to provide half the money returned by the Duke of Bedford – £212,500 – for the development of the South Kensington site.[23]

245 Sir Holburt Waring, as Vice-Chancellor, on the steps of the Imperial Institute in November 1922 announcing the victory of his fellow medic and predecessor as Vice-Chancellor, 1919–22, Sir Sydney Russell-Wells, over the great historian A.F. Pollard and the well-known personality H.G. Wells. The portly figure on the left is that of R. Mullineux Walmsley, Chairman of Convocation, 1922–4, and the founding Principal of the Northampton Institute from 1896 to 1924.

246 A photograph taken from Montague Place looking across the proposed University site towards the building for the London School of Hygiene and Tropical Medicine being constructed between 1926 and 1929. The tank, one of the first to be employed on the Somme, was used by the War Savings Association, and for a time in 1926 by the students as a mascot. It was offered to the University by the Holborn Borough Council but tactfully rejected, and so in 1931 it was sold for scrap (for £41).

247 A view across the future Senate House site soon after the completion of the building of the London School of Hygiene and Tropical Medicine in 1929.

A week later Beveridge was elected Vice-Chancellor of the University. His own account of the election and the issues involved deserves quotation in full.[24]

The leader of the External party, Graham Little, had succeeded in winning the London University seat in Parliament at the General Election of 1924. He was now put forward for election by the Senate as Vice-Chancellor in June 1926. His election would mean good-bye to Bloomsbury for all time.

The Internalists on the Senate considered anxiously whom they could nominate to beat this move of the Externalists. The obvious nominee was Sir Gregory Foster, Provost of the University College, head of the largest College of the University, with many years of service on the Senate. But the very importance of University College weakened the election prospects of its Provost; the other Colleges, beginning with King's College,

248 A rough sketch of possible quasi-classical buildings for the site drawn in 1926 by Sir Albert Richardson, the epicurean Professor of Architecture at University College, 1919–46, and later President of the Royal Academy.

249 The plaque in the entrance hall of the London School of Hygiene and Tropical Medicine to Sir Patrick Manson (1844–1922). The work of 'Mosquito Manson' in China in the 1870s and his manual on *Tropical Diseases* (1898) led to great advances in the control of malaria and yellow fever, and to the foundation in 1899 of the London School of Tropical Medicine, expanded to include hygiene and rebuilt with Rockefeller money in the 1920s.

would be jealous and afraid of him. Gregory Foster would have liked to be Vice-Chancellor, but he was against standing himself on this occasion. He and others with him came to the conclusion that the strongest candidate that they could put up to keep Graham Little out was myself – hardly known in the Senate either for good or evil after six years there, though well known outside. Having reached this conclusion, Gregory Foster, above all, worked to secure my return.

It proved to be a desperate fight. With the Faculty and the Convocation members lined up all but equally on opposite sides, success depended on the *tertium quid* and we knew that some of these – including most of the lawyers – were already in the Little camp. The election was the first business of the June meeting of the Senate. On election, the new Vice-Chancellor was in office at once; he went straight to the chair and conducted the rest of the business. To prepare for this, it had become customary for each of the rival candidates to be taken through the Senate Agenda by the Secretary of the Senate, a day or two before, on separate days. On the election day itself, we went to sit together in the Vice-Chancellor's room a few doors away from the Senate Room, while the Senate went through their first business of deciding which of us should be Vice-Chancellor, and should conduct the business that followed.

The morning's news had been bad for my prospects. Three doctors whom we had counted to be neutral at least were said to have come off the fence against me; defeat seemed likely. As my opponent and I sat in the Vice-Chancellor's room we could see through the open door the passage to the Senate Room and the senators going to their meeting. As I watched, the omens became more favourable to me. On the one hand, I saw three aged and distinguished senators whom I had never seen at a Senate meeting; I knew that most of these non-attenders, if they came at all, would, under Gregory Foster's persuasion, be for me. But I could not believe that they would come, till I saw them. On the other hand, the threatened *démarche* of doctors against me did not materialise. With my three most aged supporters, I ought to poll twenty-five votes and be safe.

Through our open door we heard the murmur of our supporters' speeches; we heard a roll-call proceeding; then silence; then at the door of

250 An amusing bird's eye view of the 'Bloomsbury site' and the surrounding area produced in 1926 by *Vincula*, which then changed its name to *New Troy* in honour of the campaign to save the site for the erection of new central buildings.

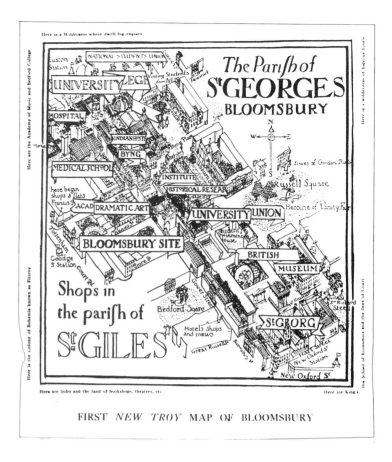

FIRST *NEW TROY* MAP OF BLOOMSBURY

our room were my proposer, Sir Wilmot Herringham, and my seconder, Professor H.G. Atkins. This meant that I was chosen. They came to conduct me to the Senate. There the former Vice-Chancellor told me of my election, put his robe round me and put me into his chair.

Beveridge was elected by twenty-six votes to twenty-one.

The election proved to be a victory also for Bloomsbury. It rapidly became clear to Beveridge that it was totally impractical to reconstruct the South Kensington premises for the additional accommodation needed by the University. An architect's report showed 'the incurable unsuitability of the Imperial Institute Building for our purposes', and Beveridge drew up a report of his own arguing 'the simple thesis that if there is to be a single University of London with any unity of spirit, its headquarters must be central. The placing of these headquarters excentrically to the main body of teaching institutions sets up a strain which weakens the whole structure, exhausting the time and energy of teachers and students in needless journeys, making them feel the University as something alien and remote, divorcing the administration of the University from its teaching and research.' The *deus ex machina* which enabled the question of the Bloomsbury site to be re-opened for a third time was the Rockefeller Foundation. Over Christmas 1926 Beveridge went to New York to seek further Rockefeller money for the LSE, and he succeeded in also persuading the Foundation to generously make £400,000 available to the University to enable it to acquire the whole site, without any of the strings that had been attached to the government offer in 1920. Opposition on the Senate was soon overcome, 'fanned by the convenient intransigence of the Office of Works' concerning the Imperial Institute, and by February 1927 it had voted narrowly (21–18) to move to Bloomsbury after all. The 'last ditchers' attempted to have the American money rejected in March, but the strength of the arguments advanced by Gregory Foster and Beveridge led to their defeat 26–10. For a time it looked as if the Duke of Bedford was now unwilling to sell, but this final hurdle was cleared by deft negotiation, and though the price had risen to £525,000, the site was finally acquired in time for the news to be announced at the University's graduation dinner in May 1927.

Meanwhile, important changes were proposed for the constitution of the University. After the war, the Haldane Report was not revived. Its Germanic ideals were discredited and the sheer growth in size of the various separate parts of the University rendered any scheme of thorough-going centralization out of the question. The minutes of the departmental committee whose proceedings had been interrupted by the outbreak of war in 1914 were being dusted when Fisher began to contemplate the offer of the Bloomsbury site in 1919. The issue was left in abeyance until 1924, when the short-lived Labour government of that year – in which Haldane himself served as Lord Chancellor – appointed a new departmental committee to 'indicate what are the principal changes now most needed in the existing constitution of the University of London and on what basis a Statutory Commission should be set up to frame new Statutes for the University'. A *frisson* of alarm went through the University. The largest attendance ever recorded (over 800) at a meeting of Convocation unanimously passed a resolution declaring that 'it would be a disaster of the first magnitude if the Haldane Report were to be resuscitated and treated as the basis of a statutory reconstruction of the University'. The scene was set for a further outbreak of controversy, over and above the controversies raging strong at the time over the Bloomsbury site question.

The first chairman of the committee, Lord Ernle, had soon to retire through ill-health, and under his successor Hilton Young (later Lord Kennet) its proceedings were conducted in a businesslike and sensible direction. Young was himself the son of Sir George Young,

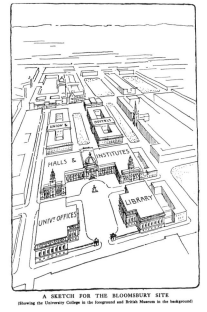

A SKETCH FOR THE BLOOMSBURY SITE
(Showing the University College in the foreground and British Museum in the background)

251 A preliminary sketch by H.V. Lanchester, the University's architect, for the 'Bloomsbury site' in 1926.

252 Sir Ernest Graham-Little (1868–1950), the University's very independent and highly individualistic MP from 1924 until the abolition of the university franchise in 1950. Originally a dermatologist at St Mary's Hospital Medical School, he was a member of the Senate from 1906 to 1950, a stalwart of the 'external party', and President for many years of the University of London Graduates Association, an organized pressure-group in Convocation.

who had played a leading part in the campaign for a teaching university in London in the 1880s and 1890s, and the seven other members of the committee included some members of the University who were fully aware of its problems and the changes there had been since 1913 – the former Principal, Sir Henry Miers, the future Vice-Chancellor and Principal, Sir Herbert Eason, and the powerful historian, A.F. Pollard. The need for some measure of reform was unmistakable. The Senate as constituted in 1900 had proved inadequate to control what had become a large and complex university. In a draft memorandum in 1918 H.A.L. Fisher had, in a phrase suppressed from the final version, described meetings of the Senate as presenting 'a scene of Polish anarchy which involves the whole University in discredit'. It was estimated that the Senate had an average of four and a half seconds to consider each of the 5,000 or more resolutions coming before it each year.[25] The machinery of the University was evidently inappropriately constituted, involved the wrong people, and was swamped in detail.

The Hilton Young Report was issued in 1926. It was neither so large nor so revolutionary a document as the Haldane Report had been. 'We are convinced', the committee said, 'that with the lapse of time and material change of circumstances some of the main recommendations of the Haldane Report have lost their force, and that the ground for attempting to impose such an entirely new constitution on the University as the Report proposed no longer exists'. 'A practicable scheme of reform and reorganisation', they went on, 'must, in our opinion, be evolutionary rather than revolutionary and build as far as possible on existing foundations. Certain characteristics peculiar to the University of London have become firmly established, the University has developed greatly during the past twenty-five years, even though hampered by serious constitutional defects.' Proposals were made to remedy the defects. A new body was proposed in the form of a University 'Council' to control the finances, having 'final authority in the allocation of university funds' and the power to negotiate with grant-giving bodies on behalf of the University as a whole. The Senate was to be reduced in size; 'we can find no justification for the system whereby so many Senators are nominated by bodies none of which has an organic connexion with the University', and more members of the Senate were to be appointed by the constituent schools. 'We also think that in general the University has too many statutes, and that the cumulative effect of some of them is to tie the hands of important bodies by preventing them coming to decisions without receiving reports from numerous subordinate bodies.' Various proposals were made for streamlining the constitutional structure of the University, recognizing it more fully as a federal university, while retaining the reprieved external side, not now to be restricted or diminished in any way.[26]

The Senate and Convocation both lost no time in proceeding to vote in rejection of the report, but the government – tired by now of the affairs of the University of London – moved quickly to get legislation carried. The University of London Act, 1926, was passed within the year, despite the determined opposition of the University's MP, Ernest Graham-Little. Commissioners were to be imposed on the University to make new statutes 'in general accordance with the recommendations contained in the Report of the Committee'. Four members of the Senate resigned in protest. The Commissioners, under the chairmanship of Mr Justice Tomlin, included Sir Cooper Perry, recently retired as Principal, and T.P. Nunn, the Professor of Education. They worked diplomatically and were accommodating towards various modifications proposed by the University. The resulting new statutes were duly sealed in July 1928, and approved to come into effect by the Privy Council in March 1929. By 1929, with a new central site and a reconditioned constitution, the University was geared up to drive into a new period.

Bloomsbury and Beyond, 1929–1963

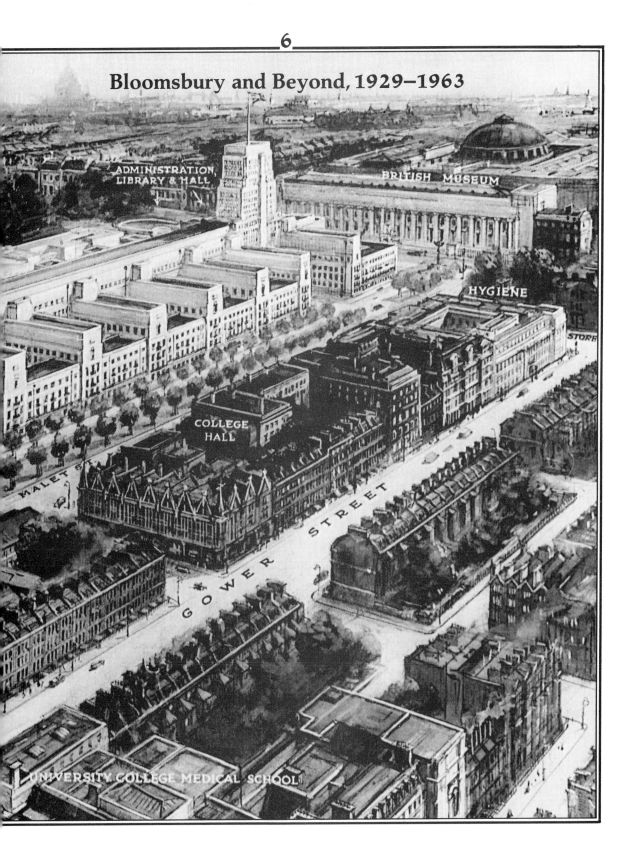

ADMINISTRATION, LIBRARY & HALL

BRITISH MUSEUM

HYGIENE

STORE

COLLEGE HALL

MALET ST

GOWER STREET

UNIVERSITY COLLEGE MEDICAL SCHOOL

253 The 'great temple of learning' to arise in Bloomsbury, drawn as a 'pictorial panorama' under Holden's supervision by Douglas Macpherson for the *Illustrated London News* in 1933, showing the 'spinal plan' for the new buildings with University College in the foreground and the British Museum in the background. *Previous page.*

254 Sir Edwin Deller (1883–1936), Principal of the University from 1929 until 1936 when he was killed as the result of an accident at the new Senate House. It was especially tragic since he had been intimately involved in planning the building and was proudly showing visitors around. He had risen through the University's central administration, becoming Academic Registrar in 1921. 'He had a quick eye for the heart of any problem, and an equability of temper that was of the utmost value in handling the often heated controversies which confronted him.'

If Bloomsbury had utterly vanished my young heart would not have mourned it. But now it is beginning to vanish little by little. Many of the squares and streets have been more or less vandalised. All of them are threatened. I gather that the arch-threatener is the University of London. I understand that there are no limits to its desire for expansion of that bleak, blank, hideous and already vast whited sepulchre which bears its name. Simultaneous tens of thousands of youths and maidens yet unborn will in the not so very far distant future be having their minds filled there and their souls starved there. Poor things!

Sir Max Beerbohm, in a radio talk in 1940; *Mainly on the Air* (1946), p.80.

The foundation of the University of London was rooted in the two movements which have last transformed the life of man: the advent of democracy, and that of science. In the spirit and tradition of this University lies infused the most indestructible soul of democracy: the love that yearns to bring the common heritage of culture to all the children of the land. In that spirit and that tradition is enshrined as well the devotion of the scientist; his religion of the quest, ever spreading and ever renewed, of disinterested knowledge. The teeming number, the variety of the learned bodies which have been grafted on this single stock, and now flourish in the light of day; the activities of the Colleges, the Schools, the Institutes, the Laboratories, the Hospitals, that are gathered in the wide-stretched arms of this Alma Mater, are a witness to the world of the great work that she does . . .

Professor Louis Cazamian, representing the University of Paris at the centenary celebrations in 1936; *University of London, 1836–1936: Centenary Commemorative Volume* (1936), p.51.

The leading item on the agenda of the new Senate and the newly-constituted Court when both bodies first met in July 1929 was the development of the Bloomsbury site. The University was now better constituted to deal with the issue, so lamentably handled in the years covered in the last chapter. The Senate was only slightly reduced in size, to fifty-four or fifty-five, but it was more appropriately composed. It consisted of seventeen members elected by the teachers in the eight Faculties (four from each of Arts and Science, three from Medicine, two from Engineering and one each from Theology, Law, Music and Economics), besides the nine heads of the largest constituent schools – University College, King's

255 Lord Macmillan (1873–1952), one of the great Scottish lawyers who shaped the University of London. A Lord of Appeal from 1930, he served as the first Chairman of the Court of the University between 1929 and 1943. He was a brilliant speaker and a tireless fund-raiser for the development of the Bloomsbury site.

College, Bedford College, Birkbeck College, East London College (which became Queen Mary College in 1934), Imperial College, LSE, Royal Holloway College and Westfield College. The Deans of the twelve general Medical Schools elected two of their number. There were also seventeen members elected by the graduates in Convocation, two appointed by University College and King's College, the two incorporated colleges, and four co-opted members. The Senate had five important standing committees: the Academic Council and the Council for External Students as before, the reconstituted University Extension and Tutorial Classes Council, the Matriculation and School Examinations Council, and a new body – the Collegiate Council, which consisted of the heads of all schools, of which there were a total of thirty-six.

The most important of the constitutional changes introduced in 1929 was the creation of the Court, as the Hilton Young Report's 'Council' came to be called. The new body was to 'have the custody, control and disposition of all the property, funds and investments of the University'. The Court was to 'control the finances of the University'. It was provided that 'before determining any question of finance which directly affects the educational policy of the University, the Court shall take into consideration any recommendation or report made by the Senate'. The Senate remained 'the supreme governing and executive body of the University in all academic matters', but it now had to share its control of the federal University under a new balanced bicameral system. The Court was to have sixteen members: six appointed by the Senate, four by the Privy Council, two by the LCC, and one was to be co-opted, plus the Chancellor, Vice-Chancellor and the Chairman of Convocation. A major change followed. The UGC and the LCC, the two biggest sources of funds for the various parts of the University, agreed to channel all their grants through the Court, rather than dealing separately and individually with the constituent parts. The schools remained independent, but the federal centre was given much greater potential power. Both the Court and the new 'Court Department' faced a sensitive and difficult task, and the sensitivities and the difficulties were handled ably and judiciously under Lord Macmillan who was elected as the first Chairman of the Court.

Sir Franklin Sibly, the geologist and former Principal of University College, Swansea, who was Principal of the University from 1926, said in 1929 that at a time of great administrative changes 'it may help us all if we remember that though we are, so to speak, changing horses, we are crossing no stream. The path of our purpose is the same . . .' His remark may have helped others, but it did not help him. He resigned soon afterwards, becoming Vice-

256 The 7th Earl Beauchamp (1872–1938), Chancellor of the University from 1929 to 1931, photographed leading the first procession of officials of the University from the Imperial Institute to the Albert Hall for the Presentation Day ceremony in May 1930. 'Nothing could be gayer,' the *Sunday Times* reported of the procession. Lord Beauchamp was a member of the Cabinet in 1910–15, and Leader of the Liberal Peers in 1924–31. To avoid scandal, he was obliged to resign all his public offices in 1931.

Chancellor of Reading where he was much happier at the helm of the youngest, smallest and financially most insecure of British universities than he had been during his three years of troubled complexity in London. The surprise choice as his successor was Edwin Deller, a member of the administrative staff, who had left school at 14 and worked as a clerk in various offices, taking his degrees in law as an evening student. He was, in fact, a born administrator as well as a man of great wisdom and *savoir-faire*. All his abilities were needed over the next few years.

Lord Rosebery had lived in semi-retirement for some years after suffering a stroke, and his death in 1929 meant that the University had to elect a new Chancellor. The choice fell upon Lord Beauchamp, another leading Liberal grandee. He had begun to apply himself actively to his duties when after only two years he abruptly resigned in mysterious circumstances on grounds of ill-health. No explanation was given at the time. Only later did it come to be known that his childless brother-in-law, the Duke of Westminster, had exposed Beauchamp's homosexual tastes to his astonished wife and children and threatened him with prosecution. George V, a close friend, was said to have remarked: 'I thought chaps were only that way abroad.' Beauchamp indeed went to live abroad for the rest of his life, providing a sort of model for Evelyn Waugh's Lord Marchmain in *Brideshead Revisited*. That the University was fully informed in confidence of the sad case against Lord Beauchamp is revealed in a private file kept by Deller marked 'De Bello Campo', the form of his name suggested by Lord Beauchamp for the Latin announcement at his inauguration ceremony as Chancellor in 1929.[1] His successor in 1931 was Lord Athlone, a member of the

257 Charles Holden (1875–1960), the architect chosen by the University in 1931 for its new buildings: plaque by Paul Vincze in the entrance to the University Library on the fourth floor of the Senate House. 'I have designed it,' Holden said, 'to last five hundred years.'

258 The Earl of Athlone (1874–1957), Chancellor of the University from 1932 to 1955, painted in the chancellorial robes by Augustus John. Born Prince Alexander of Teck, the brother of Queen Mary, he was a soldier who became Governor-General of South Africa, 1923–31, and of Canada, 1940–6. He brought distinction to many University functions, together with his wife, Princess Alice.

royal family above reproach, who was to serve as Chancellor during nearly a quarter-century of enormous change.

The first task on the Bloomsbury site was to make the complicated legal arrangements to close the roads which divided it. Two years were taken to extinguish the rights of way, though it was agreed with Holborn Borough Council to maintain a passage way across the former route of Keppel Street. The major task was to select an architect. It was agreed that the buildings should be characteristic of London and of the time. The design, Beveridge pronounced, 'should recall to us the clear-cut relevance of science, the light-heartedness and the solemnity of youth, the enchanted garden of the arts'.[2] The proposition was a challenging one. The Court decided to choose the architect itself rather than holding a public competition, and to make the selection by two methods – inspection of buildings *in situ* and inspection of architects round a dinner-table. In February 1931 Beveridge and Deller were despatched to examine various buildings. 'We went up and down the length and breadth of England and Wales, seeing town halls and academic buildings, schools, hospitals and cathedrals. We enjoyed ourselves hugely.' A short-list of four architects was drawn up, and four dinner-parties were arranged for their inspection at the Athenaeum, presided over by Lord Macmillan.[3] The architect who passed both tests was Charles Holden.

Holden had been involved in designing the building for the King's College of Household and Social Science (see **230**), and had subsequently achieved acclaim for his design of some forty 'modern' underground stations (Arnos Grove was his own favourite) and for the headquarters of the London Passenger Transport Board near St James's Park, a building for which he was awarded a medal by the Royal Institute of British Architects in 1929. Holden took on the University buildings as his greatest work. He had produced a first sketch before dining at the Athenaeum, and in 1931–2 his impressive plan for the whole site took shape. A massive spine of Portland masonry was to stride the whole length from Gordon Square to Montague Place, culminating in a great tower, to be the tallest building in London. Accommodation was to be provided for the administrative offices, the University Library, a Great Hall, and the Students' Union, as well as for the Institute of Education, the School of Slavonic Studies, the Institute of Historical Research, the Courtauld Institute of Art and the Institute of Archaeology, five parts of the University planned to be rehoused on the site.

'From an architectural point of view', Holden said in 1932, 'this type of plan offers very great possibilities for an impressive composition of the masses into one great whole, and one that would yet be

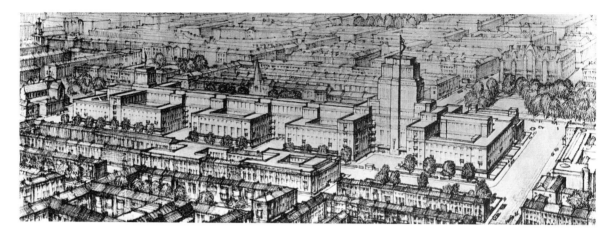

259 A perspective drawing by Charles Holden of the 'spinal plan' for the buildings originally intended to cover the whole site. 'It's exactly like a battleship,' said King George V when Macmillan, Deller and Holden showed him the plans and drawings in 1932.

260 The Senate House site as it appeared surrounded by hoardings in 1931 after the closing of Keppel Street and British Museum Avenue and the removal of the tank . Across the allotments on which local policemen raised vegetables can be seen (top left) the huts occupied by the Union from 1922.

impressive while still incomplete . . . The design for the buildings is mainly of our own time, arising out of the natural expression of the plan. The very orderly disposition of the parts and the strong horizontal character of the whole would give to the mass a classical bias, which, together with the rhythmical disposition of the window and door openings and other essential features, may be relied upon to present a neighbourly front to the British Museum and to the surrounding buildings.'[4] It was envisaged that it might take twenty or thirty years to complete the whole plan, at an estimated cost of about three million pounds.

The plans met with the University's immediate formal approval and with general approbation. It was widely accepted that it achieved what Deller called its 'twofold purpose': as the 'focus of our manifold activities and the visible sign and symbol of the pursuit of learning and the things of the mind and the spirit in a vast city'. 'London', the *Manchester Guardian* said in 1931, 'is favoured beyond other British cities in most things, but its university has not yet figured in the eyes of the world with the prestige natural to its position.' The University of London would now be not so easily overlooked. The press in 1932 was unanimous in recognizing the stamp of modernity and dignity to be given to the University by the projected buildings. 'It is clear', one architectural critic declared in *Country Life*, for example, 'that the most important London building of this generation will be unmistakeably modern, and worthy in every way of the institution it is to house.'[5]

Given the controversy that had long raged about the location, it would not be expected that this unanimity of acclaim was shared throughout the University. From the start some thought it a monstrosity. T.L. Humberstone, a former member of the administrative staff who had become a Holborn borough councillor and who took it upon himself to become a thorn in the University's side, considered it 'fantastically silly and megalomaniacal'. Pevsner was less extravagant in his criticism. The style, he said later, is 'of a strangely semi-traditional, undecided modernism', with 'odd broad buttresses' and small balconies which he found 'baffling'. His judgment was acid: 'The design certainly does not possess the vigour and directness of Charles Holden's smaller Underground stations.'[6] While architectural opinion has now become more sympathetic to the elegances of the Senate House, opinion in the University remains divided. Some admire it, others hate it. There is an important point to note in an historical perspective: no one since the 1930s has been able to ignore it.

The first sod was cut at the southern end of the site two days before the close of 1932. There was no ceremony, but the first pictures were taken in a full photographic and fitful film record of the building process. Bore-holes were made as a preliminary to the excavation for the foundations, and it was discovered that the gravel stratum above the bed of London blue clay was waterlogged. Piles had to be driven well into the clay to a depth of thirty feet below the basement level to carry the reinforced concrete on which the walls were to be constructed. The work was sufficiently advanced by June 1933 to enable a ceremonial laying of the foundation stone by King George V. It was a memorable occasion. The Union proposed that the students present should sing the Lutheran hymn *'Eine feste Burg ist unser Gott'*. The Vice-Chancellor did not see the joke, and agitatedly wrote to the heads of schools to ensure that what was sung was 'All people that on earth do dwell'. All passed off smoothly. 'The brilliance of the scene', wrote Deller, 'and the orderliness and symmetry with which it was composed will remain fresh for many a year in the minds of all who were present.'[7]

The building work proceeded rapidly. The lowest tender was

261 King's College celebrated the centenary of its foundation in 1929, and the cover of its *Review* was one of the many designed by Fougasse (C.K. Bird), a former student of engineering at the College who became Art Editor of *Punch* and well-known as a cartoonist.

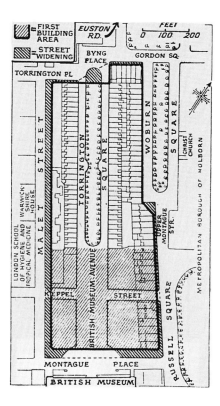

262 A plan of the Bloomsbury site in 1931 showing the areas allocated to street widening and the 10½-acre site available for the new University buildings.

263 The stand erected on the Senate House site for the 3,000 guests attending the ceremony for the laying of the foundation stone on 26 June 1933. Representatives of 164 universities and learned societies throughout the world were present.

received from Holland & Hannen and Cubitts, and this was accepted. A condition of the contract was that all the materials had to be obtained from sources in the British Empire. Lord Macmillan, as Chairman of the Court of the University, had worked hard to ensure that the financing was arranged. He was remarkably successful at a time of deepening worldwide economic depression. University College had celebrated its centenary in 1927 (postponed from 1926 for essentially economic reasons) and its appeal for half a million pounds then launched was forced to close in 1930 with less than half the total raised. The centenary appeal at King's College for £350,000 in 1929 realized only £65,538 when it was closed in 1933. Macmillan appealed forcefully to the City of London, and his vigour was rewarded. The Corporation of the City gave £100,000 towards the Great Hall, 'a truly magnificent pledge of the City's interest in its University'. Gifts from fifty of the City livery companies followed, totalling over £75,000, besides which the Goldsmiths' Company contributed £50,000 towards the housing of the library which they had presented in 1903. London business firms gave some £120,000, and the Marks family (of Marks & Spencer) gave £15,000, by far the biggest private donation. The LCC made a major contribution, giving a total of £250,000, plus £200,000 for the Institute of Education and Birkbeck College. Middlesex County Council gave £100,000, especially for library accommodation. Other local authorities provided over £150,000. Some £125,000 of the £212,500 provided by the government in 1926 had been used to top up the Rockefeller money which bought the site (see above pp.207 and 211); the remainder was applied to the cost of the new buildings. Over a million pounds from various

264 King George V and Queen Mary arriving for the foundation stone laying, with the OTC providing a guard of honour. They were greeted by Lord Athlone as Chancellor and by Louis Napoleon George Filon as Vice-Chancellor, 1933–5. Filon's given names recall that his father had been tutor to the Prince Imperial; he was Professor of Applied Mathematics at UCL and Director of the University Observatory at Mill Hill, opened in 1929.

265 The inscription on the foundation stone of the Senate House.

THIS STONE WAS LAID BY
HIS MAJESTY KING GEORGE V
ON THE TWENTY-SIXTH DAY OF JUNE 1933
IN THE TWENTY-FOURTH YEAR OF HIS REIGN
HER MAJESTY QUEEN MARY
BEING PRESENT ON THE OCCASION

266 King George V laying the foundation stone.

public and private sources was thus channelled into the Senate House, enabling it to be raised above Bloomsbury in 1933–8.

It had been hoped that the first stage would be complete by the time of the centenary of the University in 1936. In the event, the building was not ready, and so the celebrations had to take place without their centre-piece. The anniversary events were brought forward from November to the beginning of the summer vacation, partly for the convenience of the many representatives of other universities who were to attend, and partly to suit King George V who had agreed to open the buildings. George V's death early in the year cast a blight over the arrangements, but the celebrations went ahead between 27 June and 3 July 1936. Some 190 official delegates attended, including many from overseas, and there were dinners, receptions, garden parties, and a service of thanksgiving at St Paul's. Honorary degrees were presented to a number of public figures, including G.M. Trevelyan, H.G. Wells, Vaughan Williams, Sir William Bragg, Max Planck and (in absentia) Albert Einstein. Not until some weeks later was the first part of the new buildings finished, and in August 1936 the heroic move of the administrative offices from the Imperial Institute took place. In October the Court met for the first time in the new building, as in November did the

267 The handsome casket, the gift of Lord Hayter of the lock and safe firm of Chubb & Sons, which was placed in a cavity underneath the foundation stone containing a copy of the *University Calendar*, the programme of the day's ceremonial, newspapers and one of the only six pennies minted in 1933 – items that so fascinated the King that he packed them himself. The casket, it was said, 'may interest posterity when posterity comes upon it among the ruins of London'.

Senate. The two main halls on either side of the entrance hall were named the Macmillan Hall and the William Beveridge Hall after the two men most responsible for enabling the building to be built. It was explained to Beveridge at the time that identifying the hall by his surname only might lead to misunderstanding about its purpose.

On the day before the actual hundredth anniversary of the sealing of the original Charter at the end of November 1936 a final tragedy cast a further shadow over the University's centenary year. Sir Edwin Deller, the newly-knighted Principal, still only 53, was fatally injured in an accident at the Senate House when a builder's truck fell down an unfinished lift-shaft on top of him. Without recovering consciousness he died three days later.[8] The University was totally unprepared for such a disaster. The Academic Registrar, S.J. Worsley, served as Acting Principal until July 1937, when it was

268 The building of the Senate House proceeded rapidly: a view from the roof of the British Museum in September 1934, fifteen months after the foundation stone was laid.

269 A view from more or less the same position in May 1935.

270 A view from Malet Street in early 1937. The tower, 210 feet in height when completed, was dubbed 'London's first skyscraper' in the press, and soon 'the dummy skyscraper' when it was realized that building regulations initially prevented occupancy above the eighth floor.

271 The Senate House tower nearing completion in March 1937. The 70-foot flag-staff was added in August 1937. The southern administrative block was occupied from August 1936.

272 The Senate House was built by traditional labour-intensive methods, employing over 600 men. The load-bearing walls were of numbered blocks of Portland stone with a brick and mortar core. The tower was given a steel frame, not for structural reasons, but to bear the great weight of the books to be stored in it.

decided that the Vice-Chancellor, Sir Herbert Eason, would succeed as Principal when his term of office in the Vice-Chancellorship ended.

By then, the hopes of completing the whole of Holden's great 'spinal plan', on however long a timetable, had to be abandoned. During 1937 it became clear that funds would not be forthcoming to complete the scheme in its entirety. Holden was asked to re-design the plan incorporating many modifications in the interest of financial stringency. The so-called 'balanced scheme' was devised, leaving the Portland stone buildings at the southern end of the site with the Senate House tower in the centre, and envisaging a series

273 The ambitious, not to say grandiose, 'spinal plan' was abandoned in 1937 and replaced by the so-called 'balanced plan' involving separate buildings to the north of the Senate House designed more economically without Portland stone. Further modifications were made later.

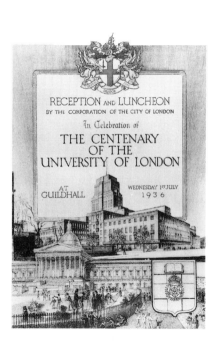

274 The University's centenary was celebrated at the end of summer term in 1936 before the building of the Senate House was completed. The cover of the menu for a luncheon given by the City of London juxtaposed an architectural drawing of the Senate House with George Scharf's drawing of University College when it was the University of London Mark I between 1828 and 1836.

of separate buildings in more economical brick to the north, retaining Torrington Square as the 'University Garden'.

The building of the tower was completed. The flagstaff was added to the top in August 1937, and in November 1937 the whole building was impressively floodlit by night for the first time, just before an honorary degree was to be presented to the lady who had become Queen Elizabeth after dramatic events outside the University in 1936. Part of the Library was occupied in 1937, but it was not until October 1938 that the bulk of the books were moved from South Kensington, a transfer requiring 161 pantechnicon loads (and seven taxi journeys for the most valuable items, including the original Charter). The leases of the houses facing on to Russell Square fell in on Lady Day 1939 and the houses were quickly demolished to make way for the Ceremonial Hall which was to complete the modified 'balanced scheme'. The Hall, however, was to elude the University. With the outbreak of war in 1939 the work on the foundations was suspended and never resumed.

For a time during the academic year 1938–9 the Senate House enjoyed a splendid but brief period of glory, illuminated by floodlighting outside and by cleverly concealed lighting inside, all the elements of its striking décor carefully co-ordinated by Charles Holden, floral displays beautifully arranged at receptions, brass-buttoned and white-gloved page-boys alert in the entrance hall. George V had said that the plan was 'exactly like a battleship'; the resulting building was more like a lavishly equipped ocean liner, cruising in its first season, however, to war. In use but uncompleted in 1939, the Senate House was destined never to be formally opened.

The decade between the adoption of the new constitution in 1929 and the outbreak of the war in 1939 was the period in which the University achieved maturity in the public mind and in its own consciousness. It became evident that the University was more than

275 A perspective drawing of Holden's design for the western front of the Senate House facing Malet Street in the 'balanced scheme' of 1937.

276 A perspective drawing of Holden's design for the eastern front of the Senate House facing Russell Square in the 'balanced scheme' of 1937, showing on the right the projected 'University Hall' that was never to be built.

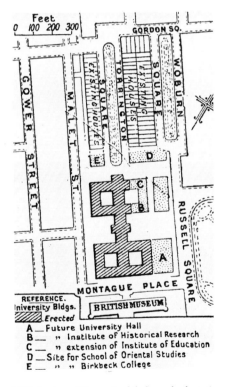

277 A plan of the revised 'balanced scheme' showing what had been built and what was proposed in December 1937.

REFERENCE.
University Bldgs.
////// Erected
A — Future University Hall
B — ,, Institute of Historical Research
C — ,, extension of Institute of Education
D — Site for School of Oriental Studies
E — ,, ,, Birkbeck College

the sum of its separate parts, despite their increasing range.

Birkbeck College had become a school of the University in 1920. Housed from 1885 off Fetter Lane, it had begun to concentrate more on university-level teaching, shedding book-keeping and elocution and the other miscellaneous subjects increasingly taught in the polytechnics. From 1920 Birkbeck accepted only part-time and evening students, finding an important niche in the University's provision. It also became the only college of the University located in the City of London. Another long-established teaching institution, the School of Pharmacy, joined the University as a school in 1925. It had been established by the Pharmaceutical Society of Great Britain in 1842 to provide trained practical pharmacists. Also in 1925 the degree of BPharm was established.

Two new postgraduate medical institutions were created as a result of the Athlone Report in 1921, produced by a committee chaired by the University's future Chancellor. On it 'Public Health was represented by Sir George Newman and commonsense by Sir Cooper Perry'. A new Institute of State Medicine was proposed, and somehow this became linked to the London School of Tropical Medicine which had existed in connection with the Seamen's Hospital since 1899. 'It has remained something of a mystery how the ultimate fusion with hygiene came into being,' wrote Sir Philip Manson-Bahr in a compelling sentence, 'but, as is so often the case,

278 The Goldsmiths' Library photographed in the course of construction in 1937, with the arms of the Goldsmiths' Company already installed in the stained glass of the window at the south end.

279 The Middlesex Library South after its completion in 1938.

280 The Principal's room in the Senate House in 1938, with the building's only coal fire in a fireplace of Ashburton marble designed at the request of Sir Edwin Deller, a Devon man by origin.

281 Sir Herbert Eason (1874–1950), the ophthalmic surgeon, Dean of Guy's Hospital Medical School, 1904–12, and Superintendent of Guy's Hospital, 1920–37, who served as Vice-Chancellor of the University in 1935–7 and became Principal in 1937–41. 'Completely self-assured, a little intolerant of the slower moving minds of some of his colleagues, and master of a dangerously witty tongue.'

282 The ceremonial staircase in the Senate House, with floral decorations, in 1938. The walls were lined with Travertine marble, the ceiling having mouldings in which the London plane-tree provided the main motif.

283 A view of the Senate House across Torrington Square, drawn by Dennis Flanders as it appeared on the eve of war in 1939.

UNIVERSITY of LONDON
SITE for NEW BUILDINGS.

"We had it built nice and high because we want our students to look down on Oxford and Cambridge."

284 A cartoon appearing in the *Evening News* in May 1938.

285 The Senate Room when it was first used in 1938, panelled in English walnut and with the walls covered in tapestry incorporating the 'UL' monogram.

various non-related incidents, moving in a mysterious way, performed this miracle'.[9] The result was the London School of Hygiene and Tropical Medicine, opened in the handsome new building built with a generous injection of Rockefeller money in 1929 across Malet Street from the Senate House site. An entirely new school was the British Postgraduate Medical School, as it was originally called, incorporated in 1931 and opened in 1935. It was attached to a general hospital, the Hammersmith Hospital, and it was to be unique among medical schools not only in being exclusively concerned with postgraduates, but also in having whole-time members of the academic staff with a commitment to research. The medical schools in general continued to be very differently organized to the other colleges of the University. The recommendations of the Haldane Report were scorned, though a few of the professorial units envisaged by Haldane did begin to be established after 1920, first at St Bartholomew's, St Thomas's, the London School of Medicine for Women, and St Mary's.

Three institutes were added to the University in 1932. Sir Bernard Pares achieved independence for the School of Slavonic and East European Studies which had begun at King's College in 1915. For a time it had been housed in the hut of the Institute of Historical Research, but in 1928 it moved into a house in Torrington Square and ten years later — with financial support from Czechoslovakia — into part of the Senate House building. The London Day Training College, since 1902 a leading centre for the training of teachers and for the study of educational issues, became the Institute of Education. It had been a school of the University, but legally and financially it had been under the control of the LCC. Under Sir Percy Nunn it flowered into a focus for 'higher pedagogical teaching and research' with the status of a University institute from 1932. It was to be rehoused in the Senate House building in 1938. The Courtauld Institute of Art was an entirely new foundation, opened in 1932 and endowed by Samuel Courtauld with the support of Sir Robert Witt and Lord Lee of Fareham, who had suggested the Institute. Degrees in the history of art were offered for the first time in Britain, and a teaching tradition was established combining the best of the British tradition of connoisseurship and antiquarianism with the achievements of continental art-historical scholarship. Courtauld himself gave the lease of his fine house in Portman Square. In 1937 another institute was founded, modestly funded but equally splendidly housed in St John's Lodge in Regent's Park. The Institute of Archaeology was the creation of Sir Mortimer Wheeler and his first wife Tessa Wheeler; it rapidly became a hub of archaeological research.

286 The Senate House as it appeared during the 1939–45 war, with to the north the building for the School of Oriental and African Studies virtually completed and the skeleton of Birkbeck College left uncompleted, and the vacant sites for the Great Hall (right) and for the Union building (top left).

287 The Courtauld Institute of Art was opened in 1932 at 20 Portman Square, one of Robert Adam's finest town houses, built in the 1770s and 'dedicated to the use of the Arts in 1932 by Samuel Courtauld in memory of Elizabeth Theresa Frances, his wife, who devoted her life to Music and other Modes of Beauty and died here in mid-career on 25 December 1931'.

231

288 Sir Bernard Pares (1867–1949), Professor of Russian History, Language and Literature, 1919–36, and Director between 1922 and 1939 of what under his guidance became the School of Slavonic and East European Studies, separated from King's College as an institute of the University from 1932.

289 R.W. Seton-Watson, FBA (1879–1951), the first Masaryk Professor of Central European History, 1922–45: the companion piece of the plaque to Pares in the entrance hall of SSEES in the Senate House. He was acclaimed throughout eastern Europe, but: 'For university business he found no time; he was unpunctual, untidy, and far too pre-occupied with more important matters.'

The number of students registered at the University expanded majestically. From just over 8000 in 1920–1 the total grew to well over 14,000 in 1938–9. The total output of graduates nearly doubled over the same period, reaching nearly 5000 per year on the eve of the Second World War. By the early 1930s, a third of all university students in England were London students, and the University of London became bigger than the universities of Oxford and Cambridge combined.

Increasing efforts were made to provide ceremonial occasions to symbolize the unity of the federal university. In the 1920s Presentation Day outgrew the University's pathetic Great Hall at the Imperial Institute, and the annual occasion in May became a regular feature at the Albert Hall. By the late 1930s over 1500 presentees had to be coped with. From 1930 an additional ceremony was added when Foundation Day was formally instituted in November, first for the presentation of graduates with higher degrees and then for the awarding of honorary degrees. Besides the four awarded in 1903 (see p.176), the only other honorary graduand had been the Prince of Wales (later Edward VIII, and later still the Duke of Windsor). In 1921 he had been invested with the degrees of DSc and MCom at the time when the new degrees in Commerce were being launched. (The BCom and the MCom, never a great success, were eventually abolished in 1954.) In 1931 honorary doctorates were presented to Lord Beauchamp and Lord Macmillan, and at a special ceremony marking the centenary of the British Association for the Advancement of Science, to a number of distinguished scientists and to Field Marshal Smuts as President of the Association. The presentation of a small and carefully selected number of honorary degrees subsequently became an annual event.

A further focus for the University as a whole was provided in 1931 by the opening of the University sports ground at Motspur Park, nineteen minutes by train from Waterloo. A variety of sports could now be played on the University's own ground. An appeal had been launched in 1926 for the sports ground and for a University boat-house in order to 'encourage both that corporate spirit among its students which exists nowhere so finely as on the river and the sports ground, and the cult of true sportsmanship'. One of Lord Rosebery's last acts as Chancellor was to donate £5000 for these purposes.[10] The University boat-house at Chiswick was opened in 1937. In 1933 the Principal said: 'The problem of encouraging a corporate University life among the students of such varied nationalities and belonging to colleges scattered over so wide an area is one that faces us continually.' The sports ground and the boat-house joined the University Union and the OTC as the

290 The Institute of Archaeology was established in 1937 and originally housed in the splendid St John's Lodge in Regent's Park, which later – after the Institute moved to Gordon Square in 1958 – housed departments of Bedford College until 1984.

291 The founder of the Institute of Archaeology was Sir Mortimer Wheeler, FBA FRS, (1890–1976), seen here looking characteristically raffish during a break from the excavation of Maiden Castle in the mid 1930s. Formerly Director of the National Museum of Wales and Keeper of the London Museum, Wheeler was to become Director-General of Antiquities in India and Secretary of the British Academy, as well as a well-known publicist for archaeology and pioneer telly don.

main intercollegiate 'centres of social intercourse'. Efforts were also made to provide halls of residence. The Duke of Connaught presented his virtually bankrupt hostel for Canadian students, and the University reopened Connaught Hall as the first intercollegiate hall for men students in Torrington Square in 1931. College Hall, the independent hall of residence for women students, was rebuilt in Malet Street in 1932. A move towards the inspection and registration of student lodgings was made in 1931 with the opening of the Lodgings Bureau at the premises of the Union, then temporarily housed in Torrington Square.

Thus there were other developments in Bloomsbury while the plans for building the new headquarters for the University were pressing ahead, and in a variety of ways the University was beginning at last to mean something to itself. A symbolic development was the Central Research Fund, established in 1937, with £5000 a year to distribute throughout the University for assisting specific research projects. By 1938 the Principal could say that 'the progress of the University – both material and intellectual – is steady and

292 In 1931 the University athletic ground at Motspur Park was opened by Lord Beauchamp. The 28-acre site near Wimbledon was bought 1926, and a pavilion and covered stand, were erected in 1932. The ground soon became a showpiece.

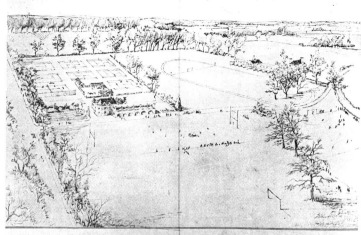

SKETCH VIEW SHEWING LAY-OUT OF SPORTS GROUND

293 The Inter-Universities Sports took place at Motspur Park in May 1932; competitors in the half-mile heat are shown here. In 1937 Sidney Wooderson chose the ground as the best in the south of England for his successful attempt on the world one-mile record (4 mins. 6.6 secs.).

294 In 1939 most of the colleges of the University were evacuated from London and billeted on universities all over the provinces. King's College went to Bristol, apart from the Faculty of Medical Sciences, which went to Glasgow. The Great Hall of Bristol University became the temporary library for war-time King's students.

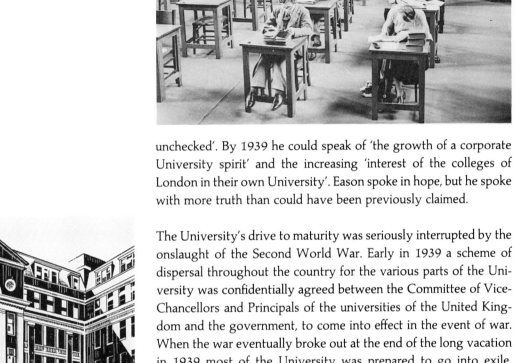

295 The Middlesex Hospital, of which the Medical School was an integral part, as rebuilt in 1935.

unchecked'. By 1939 he could speak of 'the growth of a corporate University spirit' and the increasing 'interest of the colleges of London in their own University'. Eason spoke in hope, but he spoke with more truth than could have been previously claimed.

The University's drive to maturity was seriously interrupted by the onslaught of the Second World War. Early in 1939 a scheme of dispersal throughout the country for the various parts of the University was confidentially agreed between the Committee of Vice-Chancellors and Principals of the universities of the United Kingdom and the government, to come into effect in the event of war. When the war eventually broke out at the end of the long vacation in 1939 most of the University was prepared to go into exile. University College was the most widely dispersed. The Faculty of Arts went to Aberystwyth, the Faculty of Science to Bangor, the Faculty of Engineering to Swansea; the Faculty of Medicine was initially split between Bangor, Cardiff and Sheffield. The Slade School of Fine Art was billeted on the Ruskin School in Oxford and the Bartlett School of Architecture on Cambridge. Most of King's College went to the University of Bristol, while its Faculty of Medical Sciences went to Glasgow. Cambridge provided a place of evacuation for several colleges: Bedford went to Newnham, LSE to Peterhouse, QMC to King's and SOAS to Christ's. Westfield went to St Peter's Hall in Oxford. Goldsmiths' College and the Institute of Education went to the University of Nottingham. The medical schools of necessity had to stay close to their clinical centres, but pre-clinical teaching was scattered up and down the country in a

296 Much destruction was wrought on various parts of the University by bombing during the Second World War. University College was among the most extensively damaged. Bombs in 1940 and 1941 gutted the library and several lecture theatres and burnt the dome.

297 Charles Wilson, from 1943 Lord Moran (1882–1977), the great Dean of St Mary's Hospital Medical School from 1920 to 1945, a powerful figure in the world of medicine and medical adviser to Sir Winston Churchill.

variety of strange places from Aberdeen to Tunbridge Wells. There was an enormous amount of dislocation. 'Speaking generally,' the Principal reported blandly in 1940, 'the work of the University has continued satisfactorily, although the temporary arrangements have thrown much additional work on the teaching and administrative staffs of the Schools and of the University itself.'

The new Senate House was taken over by the Ministry of Information for the duration of the war, with the roof providing an indispensable observation post for the Royal Observer Corps. It became the home of a bureaucracy on a wholly new scale, for which one of the many intellectuals temporarily employed, the poet Cecil Day-Lewis, suggested the motto 'A Minute every Second'. The Senate House came to figure in literature. 'It was not until he was under its shadow and saw the vast bulk of London University insulting the autumnal sky, that he remembered that here was the Ministry of Information . . .' Evelyn Waugh's character in *Put Out More Flags* (1942) had difficulty in obtaining entrance: 'It was far from easy to gain admission; only once in his life, when he had had an appointment in a cinema studio in the outer suburbs, had Ambrose met such formidable obstruction. All the secrets of all the services might have been hidden in that gross mass of masonry.'

Graham Greene provided an even more graphic description of 'the Ministry' in *Penguin New Writing* in 1941: 'the high heartless building with complicated lifts and long passages like those of a liner and lavatories where the water never ran hot and the nail-brushes were chained like Bibles. Central heating gave it the stuffy smell of mid-Atlantic except in the passages where the windows were always open for fear of blast and the cold winds whistled in. One expected to see people wrapped in rugs lying in deck-chairs, and the messengers carried round minutes like soup.' Greene's character 'stood aside for an odd little procession of old men in robes, led by a mace-bearer. They passed – one of them sneezing – towards the Chancellor's Hall, like humble ghosts still carrying out the ritual of another age. They had once been kings in this place, the gigantic building built to house them, and now the civil servants passed up and down through their procession as though it had no more consistency than smoke.'

The most poetic encounter of all at the Senate House during its Ministry of Information period was that between Sir John Betjeman and Joan Hunter Dunn, deputy manageress of the catering department inherited by the Ministry from the University.

> Miss J. Hunter Dunn, Miss J. Hunter Dunn,
> Furnish'd and burnish'd by Aldershot sun,
> What strenuous singles we played after tea,
> We in the tournament – you against me!

298 College Hall, the original hall of residence for women students, was rebuilt in Malet Street in 1931–2. 'The provision of running water in the rooms removed the need for maids to carry cans of hot water around the house in the morning and in the evening before dinner.'

299 Harold Laski (1893–1950), Professor of Political Science at the London School of Economics, 1926–50, in a *Vincula* cartoon of 1925. A staunch socialist and later Chairman of the Labour Party, he was one of the most influential teachers of his time. 'His lectures, brilliantly delivered and based on great erudition and a memory of extraordinary power, were always crowded.'

Saint Harold slayeth the Dragon of Injustice.

Design for Window in a Chapel of Progressive People at the School of Economics. See Auntie Aggie's Painting Competition, page 25.

Miss Hunter Dunn had a diploma from King's College of Household and Social Science. 'When the bombs fell she bound up our wounds unperturbed,' Betjeman later recalled. 'She was so marvellous at first aid. I used to wish desperately for a small wound from a bomb so that she would minister to me.'[11]

The central administration moved out of the Senate House only three years after it had moved in. The central offices moved first to the monumental buildings of an earlier age at Royal Holloway College, and then in 1941, when the War Office requisitioned most of Royal Holloway, they moved on to Richmond College. The Methodist Conference had been obliged to close the College, and it became the home of the administration for the rest of the war. The number of students fell sharply, as military service made its demands upon the age-group. Work of national importance was undertaken by many of the teachers. A cohort of the remaining students completed their studies under a skeleton academic staff without ever entering the London buildings of their colleges, several of which were seriously damaged in air-raids. For some there were great benefits obtained from the close relations with the host institutions. The Principal of Westfield College, for example, noted in 1942 that her college was able to offer the best of two worlds, 'a combination of Oxford University life, and London syllabuses and London fees'.

The colleges began to return to London in 1944 when the advent of V-bombs coincided with the summer examinations. It was decided to carry on, while warning all candidates that conditions were 'not pleasant'. A variety of unusual locations were employed in order to avoid the concentration of many candidates in one spot, and the Principal was able to report that the exams 'were carried through without casualties – other than those normally caused by

300 Birkbeck College temporarily closed in 1939, but soon re-opened to continue teaching for part-time students who could not be evacuated. Classes continued on a makeshift basis after the destruction of the library. 'We have no panes, dear mother, now' read a notice in nearby Fleet Street.

these exacting but essential tests'. It was noted that exam performance did not deteriorate during the war, despite the arduous conditions.

While the number of 'internal students' fell, the number of 'external students' increased markedly. It was estimated before the war that about a third of external students carried out their studies at teaching institutions in London, about a third at university colleges and technical colleges in the provinces, and about a third carried out their studies privately. About a tenth of them were resident overseas, with Ceylon providing the largest proportion. In 1919 examinations were conducted at thirty overseas centres scattered throughout the Empire. From 1920, at the request of the Foreign Office, examinations were held widely throughout the rest of the world: at Jerusalem and Shanghai in that year, in 1922 at Tientsin, in 1923 at Baghdad and Istanbul, and subsequently in Alexandria, Bangkok, Isfahan, Buenos Aires, Athens, Jedda, Peking, Cairo and elsewhere. It was not only the internal side of the University which expanded in the 1930s. By 1937 there were seventy-nine overseas centres for London degree and matriculation examinations, dealing with a total of 4908 candidates.

At the outbreak of war it was assumed that the external side 'might be at a standstill for some time', but enquiries from external students immediately 'came in at the rate of some hundreds a day'. Many students who otherwise would have become internal students took advantage of the external arrangements for decentral-

301 During the war the Senate House became the Ministry of Information, with Lord Macmillan, Chairman of the Court of the University, as the first Minister in 1939–40, and Sir John Reith as Minister briefly in 1940, and Duff Cooper in 1940–1. 'Mr Duff Cooper's room at the Ministry of Information is the central clearing house for news', read the original caption for this strange photograph.

302 General Dwight D. Eisenhower, later President of the United States, photographed leaving the sandbagged Senate House after a press conference in 1944 with Churchill's protégé Brendan Bracken, Minister of Information, 1941–5.

ized examinations, and the war produced a great boom in external students. Their number exceeded those of internal students in 1941, a situation that, as it transpired, was to obtain until 1957 (see tables 6.1, 6.2). Hundreds of service personnel found it was a way to continue their studies, and with the help of the Red Cross even prisoners of war – as in the First World War – were provided for. In the first year of the war 'many thousands of printed papers were . . . insured, despatched and delivered all over the world. Thousands of scripts were collected and returned to the University, marked by examiners and the results cabled back to the centres.' Only two scripts were lost. The University congratulated itself. 'That these cultural bonds of Empire could be thus maintained in war-time is a tribute to the University Staff, the Overseas Education Authorities, the Post Office, and ultimately to the ceaseless vigilance of the Royal and merchant Navies.'

In 1941 Sir Harold Claughton (1882–1969) succeeded as Principal of the University. He had been the first Clerk of the Court since 1929, having previously been Financial Officer and Secretary to the Senate from 1924, and before that in the Imperial Record Department in India, in Military Intelligence during the First World War and Secretary of the Surplus Government Property Disposals Board after the war. He was an influential figure in the University, but his successor as Clerk of the Court in 1944 and subsequently as Principal in 1948 was to be vastly more influential. Dr D.W. Logan (Sir Douglas Logan as he became in 1959) was to be the central figure in the post-war development of the University. He had taken degrees in Greats and in Jurisprudence at Oxford and spent a year at the Harvard Law School before becoming an Assistant Lecturer in Law at the LSE in 1936. A year later he went as a Fellow to Trinity College, Cambridge, and then after the outbreak of war, into the Ministry of Supply. The head of the Law Department at LSE was Sir David Hughes Parry; he was also an admired and commanding figure in the University as Chairman of the Academic Council from 1939 to 1945, Vice-Chancellor from 1945 to 1948, and a member of the Court from 1938 to 1970 (and its Chairman from 1962). Hughes Parry was influential in appointing Logan.[12]

One day in 1943 he walked into my office and asked whether I was interested in the post of Clerk of the Court of the University of London. Eventually I put in an application and, rather to my surprise, I was offered the appointment which I took up in January 1944. In the following year he became Vice-Chancellor and in that capacity he later chaired the committee to find a successor to Sir Harold Claughton as Principal – and the lot 'fell upon me'. I moved along the corridor in January 1948 and Hughes Parry was the first of the twelve Vice-Chancellors under whom I have served. He initiated me into the mysteries of the academic side of the University and remained my mentor in university and many other matters for the rest of his life.

Logan was Principal from 1948 until 1975. It was to be an era of growth and expansion for the University.

Planning for the post-war period began in 1943. The Court began visiting bombed premises and collecting information about the needs of the schools on their return to London. The difficulties were evident, quite apart from a variety of new problems that revealed the shape of things to come. 'We pass from the house of war', wrote the Principal in 1945, 'to find our garden strewn with reports, commissions and committees, white papers, and the new Education

303 The Royal Postgraduate Medical School organized 'refresher' and other specialist courses for medical practitioners from the time of its opening in 1935, and during the war provided a variety of courses for military doctors from many countries. Here Sir Reginald Watson-Jones (1902–72), the distinguished orthopaedic surgeon, is seen demonstrating a method of plastering for fractures of the spine under field conditions, with the weight of the body being supported by a tin bowl and a brick.

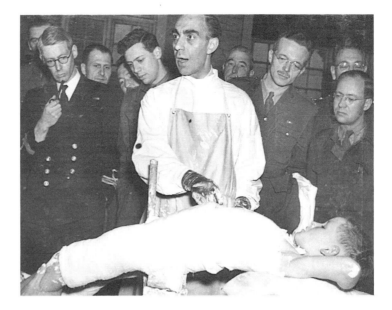

Act.' There was an immediate post-war boom in students. From 11,451 internal students in 1944–5, the number nearly doubled to 20,405 in 1947–8. Trends in the total numbers of students in the whole period covered by this chapter are given in table 6.1, and the total numbers of graduates are given in table 6.2. The rapid growth in the years after the war gave on to a period of expansion that was to last until the early 1980s.

Table 6.1 Number of Students, 1930–65[13]

	Internal Total	Internal Full-time	External
1930–31	11,152	10,791	n.a.
1935–36	13,579	12,864	10.943
1938–39	14,587	14,587	10,839
1940–41	8,960	9,121	8,902
1945–46	14,993	12,894	19,257
1950–51	23,202	18,412	27,780
1955–56	22,214	19,029	24,957
1960–61	26,762	21,995	26,953
1965–66	32,802	26,389	29,524

Table 6.2 Number of Graduates, 1930–65[14]

	Bachelor's Degrees			Higher Degrees			Total
	Internal	External	Total	Internal	External	Total	
1930–31	2051	1285	3336	372	106	478	3814
1935–36	2429	1557	3986	409	88	497	4483
1940–41	1461	893	2354	174	36	210	2564
1945–46	1971	1206	3177	193	101	294	3471
1950–51	3586	2799	6385	746	150	896	7281
1955–56	3638	1855	5493	784	181	965	6458
1960–61	4488	1415	5903	1010	123	1133	7036
1965–66	5248	2513	7761	1744	148	1892	9653

304 In 1943 an honorary LLD was conferred on President Franklin D. Roosevelt in a special ceremony at Government House in Ottawa when the Chancellor, Lord Athlone, was Governor-General of Canada.

305 The Warburg Institute took refuge in London in 1933 and became an institute of the University in 1944. It grew out of the Hamburg library of Aby Warburg (1866–1929), photographed here in Rome shortly before his death, surrounded by his travelling scholarly apparatus, his amanuensis and valet Alber, and his assistant Gertrud Bing, herself later Director of the Institute, 1955–9.

The post-war years saw two schools added to the University. One, the Royal Veterinary College, the oldest of its type in the country, was well-established before it joined the University in 1949 following an inter-departmental report in 1944. Degrees in veterinary medicine were introduced at the same time. The other was a new foundation, also resulting from a war-time report. The recommendations of the committee on medical education chaired by Sir William Goodenough led to the establishment of the British Postgraduate Medical Federation by the Senate in 1945, and it was incorporated by Charter and admitted as a school of the University in 1947. It was to link together the work of a series of institutes for

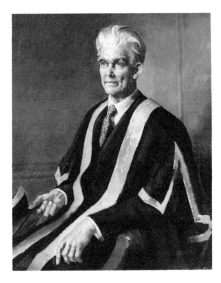

specialist postgraduate work in medicine. The British Postgraduate Medical School became a constituent institute, as did the research aspects of three other institutions which had been schools of the University – the Royal Cancer Hospital, a school since 1927, which evolved into the Institute of Cancer Research in 1951, and the Maudsley Hospital and the Bethlem Royal Hospital, schools since 1924, evolved into the Institute of Psychiatry in 1948. Seven other institutes were formed between 1949 and 1951, such as the Institute of Child Health where the Nuffield endowment of a chair boosted the research work of the Hospital for Sick Children in Great Ormond Street. Between 1954 and 1959 six further institutes were added to the Federation. A central headquarters building was provided in Guilford Street in 1955, and the postgraduate work of a number of different specialist hospitals was provided with a useful if complicated structure within the University.

306 Sir David Hughes Parry (1893–1973), Professor of English Law at LSE, 1930–59, the first Director of the Institute of Advanced Legal Studies, 1947–59, Vice-Chancellor, 1945–8, and Chairman of the Court, 1962–70 – to mention only the main offices he held during a life of unparalleled service in the University to which (as to his native Wales) he was devoted. 'He satisfied Kipling's exacting criterion and could walk with Kings without losing the common touch.'

307 The carriage used by Florence Nightingale (1820–1910) during the Crimean War in the 1850s – known as 'Florrie's lorry' – moved by medical students at St Thomas's in 1946 to block the entrance to the nurses' home. Her 'institution for the training, sustenance and protection of nurses' was established at St Thomas's Hospital in 1860, and an appeal is currently under way to establish a museum of Nightingalia there.

308 Triumph over austerity: seven graduates of the University photographed outside the Albert Hall at Presentation Day in 1947.

309 Sir Winston Churchill had an honorary degree conferred upon him *in absentia* in 1945, but in 1948 he spoke at Foundation Day. To his left, underneath the maces, is Sir Douglas Logan in his first year of office as Principal. To the left of Lord Athlone in the chair as Chancellor is Dame Lillian Penson (1896–1963), from 1939 a formidable Professor of History at Bedford College and the first (and only) woman to serve as Vice-Chancellor, 1948–51.

Several new research centres in the humanities were also established as institutes under the direct control of the Senate. The Warburg Institute joined the University in 1944. Its concern with the study of the classical tradition, with those elements of European thought, literature and art which derive from the ancient world, originated in the library built up in Hamburg by Aby Warburg, the historian of Renaissance art and civilization. The library grew into a research institute and a seminar of Hamburg University. With the coming to power of the Nazis in 1933 and the consequent 'burning of books', the whole library was stealthily packed into two little ships and transferred in its entirety to London. Temporary accommodation was found in the Imperial Institute in 1937 after the

310 Lord Birkett (1883–1962) as painted by Claude Rogers: a leading KC before the war and a leading judge during and after the war, he served as Chairman of the Court of the University from 1948 to 1962.

311 Professor L.A. Willoughby (1885–1977), Professor of German at UCL, 1931–50, and then the first Director of the Institute of Germanic Languages and Literature (later renamed Institute of Germanic Studies), the plan for which he conceived during the war. 'There were many who noted with awe in Leonard Willoughby a striking facial resemblance to Goethe.'

312 Professor R.H. Tawney (1880–1962) in Claude Rogers' 70th birthday portrait which hangs in the Senior Common Room at the LSE where he was an influential teacher of economic history from 1913. He had a wider pervasive influence through his pioneer WEA classes and his writings such as *The Acquisitive Society* (1921) and *Equality* (1931) as well as *Religion and the Rise of Capitalism* (1926), all informed by his conviction as a Christian and as a socialist. 'All flesh is grass,' he said, 'and historians wither, poor things, sooner than most.'

313 The Royal Veterinary College, founded in 1791, became a school of the University in 1949. A new building was erected on its original site in Camden Town in 1937, seen here in a drawing of that year. Since 1959 the College has also occupied a large second site at Hawkshead near Potters Bar in Hertfordshire.

KING'S COLLEGE LONDON

IMPORTANT NOTICE

The University has asked all College Authorities to direct the notice of all students to the following resolution of the Senate:

"The University has been informed by the Metropolitan Police that, in view of the fact that no adequate site can be provided for student celebrations on 5th November, 1954, they are not prepared to give facilities for or protection to any procession or demonstration by students on that day. Students are therefore warned that arrangements of the kind customary in previous years should not be made. A student who is found to have taken part in any form of procession or demonstration on 5th November next, or otherwise to have misbehaved himself or herself, will be liable to appear before a College Board of Discipline and a student convicted of any offence in a court of justice will be summoned to appear before a University Board of Discipline. Any student, therefore, who takes part in such activities, is liable to be sent down by his School either temporarily or permanently and may have his registration for the University examination he proposes to take cancelled or he may be debarred from sitting for that examination for such period as the Senate deems necessary.

Schools should draw the attention of their students to the general undesirability of demonstrations in the streets of London and of inter-collegiate "rags" which often result in wanton and unnecessary damage to persons or property. Students should be warned that participation in such activities will be regarded as a serious disciplinary offence."

P. S. NOBLE, Principal.

October, 1954.   E. S. ABBOTT, Dean.

314 Unruly scenes and several arrests on bonfire night in 1953 led to the banning of the occasion in 1954. Rags had their heyday between 1907 and 1953, and the great age of ragging began to fade, though it was some years before 'Reggie', the lion mascot of King's students, or 'Phineas', the highlander mascot of UCL, were safe from japes of one kind or another.

315 All over London important University work was carried out in a variety of 'temporary' buildings. This hut at the back of Hammersmith Hospital used in the First World War by Sir Robert Jones for making pioneer artificial limbs, became the refectory of the Royal Postgraduate Medical School after 1935, and was still in use *c.*1956, with the new MRC Cyclotron Building behind.

316 The University of London Union, formally amalgamated with the Athletic Union in 1952, was eventually provided with a permanent home in Malet Street, built to Charles Holden's design in 1951–7, seen here after it came into use in 1955. It was described in the following year as 'the finest building of its type in the country with facilities exceeding the most optimistic hopes of the members who founded the Union thirty-five years ago'.

University administration moved out and the *Kulturwissenschaftliche Bibliothek Warburg* was transformed into the Warburg Institute of the University of London.[15] The University was enriched by the addition of many individual scholars who were refugees from the *Hitlerzeit* in Germany; it was also enriched by an institutional refugee.

The Institute of Advanced Legal Studies was founded in 1947 on the model of the Institute of Historical Research. It had been proposed before the war to provide a centre 'for the encouragement of the study of the higher branches of legal science and for making available to scholars not only in this country but throughout the British Commonwealth and abroad the unrivalled materials which exist in London for legal research'. Under Sir David Hughes Parry as

317 The ULU bar at the time of the opening of the building by the Queen Mother in 1957, with its 'contemporary' decoration. It came to have one of the highest turnovers of any student union bar. In 1984 it was transformed – briefly – to 'Quirks' and then to 'Mergers', and now has a quite different appearance.

318 The 'Bloomsbury site' of the 1920s and 1930s expanded into the 'University Precinct' of the 1950s. At the northern end of Gordon Square a new building was provided for new Examination Halls, and for the two Institutes of Archaeology and of Classical Studies, seen here under construction in 1957.

the first Director the Institute rapidly established itself as such a focus. The proposed Institute of Empire Studies was opened in 1949 as the Institute of Commonwealth Studies 'to act as the focal point of the University's activities relating to the Dominions and Colonies'. Similar objects with regard to Germanic languages and literatures motivated the establishment of the Institute of Germanic Studies in 1950. The Institute of Classical Studies – the University's tenth institute – followed in 1953, incorporating the libraries of the Society for the Promotion of Hellenic Studies and the Society for the Promotion of Roman Studies. Like the other institutes, it was to be not only a workplace, but 'a marketplace for ideas and for the examination of new work'.

The new institutes were all housed on the Bloomsbury site which grew into the long-envisaged 'University Precinct'. Various buildings, handsomely designed in brick by Charles Holden, were built to the north of the Senate House in a modified version of the

SENNET

March 3, 1959   University of London Union   No. 104. 3d.

MARTIN PLANS FOR AN OPEN PRECINCT

Ambitious scheme for the Bloomsbury site

AN imaginative idea for merging the buildings of the original "Holden" scheme into a larger, secluded University precinct which will retain much of its traditional Bloomsbury character, was the chief feature of Sir Leslie Martin's Outline Development Plan for the University Precinct announced last week.

Other recommendations in the plan, which does not embrace the designing of any specific buildings, but only suggests the allotting of space and the general outline they might take, include the closing of all roads within the precinct, the extension of garden areas, first floor access terraces for pedestrian use in the new buildings, and the preservation of some of the older houses in the area.

Also emerging from his preliminary report is the fact that most of the new buildings in the precinct will be devoted either to post-graduate studies (the expansion of S.O.A.S. and the Institute of Education particularly) or to growth of University College, which Sir Leslie Martin described as "a cramped college at present."

There will be no large halls of residence within the area.

Cass more to change colour

The Woolwich International

FILM shows, an exhibition, a concert, and finally a grand ball will be the pattern of events at Woolwich in the next few days during the annual International Week.

All leading national Clubs in the Polytechnic will either be presenting films from their countries or staging exhibits in the main hall, or both. "Punch" cartoons will represent the English way of life.

The Cabaret on Friday evening will be run on a competitive basis, the three judges being the Mayor of Woolwich, the Principal, Dr. H. Heywood, and Past Union President Ian Baldwin. Each country has been allowed to spend only 4/- on its performance, with marks deducted if this sum is overspent, or if students from other Colleges are brought in.

The Arab students are staging a series of typical songs, the Polish students will be dancing, and the Chinese have the customary show of magic. A play is planned by West African students.

A model of the Bloomsbury area showing Sir Leslie Martin's suggestions for the development of the University Precinct. The Senate House is in the foreground.

319 *Sennet* was the ULU newspaper from 1954 to 1979, in succession to *Vincula* (1922–6) and *New Troy* (1926–30; briefly revived in 1947). It gave way in 1980 to *London Student*. The front page of this issue in 1959 highlighted the Martin plan for the University Precinct in Bloomsbury.

'balanced scheme' agreed before the war. The first to come into use was that for the School of Oriental and African Studies, as the School of Oriental Studies was expanded to become in 1938, the first stage of which was completed for the Ministry of Information in 1943. In 1947 the Institute of Historical Research at last moved into its permanent home in the north-east wing of the Senate House building, also completed for the use of the Ministry of Information during the war. In 1951 Birkbeck College was provided with its new building, left as a steel frame since the outbreak of the war. The University of London Union building was erected between 1951 and 1957, most of it coming into use in 1955. In 1958 the Warburg Institute was also to move into its new building at the northern end of the site, a building which also housed the Courtauld Institute Galleries – 'a wonderful addition to the cultural facilities of the University Precinct'. The Courtauld Institute itself was planned to follow, but this was never to be.

320 The School of Pharmacy was founded in Bloomsbury Square in 1842 by the Pharmaceutical Society of Great Britain to 'elevate the profession of pharmacy by furnishing the means of proper instruction'. This photograph shows the building as it appeared c.1910. It became a school of the University in 1925.

321 In 1929 the Pharmaceutical Society purchased a new site in Brunswick Square for the rebuilding of the School of Pharmacy. Begun in 1938, the University took it over in 1949 and the new building was completed in 1951–9. At the time of the opening in 1960 it was described as 'the oldest new building in London'.

Additional land was purchased from the Bedford Estate, a further thirteen acres of Bloomsbury in 1951, acquired for £1,619,000 after difficult negotiations. University College grew on the neighbouring site to own virtually all of the 'rectangle'. In 1958 a new building at the northern end of Gordon Square was opened for the Institute of Archaeology, the Institute of Classical Studies, and for Examination Halls which finally enabled the University's remaining use of the Imperial Institute building to be vacated. In 1959 Sir Leslie Martin, Professor of Archaeology at Cambridge and formerly Architect to the LCC produced, at the University's request, his comprehensive plan for the development of the whole Precinct. The LCC and the Royal Fine Art Commission gave their approval, but problems of financing meant that the realization of the plan was in the ensuing years to be patchy.

322 In 1952 the government decided that Imperial College should be considerably expanded to help supply the nation's needs for technological manpower, and in the mid-1950s many plans were drawn up and torn up before new buildings proliferated in the late 1950s and throughout the 1960s, virtually covering the area between the Natural History Museum and the Albert Hall.

Many developments took place beyond Bloomsbury too. In 1945 the South Eastern Agricultural College was renamed Wye College, amalgamated with Swanley Horticultural College and transformed under a great Principal, Dunstan Skilbeck. In 1953 King's College of Household and Social Science flowered into Queen Elizabeth College, named in honour of the Queen Mother, and it became the first of the women's colleges to admit men. The entrance of women to the medical schools – all exclusively male, apart from the school for women – was enforced in the aftermath of the considerable changes in the structure of medical education consequent upon the introduction of the National Health Service in 1948. The voluntary hospitals as well as the municipal hospitals became the responsibility of the government, and the medical schools had to be constitutionally separated from their parent hospitals. Only St Bartholomew's Hospital Medical College (since 1921) and the London School of Medicine for Women (since its inception in 1874) were previously constituted as legally separate bodies. After 1948 the medical schools began – gradually and often reluctantly – to be organized more as parts of the University.

The largest scale developments outside Bloomsbury in the 1950s took place in South Kensington. The post-war discussions about the nation's needs for technologically skilled manpower led to a decision that Imperial College should be substantially expanded. In 1952 the government, considering that 'a most important means of increasing productivity in industry is to improve facilities in higher technological education', announced that the number of students at

Imperial College should be doubled to 3000 within a few years. Special financial allocations were subsequently made to the College to enable the provision of considerable additional buildings, expansion which involved the demolition of the Imperial Institute building. 'It is symbolic of the needs of the times that we can no longer rest on the memorials of past greatness,' said the Rector of Imperial College, 'but must prepare for a new but different greatness in the future.' In 1956 there was a great outcry; the Imperial Institute turned out to be much admired by many who did not have to use it. The campaign for its preservation – a campaign which perhaps marked the beginning of a new age in terms of attitudes both to preservation and to Victorian architecture – resulted in the compromise that Colcutt's great tower was underpinned and retained amidst Imperial College's undistinguished new buildings, while the rest of the Imperial Institute was swept away.

The destruction of the Imperial Institute may have symbolized the decline of the Empire, but it did not mark the end of the University of London's long connection with British territories overseas. Between 1946 and 1971 several colonial university colleges were brought into 'special relation' with the University, a unique enterprise in which the University sponsored and took into partnership eight colleges in the process of becoming universities in their own right. The first was Gordon Memorial College in Khartoum, originally founded as a school by Lord Kitchener in 1898. For ten years after 1946 Sudanese students were permitted to take London degrees on the same basis as internal students and their teachers were permitted to suggest syllabuses and were appointed as examiners. Academic standards were raised and much was learnt by participating in the operations of an established university. The college became an independent university in 1956. The same special relationship was entered into with the University College of the West Indies in 1947, with the University College of Ibadan and the University College of the Gold Coast (later Ghana) in 1948, with Makerere University College in Uganda in 1949. The relationship lasted until 1961–3, by which time three further colleges were added: the University College of Rhodesia and Nyasaland in 1957–71, and the Royal College of Nairobi and the University College of Dar-es-Salaam in 1961–3. Altogether some 7000 London graduates were produced in this way.[16]

The University College of Southampton in 1949 seized the opportunity of the same sort of 'special relationship' with the University of London, and until the University of Southampton was chartered in 1952 its students took London degrees and its academic staff was brought into partnership in examining so that

323 Sir Ifor Evans, later Lord Evans of Hungershall (1899–1982), as meticulously painted by Sir William Coldstream, the Slade Professor of Fine Art: founder of ULU in 1921, Professor of English at Queen Mary College, 1933–44, Principal of QMC, 1944–51, and Provost of University College, 1951–66 – a much admired and much loved figure.

324 HM Queen Elizabeth the Queen Mother in the Royal Festival Hall reading the affirmation on the occasion of her installation in November 1955 at the beginning of her twenty-five-year period of service as Chancellor of the University. Among the honorary graduands can be seen Mrs Pandit, Lord Salisbury and Sir William Walton.

325 The Queen Mother leaving the Royal Festival Hall in November 1955 after having been installed as Chancellor, accompanied by Sir John Lockwood (1903–65), Master of Birkbeck College, 1951–65, and Vice-Chancellor, 1955–8.

the degrees were not merely 'external'.[17] The benefits of the arrangement were subsequently extended to the remaining university colleges at Hull, Exeter and Leicester. The University College of North Staffordshire (founded 1949) was the first English provincial university not to grow up under the aegis of the London degree syllabus, even before it became the University of Keele in 1962. The new universities of the 1960s, starting with the University of Sussex, were launched without a London apprenticeship. For long after the University of London Mark III had become the university *for* London, it thus continued to perform some of the wider national and imperial aims of its nineteenth-century origins.

Lord Athlone retired as Chancellor in 1955 and was succeeded by Queen Elizabeth the Queen Mother. The University had presented her with her first honorary degree in 1937 when she was described as 'one of Scotland's gifts to England'. Many such gifts had played a fundamental role in the development of the University of London and so it was entirely fitting that one should take the form of the first woman Chancellor. The Queen Mother was to carry out her ceremonial duties with much admired style for the next twenty-five years. The University had already had its first woman Vice-

Chancellor – the first in the Commonwealth – in the formidable form of Dame Lillian Penson in 1948–51. There had been a small number of women professors since Caroline Spurgeon became Professor of English Literature at Bedford College in 1913 – the first woman in the country to become a professor.[18]

By the time of the installation of the Queen Mother as Chancellor, the University's post-war growth had made it so large and complicated that the Principal had to write a booklet to explain it. Sir Douglas Logan's *The University of London: An Introduction* grew through three editions (1955, 1962, 1971) into an indispensable guide to the structure of the University, a federal structure that few members of the University could fully comprehend. The University, after all, contained 22 per cent of the full-time students of the whole country, 32 per cent of all postgraduate students, and 40 per cent of all medical students. The provision of accommodation of all sorts had by no means kept up with the growth in numbers of students since the war. Behind this lay the central problem of finance.

The increase in the flow of funds provided by the Treasury and allocated by the UGC in the post-war years is shown in table 6.3. The growth was substantial, especially when compared with the pre-war levels. In 1930–5, the first quinquennium for which the Court of the University was responsible, the total provided by the UGC was £556, 000 per annum. It had been increased to £621,000 per annum in the 1936–41 quinquennium. Before the war a considerable proportion of total income came from the LCC – £125,000 per annum in 1930–5 (some of which was foregone in the financial crisis of 1931–3) and £129,000 per annum in 1935–40. After the war the LCC contribution remained at this level, increased to £175,000 in 1947–8, to £200,000 in 1949–50 and to £250,000 in 1957–8. The home counties and neighbouring county boroughs provided additional grants (as they had since 1921) and in 1948–52 they totalled £143,000 per annum. The contribution of local authorities, significant in the inter-war period, dwindled after 1945 as the UGC increasingly became the dominating source of finance for the University.

By the 1950s the UGC was providing about three-quarters of the University's funds. Their distribution among the colleges, medical schools and institutes of the University is shown for 1960–1 in table 6.4, which also indicates other sources of income. The changing pattern of funding since 1920–1 (given in table 5.2, p.199) is evident. In 1920, the UGC provided only 30 per cent of the University's funding, while fees accounted for 38 per cent. By 1960, fee income had shrunk to only 8 per cent, and the UGC was directly

Table 6.3   Provision of Funds by UGC, 1945–64[19]

	Recurrent Grants	Capital Grants	Special Allocations for Imperial College	Total Capital Grants	Total Allocation
	£000s	£000s	£000s	£000s	£000s
1945–46	1,704	557	–	557	2,261
1946–47	2,115	462	–	462	2,577
1947–48	2,913	1,033	–	1,033	3,946
1948–49	3,273	2,012	–	2,012	5,285
1949–50	4,171	1,323	–	1,323	5,494
1950–51	4,784	1,710	–	1,710	6,494
1951–52	5,235	2,915*	–	2,915	8,150
1952–53	6,280	913	–	913	7,193
1953–54	6,573	1,536	386	1,922	8,495
1954–55	7,454	818	438	1,256	8,710
1955–56	7,984	1,698	1,539	3,237	11,221
1956–57	8,511	2,134	1,629	3,763	12,274
1957–58	10,240	3,112	2,031	5,143	15,383
1958–59	10,649	3,119	1,042	4,160	14,810
1959–60	12,221	2,923	3,505	6,428	18,649
1960–61	13,730	2,497	2,678	5,175	18,906
1961–62	14,453	2,500	1,655	4,155	18,609
1962–63	15,687	5,503	2,897	8,400	24,087
1963–64	17,228	5,358	1,841	7,199	24,427

*Includes contribution of £1,018,000 towards the cost of purchasing property in Bloomsbury from the Bedford Estate.

providing 75 per cent of income. The level of fees became increasingly a book transaction, as they came to be automatically paid on behalf of students by local education authorities, which also increasingly provided maintenance grants (to over 70 per cent of students by the early 1950s). After 1945 the UGC also provided funds for capital as well as recurrent purposes, as it had not generally done before the war when new buildings had to depend on private benefactions. The increasing direct dependence on the state for university funds for all purposes meant that the quinquennial estimates became, as Logan put it in 1953, 'almost a matter of life and death'.

The money flowed in, but it did not flow as rapidly as the University would have liked or as rapidly as it needed. Only one-sixth of the schemes put forward by schools and institutes could be included in the University's building programme in 1950–1. Ten years later the Principal wrote of 'the chronic deficiencies in the resources put at our disposal in the post-war period for capital development'. Targets for increases in student numbers were always met, but the increase in resources was 'woefully inadequate'. 'There has been no dearth of ministerial pronouncements', wrote Logan in 1961, 'about the importance of extending the facilities for

Table 6.4   Sources of Income, 1960–61[20]

	Endowments		Donations		Grants from Central University		Fees		Grants for Research Govt. Depts	Other Bodies
	£	%	£	%	£	%	£	%	£	£
Bedford College	3,915	0.8	1,216	0.3	411,270	86.7	44,966	9.5	2,419	1,101
Birkbeck College	397	0.1	1,112	0.2	444,241	83.2	24,716	4.6	28,689	31,539
Imperial College	23,552	0.9	31,050	1.1	2,036,532	74.9	148,370	5.5	297,585	148,665
King's College	2,971	0.3	2,914	0.3	822,850	81.6	107,989	10.7	27,738	28,918
LSE	24,806	2.8	12,079	1.4	641,380	72.6	119,386	13.5	10,758	68,925
QEC	3,799	1.7	–	–	188,479	83.7	15,842	7.0	4,104	11,465
QMC	800	0.1	–	–	602,324	82.6	67,028	9.2	35,725	18,603
Royal Holloway College	3,333	1.2	–	–	238,834	84.0	19,519	6.9	13,088	6,124
Royal Veterinary College	2,603	0.7	1,848	0.5	299,502	84.5	19,123	5.4	625	19,231
SOAS	9,304	1.7	3,499	0.6	469,251	86.5	19,603	3.6	–	29,191
School of Pharmacy	1,941	1.0	2,000	1.0	174,270	88.0	11,316	5.7	1,182	4,253
University College	50,404	2.2	14,801	0.7	1,700,072	75.5	148,015	6.6	186,570	129,230
Westfield College	1,901	1.3	–	–	124,294	86.5	13,849	9.6	871	2,531
Wye College	90	–	–	–	148,202	62.6	13,771	5.8	62,452	4,616
Charing Cross HMS	582	0.2	11	–	158,953	67.9	14,922	6.4	–	2,758
Guy's HMS	14,515	2.4	–	–	457,424	76.6	61,016	10.2	11,490	35,056
KCHMS	147	0.1	–	–	165,416	73.2	13,583	6.0	5,285	18,757
London HMC	865	0.2	–	–	341,312	78.2	31,975	7.3	13,116	36,825
Middlesex HMS	16,946	3.1	7	–	268,532	48.8	22,115	4.0	17,970	33,526
Royal Dental HS	555	0.4	–	–	115,380	90.2	9,163	7.2	–	–
RFHMS	8,052	2.7	–	–	232,066	77.8	23,901	8.0	18,148	16,100
St Bartholomew's HMC	52	–	–	–	334,282	84.7	38,422	9.7	3,638	10,133
St George's HMC	2,848	1.5	–	–	103,767	55.6	7,130	3.8	2,656	22,273
St Mary's HMS	890	0.2	–	–	294,334	66.4	24,759	5.6	16,684	59,902
St Thomas's HMS	–	–	–	–	287,705	85.7	23,269	6.9	–	16,202
UCHMS	26,711	8.4	594	0.2	237,754	71.5	18,962	6.0	7,548	29,533
Westminster MS	–	–	96	0.1	119,032	67.2	11,555	6.5	–	10,485
BPMF	14,942	0.8	46	–	1,115,216	61.8	90,907	5.0	94,018	224,199
L.S. Hygiene & Trop. Med.	12,960	3.7	15,656	4.4	254,424	71.8	13,878	3.9	19,219	26,294
Courtauld Institute of Art	5,578	0.3			72,151	81.9	3,535	4.0	788	733
Inst. of Adv. Legal Studies	–	–			20,247	91.6	75	0.3	–	1,329
Inst. of Archaeology	613	1.0	394	0.6	56,163	91.0	2,392	3.9	–	900
Inst. of Classical Studies	–	–			13,280	93.8	3	–	–	–
Inst. of Commonwealth Studies	–	–			19,491	83.1	–	–	193	3,653
Inst. of Education	10	–	3,415	0.9	266,162	71.9	87,715	23.7	–	9,081
Inst. of Germanic Studies	–	–	–	–	8,438	100.0	–	–	–	–
Inst. of Historical Research	96	0.2	730	1.6	43,210	96.4	349	0.8	–	–
SSEES	–	–			68,442	89.3	7,087	9.2	–	–
Warburg Institute	–	–			60,376	97.2	66	0.1	–	–
Computer Unit	–	–			29,757	47.0	564	0.9	–	1,321
TOTAL	284,369	1.5	91,468	0.5	14,387,498*	74.4	1,626,50	8.4	882,559	1,063,472
National Total	1,963,347	2.9	506,806	0.7	51,201,442*	74.5	6,317,603	9.2	3,212,605	3,002,795

*The London total comprehends the Treasury (UGC) grant of £13,945,464, grants from other government departments of £17,034, and grants from local authorities totalling £425,000 (2.2% of total income). The national total includes £48,399,076 from the Treasury (UGC), £1,224,802 from other government departments and £1,577,564 from local authorities (2.3% of total income). Discrepancies in totals are accouhnted for by central University funding.

Total		Other Income		TOTAL
£	%	£	%	£
13,520	0.7	9,533	2.0	474,420
60,228	11.3	3,227	0.6	533,921
446,250	16.4	33,309	1.2	2,719,063
56,656	5.6	14,431	1.4	1,007,811
79,683	9.0	6,408	0.7	883,742
15,569	6.9	1,379	0.6	225,068
54,328	7.4	4,844	0.7	729,324
19,212	6.8	3,427	1.2	284,325
19,856	5.6	11,413	3.2	354,345
29,191	5.4	11,733	2.2	542,581
5,435	2.7	3,022	1.5	197,984
315,800	14.0	29,241	1.3	2,252,338
3,402	2.4	206	0.1	143,652
67,068	28.3	7,745	3.3	236,876
2,758	1.2	56,909	24.3	234,135
46,546	7.8	17,952	3.0	597,453
24,042	10.6	22,938	10.1	226,126
49,941	11.4	12,428	2.8	436,521
51,496	9.4	191,094	34.7	550,190
–	–	2,860	2.2	127,958
34,248	11.5	–	–	298,267
13,771	3.5	7,937	2.0	394,464
24,929	13.3	48,063	25.7	186,737
76,586	17.3	46,379	10.5	442,948
16,202	4.8	8,596	2.6	335,772
37,101	11.6	7,445	2.3	318,567
10,485	5.9	35,965	20.3	177,133
318,217	17.6	266,056	14.7	1,805,384
45,513	12.8	11,964	3.4	365,395
1,521	1.7	5,326	6.0	354,395
1,329	6.0	445·	2.0	22,096
900	1.4	1,256	2.0	61,718
–	–	872	6.2	14,155
3,846	16.4	124	0.5	23,461
9,081	2.6	3,836	1.0	370,219
–	–	–	–	8,438
–	–	434	1.0	44,819
–	–	1,093	1.4	76,622
–	–	1,660	2.7	62,102
1,321	2.1	31,630	50.0	63,272
1,946,031	10.0	1,008,023	5.2	19,343,894
6,215,400	9.1	2,501,790	3.6	68,706,388

326 The old 'temporary' Great Hall at the Imperial Institute photographed in 1959 soon before demolition, as familiar to generations of examination candidates who used it to the end, despite its leaking roof and other inadequacies. When the Imperial Institute was finally pulled down, the University gave up South Kensington entirely to Imperial College.

higher education but, when the crucial point is reached of providing universities with the necessary finance, there is an unfortunate difference between what is said and what is done.' In retrospect the rate of inflation in the 1950s and 1960s seems low, but difficulties were caused in the 1952–7 and 1957–62 quinquennia by the rate of inflation eating into the level of resources carefully planned at the start of each quinquennium and the problems of meeting agreed increases in salary scales. In 1961–2 many schools and institutes had deficits, and the University had to face what Logan called 'the complete inadequacy of the recurrent grants for the quinquennium 1962–7'. The post-war expansion was achieved at the cost of obsolescent buildings, over-crowding, inadequate equipment, and a lot of hard work. Despite its many achievements, and despite the increasing provision of funds, the University of London – along with the rest of the British university system – was under-financed at the time when Lord Robbins began to undertake a major reassessment of the role of higher education.

Robbins and After, 1963–1986

Shortly after the last May Presentation Day, a leading Sunday newspaper referred to the University as 'the vast, antique tottering empire of Sir Douglas Logan'; for this it earned a well-merited rebuke from a prominent public person and was taken to the Press Council by a senior member of the Senate for refusing to publish his letter of protest. Some months later the same newspaper, slightly chastened, referred to the University in somewhat more endearing terms as 'that shambling giant in a class by itself'.

SIR DOUGLAS LOGAN, *Report by the Principal on the Work of the University during the Year 1962–63* (1963), p.3

London is a federal university of Byzantine complexity. Don't bother about its bureaucratic structure but concentrate on its separate teaching institutions, all of which select their students themselves.

KLAUS BOEHM and NICK WELLINGS, eds, *The Student Book, 85/86* (1985), p.221

For the last twenty-three years the University of London has resounded to an almost continual salvo of reports, some originating inside the University and some exploding from outside. The first of them, the Robbins Report of 1963, was the most resonant of all. It was, as the most perceptive of recent accounts has recognized, 'one of the great state papers of this century, and possibly the last of its line'.[1] Laid down as the central axiom was recognition of the principle 'that courses of higher education should be available for all those who are qualified by ability and attainment to pursue them and who wish to do so'. Calculation of society's needs for professional and other skills was rejected as impractical, and a powerful case was advanced for a massive expansion of higher education based on the growing demand for it.

There were at the time some 113,000 students in British universities. Robbins proposed that the number should be expanded to 153,000 in 1967–8 and to 346,000 by 1980–81. Total numbers in the higher education sector as a whole were to be increased from the 216,000 of 1962–3 to 560,000 by 1980–81. In the years since the war the universities had undergone a continuous process of expansion, and several new ones were in the process of being founded. The government immediately accepted the main recommendations of the Robbins Committee. The Colleges of Advanced Technology were now to become technological universities, and the size of all universities had to be increased substantially. For universities the 1960s was to be a decade of euphoria, giving way to the disillusionment of the 1970s and then to the dismay of the 1980s. The University of London, the biggest of British universities, was fully to

327 New buildings primarily for the Institute of Education were built in Bedford Way in 1970–77, seen here from the Senate House with SOAS to the left. An entirely new appearance was given to part of the University Precinct with buildings which no longer had elegantly dated rainwater heads designed by Charles Holden. Many considered the buildings designed by Sir Denys Lasdun as monstrously ugly; to some, however, they were 'the only public monumental building in London in anything like the style of the seventies'. Only the first stage of the building and only one of the intended five terraced wings has been finished. *Previous page.*

328 Lord Robbins, FBA (1898–1984), Professor of Economics at LSE, 1929–61, and subsequently Chairman of the *Financial Times*, 1961–70, of the Governors of LSE, 1968–74, and of the famous Committee on Higher Education, 1961–3, photographed in 1973 on the occasion of the launching of the appeal for the new building of the British Library of Political and Economic Science, opened in 1978 and named after him. A lion of a man: 'Along with his gentle manner', wrote a former Secretary of the UGC, 'one sensed a giant paw from which a claw or two would sometimes make a carefully modulated appearance.'

329 Sir Douglas Logan, Principal of the University, 1948–75, as drawn by Michael Noakes at the time of his retirement. 'Logan of London' towered in the university world throughout what soon came to be seen as a golden age of expansion. He had attended Felix Frankfurter's seminar on 'Federal Jurisdiction' at Harvard, and his somewhat ornate but perceptively cogent *Annual Reports* on the work of the University between 1948 and 1973 are testimony to his devotion to the federal ideal.

share these successive national moods.

The Robbins Report recognized that a federal university on the London scale could have advantages, such as 'the sustaining of institutes for highly specialised studies, of which the Courtauld Institute and the Institute of Historical Research in London University are famous examples'.

But against these advantages must be set the fact that, as such universities grow, their very size can involve drastic and sometimes undesirable changes in the machinery of government. Power tends to become concentrated in the centre, and the link between the central authority and the places where teaching and research are actually carried on becomes increasingly tenuous. To counter this it becomes necessary to set up a system of boards and committees that consume time and distract academic staff from their primary function. Moreover, the intervention of the university between the basic academic unit, the college, and the national system makes for delay and inhibits decision. There are real anomalies in a system in which the vice-chancellor of a newly-founded university at once has access to the University Grants Committee and the right of membership of the Committee of Vice-Chancellors and Principals, while heads of long-established London colleges, each as large as a civic university of moderate size, have no such access or right of membership.[2]

At both the University of Wales and the University of London, the

Robbins Committee thought that there were 'problems and inconveniences that call for investigation and remedy'. The Report said that if the universities concerned 'cannot satisfactorily and speedily resolve their difficulties for themselves we recommend that these should be the subject of independent inquiry'.

This was a threat the University could not ignore. A process of critical self-examination was unleashed. The possibility of the dissolution of the University was being put forward in various quarters, and so the first issue that had to be addressed was whether the constituent parts of the University were in favour of preserving the basic federal structure. The views of the Schools were sought, and their replies in 1964 indicated that they all favoured the continuation of the federal link. 'We attach great importance', said Queen Mary College, for example, 'to the maintenance of the main structure of the federal system of the University with its Academic and Collegiate Councils, its Faculty Boards, its Selection Boards for the appointment of professors and readers and its central general control over the examination system of the University.' 'For many years,' said the School of Oriental and African Studies, 'in a period of rapid university growth, the University Court system has undoubtedly relieved the colleges of the University of a great burden of administration.' The Royal Free Hospital School of Medicine considered that 'continued membership of the University is essential for the School's successful development in the future'. 'Fragmentation of the University effort', said the Royal Dental Hospital of London School of Dental Surgery, 'might prove to be a disastrous step in the light of history.'[3]

Several schools made serious criticisms of the workings of various aspects of the federal arrangements. King's College considered that the business of the University at the highest level is at present conducted by far too narrow a selection of professors and readers. Many other professors have virtually no knowledge of the working of the Senate House and have little feeling that they are part of the university, which can lead to excessive regionalism, and to a dichotomy of "we" and "they".' University College was the most critical. The College drew attention to 'irksome' restrictions in the procedures for appointing professors and for planning teaching. It felt 'drastically hampered' by the restrictiveness of University-wide examination regulations. 'Reform of syllabuses is held back, obsolete material is retained, and the introduction of new material is thwarted, because common syllabuses are insisted on from all Schools of the University and for External students.' University College in particular looked enviously at the arrangement whereby Imperial College was given direct access to the UGC. Since 1953

330 An aerial view of Hammersmith Hospital in 1966, the year in which the Commonwealth Building of the Postgraduate Medical School was opened, financed by donations received from all over the Commonwealth. In the following year the School became the 'Royal Postgraduate Medical School', and in 1974 it again became an independent school of the University, having been part of the British Postgraduate Medical Federation from 1947.

Imperial College had received special earmarked capital allocations from the UGC for its expansion programme. Now it was to grow further in the post-Robbins expansion programme as a Special Institution for Scientific and Technological Education and Research, a specially favoured breed of institution briefly known by the misleading acronym SISTER. For all financial purposes (recurrent as well as capital) it was to deal directly with the UGC, bypassing the University Court. University College would have liked to follow suit in 1964. 'Should it prove that direct access to the UGC cannot for the time being be granted', the College declared, 'then it will be absolutely imperative, beyond any possibility of compromise, that the Heads of the major colleges should play a greater part in the formulation of university policy.' University College laid down various points about 'the minimum extent of reform which would be regarded as satisfactory in order that the university relationship may continue'.[4]

Serious consideration had to be given to such views, and to the other criticisms. The University approached them heartened by the clear expression of the desire to maintain the federal organization. 'What is astonishing about these submissions from the colleges', said the *Times Educational Supplement*, 'is not the string of matters they produce for dissatisfaction or dispute, which get the publicity, but the strong support they give to the organisation of the University as it is. To have listened to even part of what has been said against London University in recent years would have led one to suppose that given half a chance the constituent colleges would call the whole thing off. Instead, they testify again and again to the

331 Hughes Parry Hall was opened in Cartwright Gardens as a new intercollegiate hall of residence in 1969, originally for men students. Next door, to the right, is Canterbury Hall, built by the Church of England in 1938 and acquired by the University in 1946, providing accommodation for 223 women students.

332 In 1961 Connaught Hall was relocated in houses on the west side of Tavistock Square originally built by Cubitt in the 1820s and converted to provide accommodation for 197 men students.

benefits of its federal structure.' Once the consensus of considered opinion about the continuance of the University was established, the structural modifications that needed to be made were approached, first by the Robbins Report Steering Committee and then in 1965–6 by a Committee on Academic Organization chaired by Sir Owen Saunders, Professor of Mechanical Engineering at Imperial College and Chairman of the Academic Council (later Vice-Chancellor, 1967–9).

A number of important changes resulted. In various ways the Schools were given more control over their own teaching arrangements. 'School-based' degree syllabuses were approved. There had already been some moves in this direction, and in the Faculty of Science a new degree structure based on 'course units' was introduced. General approval was given to these developments, and subsequently 'school-based' degrees and the 'course-unit' structure enabled much greater flexibility in teaching arrangements throughout the University, replacing the previously rigid centralized system. At the same time Boards of Studies were broadened to include all permanent members of the academic staff in their membership rather than just the most senior ones. The regulations for the 'recognition' of teachers were liberalized, Schools given more freedom to choose their own postgraduate students, programmes of study for taught master's degrees were introduced, with the MPhil as a new research degree, and the academic committee structure of the University was made more responsive to the views of both Schools and teachers. What became known as the 'Saunders reforms' recognized a new flexibility in the federal relationship. 'By an effort which at the time I should not have thought to be probable,' Lord Robbins later wrote, 'a committee under the inspiration of Sir Douglas Logan, the then Principal, and Professor Saunders of Imperial College, brought about changes which in effect conferred what might be called

333 The two most recent University institutes – Latin American Studies and United States Studies – were established in 1965 in Tavistock Square. Both institutes provide centres of graduate studies within the University as well as co-ordinating wider research in their fields.

Dominion status on the larger institutions; and the movement towards separation which was very strong, has died down.'[5] This was to over-simplify a complex set of changes, but it was in essence a correct judgment.

Further changes in the constitution of the University ran up against the provisions of the University of London Act of 1926 and the statutes of 1929. Earlier efforts to make minor improvements had been resisted by Convocation. In 1951 it had been intended to add to the Senate the Director of the School of Oriental and African Studies, the Director of the British Postgraduate Medical Federation, the Principal of Wye College, and two further representatives of the medical schools, so increasing the number of institutional representatives from thirteen to eighteen. This was an obvious adjustment in the light of the growth of the University since 1929. Convocation refused to accept it unless their representation on the Senate was proportionately increased too. The matter went to the Privy Council, which rejected the Convocation case, and then to the House of Commons, which accepted it. Modest and legitimate constitutional readjustment to changing circumstances was frustrated in a way reminiscent of the battles of the 1880s and 1890s.[6] By 1965 Convocation was willing to accept an increase in the number of heads of Schools on the Senate, but they would not agree to any reduction in the number of their own seats. Other constitutional changes also involved departing from the principles of the Hilton Young Report of 1926, and thus would require amendment not only of the statutes, but also of the University's Act of Parliament. Such considerations led to the setting up of a major committee of enquiry into the governance of the University in 1970, chaired by Lord Murray of Newhaven, and appointed jointly by the University and the UGC.

The Murray Committee's Report was firmly in favour of continuing the federal system.

It is a striking feature of the evidence presented to us that there is practically unanimous support for the maintenance of the federal system and little or no sign of any desire for the dissolution of the University. It seems to us that there has been a marked change in the climate of opinion among the colleges of the University over the last 5–10 years. There are still criticisms of the central government on the score of excessive centralisation, bureaucracy, obscurity and slowness – though these criticisms are much less forceful than they were before the reforms which followed the enquiries in 1964–66 into the academic organisation of the University. There are also arguments about the right balance of power between the University and the constituent colleges. But there is a general acceptance of the federal principle and of the need for some central policy-making and planning body.

334 The clock outside the Old Theatre at the London School of Economics records the moment at which the 'student revolt' began on 31 January 1967 when the Director, Sir Sydney Caine, seen here in uncharacteristically Napoleonic stance, banned a meeting called to organize opposition to the appointment of his successor, Sir Walter Adams, while Marshall Bloom, an American graduate student, seen in more characteristic pose, was one of the leaders of frantic discussion among the gathering students, during which a porter died of heart failure. It was the first of many millenarian meetings, spreading a new mood in 1967–8 to other colleges and universities.

The thirty-four Schools of the University — sixteen medical and eighteen non-medical — formed 'an almost bewildering complex of institutions', and consideration was given to 'whether there would be advantage if the Schools were organised for certain purposes in half-a-dozen or so largish groups of roughly comparable size', groups which could evolve into separate universities. Such a reorganization was rejected, and proposals were put forward for substantial changes in the machinery of the federal organization, changes which were seen as 'evolutionary rather than revolutionary'. The proposals were aimed at remedying what were called 'the two most wide-spread criticisms of the present system of governance': 'the inadequacy of the organisation for the formulation of policy and plans and the lack of opportunity for wider participation by the academic staff'.[7]

The 'diarchy' of the Court and the Senate as the two supreme governing bodies of the University was to be maintained, but both were to be expanded in membership. It was proposed that the Court should be increased from seventeen to thirty-seven, particularly by increasing the number elected by the Senate and by introducing nominees of the Collegiate Council. The Senate itself was to be increased from 59 to 80–85, especially by introducing members elected by Boards of Studies (instead of the shadowy Faculty Boards), and by Schools, as well as student representatives. A 'strong central planning organisation' was to be based upon a joint committee of the Court and the Senate for planning and development. It was also proposed that the Vice-Chancellor should become full-time. 'A short-term, part-time, rotating Vice-Chancellorship might be apt enough if the University were no more than a confederation of colleges; but it is quite incompatible with the concepts by which we have been guided of the role and functions of the federal University. We have no doubt about the need for active and continuous academic leadership at the centre and for building up the post of Vice-Chancellor to enable him to discharge effectively the responsibility for such leadership.' The Principal would consequently become 'the chief executive of the University and head of the secretariat, with the right to attend meetings of the Court, Senate and Collegiate Council and the responsibility for giving them advice and information'. A series of other reforms were suggested, designed to strengthen the cohesiveness of the University.[8] In short, the members of the University, especially the teachers, were to be given a greater role in the central affairs of the University, and the more responsive centre was to be given greater power.

These recommendations were not greeted with any general enthusiasm. The Schools did not welcome the proposals for strengthening the central government; most of them wanted to see greater devolution of decision-making to the constituent parts of the University, and a reduction in the central administration. Much intense discussion took place throughout the University on these matters after the publication of the Murray Report in 1972. The Murray Consultative Committee consulted widely, producing five reports of its own between 1973 and 1975. The University had spurned the Haldane Report in 1913, though some of its recommendations were

335 In 1970–72 the 'Committee of Enquiry into the Governance of the University of London', jointly established by the University and the UGC, deliberated under the chairmanship of Lord Murray of Newhaven, the former Chairman of the UGC, 1953–63. He sits in the centre of this photograph of all members of the committee, with Sir William Mansfield Cooper, Vice-Chancellor of Manchester, 1956–70, to his right, and E.R. Copleston, Secretary of the Committee and formerly Secretary of the UGC, 1963–9, to his left, and next to him J.A. Lake, President of the Students' Union at Birkbeck College, 1969–70. Standing left to right are P.J. Griffiths, Assistant Secretary (now Deputy Clerk of the Court), B.C.L. Weedon, FRS, Professor of Organic Chemistry at QMC, M.V. Hoare, member of Convocation, T. Irvine Smith, member of the Court, Dr M.R. Gavin, Principal of Chelsea College, 1965–73, E. Grebenik, Principal of the Civil Service College, Lord Dainton, FRS, formerly Vice-Chancellor of Nottingham and Professor of Chemistry at Oxford, and Lord Cole, Chairman of Unilever, 1960–70.

336 One of the two boats owned by the University at the Marine Biological Station established at Millport on the Clyde in 1970 in association with the University of Glasgow to provide facilities for teaching and research in marine biology.

subsequently adopted. The Murray Report was rejected but not spurned in 1972, and its proposals influenced what eventuated. Sufficient agreement was attained by 1978 for a new University of London Act to be passed reconstructing the University, not fundamentally, but in several important respects. There was to be no University of London Mark IV. The Mark III federal form of the University introduced in 1900, which became Mark IIIB in 1929, evolved after 1978 into its Mark IIIC structure.

The evolution was not easily achieved. Attempted changes to the statutes relating to the posts of Vice-Chancellor and Principal in 1974 were disallowed by the Privy Council, following petitions lodged from within the University against what was officially proposed. The draft Bill of 1975 was opposed by some Schools and by Convocation. Further drafts in 1976 were opposed by the AUT, by other trade unions, and by the GLC. In 1977 the Bill's progress through Parliament was blocked by its opponents. On a particular point there was a petition to the Visitor. Much negotiation took place, and much re-drafting of the proposals, and eventually a measure of agreement was reached in 1978, enabling the Act to go through. New statutes had consequently to be produced, and the processes of negotiation and drafting and re-drafting were prolonged until 1981, when the first phase of the new statutes finally came into effect. Schools had to give their 'consent'; in a crucial letter from the Vice-Chancellor a typing error used the word 'comment', and so on legal advice the whole exercise had to be repeated. The creation of a full-time salaried Vice-Chancellor attracted especial difficulties, as did the proposed 'over-representation' of Convocation, and the arrangements proposed for the election of teachers to the Senate on the dual basis of constituencies based on

Boards of Studies and on Schools. At length a complex arrangement was agreed for a third electoral route to meet the problems of the teacher elections; the procedure for student elections was settled; Convocation was appeased, and the objections to the full-time Vice-Chancellorship were overcome. New charters for University College (1977) and King's College (1980) 'disincorporated' both colleges from the University, regularizing the abandonment of an earlier phase of reorganization. The University's present system of government was achieved by a process of hard-fought compromise, a process fully in keeping with the tradition of change in the University of London extending consistently back to its origins in the battles of 1826–36.

While the University endeavoured between 1964 and 1981 to put its house in constitutional order, the scale of its operations increased substantially. As in the 1880s and 1890s, and in the 1910s and 1920s, the battles concerning the constitutional superstructure took place over and above an expanding base of activities. The figures for the number of students in table 7.1 tell their own story. In the two decades of the 1960s and 1970s the total number of internal students fully doubled. The expansion in the periods before and after the First World War, and after the Second World War, rivalled this rate of growth, but now the order of magnitude was incomparably greater. The Robbins targets were exceeded. The University of London underwent a boom that made the development of the new universities elsewhere in the country look small-scale.

337 Heythrop College became a school of the University in 1970 when it moved to Palladian premises in Cavendish Square, built in the 1760s. The College was originally founded for the education of English Jesuit students in Louvain in 1614, moving to England after the French Revolution and eventually settling in 1926 near the village of Heythrop in Oxfordshire.

Table 7.1 Number of Students, 1960–85[9]

	Internal Total	Internal Full-time	External
1960–61	26,762	21,995	26,953
1965–66	32,802	26,389	29,524
1970–71	39,629	33,161	33,359
1975–76	44,641	35,940	27,470
1980–81	53,909	40,539	20,353
1984–85	51,965	40,280	16,948

All constituent parts of the University grew. University College, King's College and Imperial College in particular remained bigger in themselves than many of the provincial universities. In 1965 two new institutes were founded as the result of national reports on academic provision in their fields: the Institute of Latin American Studies and the Institute of United States Studies. Between 1964 and 1972 there was also an Institute of Computer Science. It had its origins in the Computer Unit set up in 1957 to manage the Mercury computer, replaced in 1961 by the powerful Atlas computer

338 Sir Cyril Philips, Professor of Oriental History, 1946–80, Director of the School of Oriental and African Studies, 1957–76, and Vice-Chancellor of the University, 1972–6, photographed in 1967 showing SOAS students the plans for the new buildings in Woburn Square.

operated by London University Computing Services Ltd. In 1972 the Institute was wound up, and its resources redeployed among the growing departments of computer science in the Schools of the University. The University of London Computer Centre, established in 1968, continues to provide an increasingly massive computer resource, fulfilling a regional as well as a University-wide role.

A whole new School was added in 1966 when Chelsea Polytechnic, for ten years a College of Advanced Technology, joined the University as Chelsea College. At the same time the three other London CATs became independent universities, following the recommendation of the Robbins Report. Two of them moved away to new sites as Brunel University and the University of Surrey (the former Battersea College of Technology), and one – the Northampton College of Technology – remained in London to be elevated as the City University, a name adopted despite the objections of the University of London.[10] The Royal College of Art also acquired its own degree-giving powers. After 1966 the University of London was no longer the only degree-awarding body in London, losing the one feature which had held it together in the controversies leading up to the reconstitution of 1900 when the generally held belief was that more than one university in London would create insuperable difficulties. The federal University of London in the post-Robbins years had to be on its mettle after it lost what had been considered a fundamental *raison d'être*.

The creation of the Council for National Academic Awards in 1964 also marked a major change. Another Robbins recommendation, the Council was to validate degree-level courses outside the university sector and to award degrees to students in what came

339 The Russell Square end of the Bedford Way building is Charles Clore House, the premises since 1976 of the Institute of Advanced Legal Studies – a focal point for legal practitioners and academic lawyers, containing the best legal library in the country.

340 The London Business School, founded in 1965 and housed since 1970 in fine accommodation retaining a Nash façade overlooking Regent's Park: its status as an 'institution having recognized teachers' means that internal master's and doctor's degrees can be offered, as well as a range of other courses for the business world.

confusingly to be called the 'public sector' of higher education. CNAA degrees were to replace a large part of the demand previously satisfied by the 'external' degrees of the University of London. By 1968 CNAA registrations had rapidly grown to over 15,000 and to exceed the numbers of University of London external students in the technical colleges and other institutions of further education. After 1969 the rapid development of the Open University further altered the context in which the external system operated. The long period – extending back to 1858 – when the University of London provided the only opportunity for students to obtain degrees without attending a university thus came to an end.

The University had to reassess the future of the whole external system, the examinations for which imposed a considerable burden on the administration and on the examiners.[11] It was decided in 1972 to give five years' notice of the ceasing of registration of students in public educational institutions, and that thereafter the external system should cater solely for private students. The BA General degree was examined for internal students for the last time in 1972, and it was phased out for external students over the next five years. With the development of institutions of higher education throughout the Commonwealth, the overseas examination centres were reduced, and from 1977 it was decided to accept no more overseas registrations (though in 1982 it was decided to re-open overseas registrations). From the late 1960s the number of external students of the University declined sharply, but the external system still continued to meet a need and was maintained as a special feature of the University of London.

341 J.R. Stewart, Clerk of the Court of the University, 1950–82, and Principal, 1978–83: one of the most recent of a long line of Scotsmen who have given signal service to the University of London.

342 The wing of the Senate House left unbuilt in 1939 was completed in two post-Holden styles in 1983 after the Logan Hall in the Bedford Way building replaced the plan for a Great Hall. Stewart House became the headquarters of the School Examinations Board, with over 334,000 candidates to cope with in the GCE examinations every summer.

In 1966 a ninth faculty was added to the University with the creation of the Faculty of Education. Following the McNair Report of 1944, the Institute of Education had come since 1949 to function as the 'Central Institute' under which were grouped all the colleges of education in the London region, some thirty-three of them in the 1950s. The Robbins Report recommended that a fourth-year course following the Cert Ed should lead to a BEd degree in these colleges. Much controversy about their constitutional position and their financing took place, but the University moved rapidly to establish the new degree in the new faculty. The James Report and the White Paper on *Education: A Framework for Expansion* in 1972 altered the whole pattern. Statistical projections showed that the country was heading for an over-supply of teachers and a shortage of places in general higher education. Some colleges of education were closed down, others were amalgamated with each other, new 'institutes of higher education' emerged with wider aims than the production of teachers: the 1970s were a period of chaotic change for the former colleges of education. The BEd became an entirely different degree, the new degree of BH (Bachelor of Humanities) was bizarrely introduced, and the former federal ramifications of the Institute of Education were dismembered as the successor institutions looked to the CNAA or other universities to validate their degrees. In 1979 the University decided to end provision of degrees in the former colleges of education, and the last examinations for such purpose will be held in 1988.[12] The Faculty of Education remains, a relic of the heady days of expansion in the 1960s.

The complexities of the changes in the field of education were a side-show compared to the tremendous ructions which took place in medicine. Medicine did not figure large in the Robbins Report, and in 1965–8 the whole pattern of medical education was investigated by a Royal Commission under Lord Todd, the distinguished scientist known in Cambridge as Lord Todd Almighty. Recommendations were made for a radical restructuring of the London medical schools. 'The growth of the twelve London undergraduate medical schools has been rather haphazard,' said the Todd Report; 'the schools vary widely in size and are semi-autonomous bodies whose relation to the central university authorities is less close than that of medical schools elsewhere. In our view the maintenance of twelve medical schools, each with its independent teaching hospital group and without direct contact with a single multi-faculty college of the University of London, is not compatible with a continuation of the highest standards of medical education in London in the long-term future.' A series of mergers were proposed to reduce the number of medical schools to six, each of them intended to become part

343 Clifford Wilson, Professor of Medicine at the London Hospital Medical College, 1946–71, painted by John Ward while engaged in clinical teaching. He was the first professor in a Professorial Unit to serve until the age of retirement, and had the distinction – rare in his generation – of having a disease named after him.

344 Sir Nikolaus Pevsner, FBA (1902–83), who taught at Birkbeck College, becoming Professor of the History of Art, 1959–69, one of the many refugees in the 1930s who became ornaments of the University of London. Pevsner's *Buildings of England* series forms one of the great achievements of the last generation; the volume on *The Cities of London and Westminster* (1957) was dedicated to G.F. Troup Horne, the Secretary of Birkbeck College, 1919–52, in memory of 'the nights of 1941–4 at the old Birkbeck College in Bream's Buildings'.

of a multi-faculty college. St Bartholomew's Hospital Medical College and the London Hospital Medical College were to be merged and linked as the medical faculty of Queen Mary College; University College Hospital Medical School and the Royal Free Hospital School of Medicine were to be merged with University College; St Mary's Hospital Medical School and the Middlesex Hospital Medical School were to be linked with Bedford College; Guy's Hospital Medical School and King's College Hospital Medical School were to be integrated with King's College; the Westminster Medical School and Charing Cross Hospital Medical School 'might well aim to become in due course the medical faculty of Imperial College', and St Thomas's Hospital Medical School and St George's Hospital Medical School could 'reasonably hope to become in the course of time the medical faculty of a new multi-faculty institution in south-west London', perhaps developing out of Chelsea College.[13]

Such proposals, Todd argued, represented a 'logical and practicable reorganisation' which would produce a more integrated pattern of medical education in place of the structure which had grown up because of 'a variety of past circumstances' and which was 'educationally indefensible as well as uneconomic'. The University found the proposals neat on paper but inflexible once the practical considerations were examined, and the medical schools themselves were generally unenthusiastic about the twinning proposals, though the force of some of the Todd criticisms was accepted.[14] Years of discussion and negotiation ensued, mostly fruitless in their result. A new urgency was provided by the magnitude of the financial recession of the late 1970s, coming after the reorganization of

345 The Viennese-born Professor Sir Ernst Gombrich, FBA, seen in the magnificent library of the Warburg Institute, of which he was Director, 1959–76.

346 Sir Andrew Huxley, OM, FRS, Jodrell Professor of Physiology, 1960–69, and Royal Society Research Professor of Physiology, 1969–83, at UCL; Nobel prizewinner in 1963, and President of the Royal Society, 1980–85. Since 1984 Master of Trinity College, Cambridge, the college which provided several of the original members of the Senate of the University of London in 1836.

the National Health Service in 1974. In 1979 the University set up a new working party charged with the task of settling the framework for medical education in London, under the chairmanship of Lord Flowers, then Rector of Imperial College. The Flowers Report in 1980 recognized that the financial climate was 'to say the least, overcast, and whilst there might be the occasional ray of fiscal sunshine there was certainly no prospect of a pot of gold at the end of the day'. The Report took as its starting-point the fact that the proportion of the total University resources made available to medicine by the Court had risen from 30 per cent in 1969–70 to 35 per cent in 1978–9. In the full realization that 'fierce loyalties' to the existing institutions would be strained to the point of rebellion, new restructuring proposals were put forward.[15]

The medical schools of St George's Hospital and of Charing Cross had already been rebuilt as single schools not linked to multi-faculty colleges, the recommendations of the Todd Report notwithstanding. It was proposed that they should both have other institutions linked with them, and proposals were made to group the total of thirty-four existing separate institutions concerned with medical education and research within the University into six Schools of Medicine and Dentistry. A University College School of Medicine was to incorporate not only University College Hospital Medical School, but also the Middlesex Hospital Medical School and the Royal Free Hospital School of Medicine, the London School of Hygiene and Tropical Medicine and several of the institutes of the British Postgraduate Medical Federation, including the Institute

347 Sir Karl Popper, the Austrian-born Professor of Logic and Scientific Method at LSE, 1949–69: his writings such as *The Open Society and its Enemies* (1945) and *The Logic of Scientific Discovery* (1959) have made him a major contemporary philosophical and methodological force.

348 Sir Geoffrey Wilkinson, FRS, one of the scientific giants of Imperial College where he has been Professor of Inorganic Chemistry since 1956. He was awarded the Nobel prize for Chemistry in 1973.

349 St George's Hospital Medical School moved from Hyde Park Corner in 1976 into new buildings at Tooting completed in 1984.

of Child Health; a Lister and St Thomas's Joint School of Medicine was to link King's College Hospital Medical School, Guy's and St Thomas's, as well as the Institute of Psychiatry; a Harvey School of Medicine was to link St Bart's and the London as well as the Institutes of Urology and Opthalmology; St Mary's was to be linked with the Royal Postgraduate Medical School and the Institute of Dental Surgery. St George's was to be linked with the Royal Dental Hospital of London School of Dental Surgery and the Institutes of Cancer Research and Dermatology, and Charing Cross Hospital Medical School was to include the Cardiothoracic Institute. Westminster Medical School was to cease to exist: 'We believe that in all the circumstances Westminster Medical School does not have a viable future and we regretfully propose that it

350 An architect's drawing of the new St Mary's Hospital being built behind the existing premises in Paddington: it will incorporate new facilities for the Medical School.

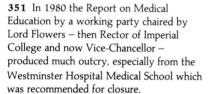

351 In 1980 the Report on Medical Education by a working party chaired by Lord Flowers – then Rector of Imperial College and now Vice-Chancellor – produced much outcry, especially from the Westminster Hospital Medical School which was recommended for closure.

should close and its academic activities should be transferred to schools expanding their student numbers.'[16]

The Flowers Report produced an even greater storm of criticism than the Todd Report had caused, even though it was more firmly grounded in an understanding of the complexities of the London situation in the new financial climate. What eventuated departed significantly from the proposals. In 1980 University College Hospital Medical School was reunited with University College to form the new Faculty of Clinical Sciences, and amalgamation is planned with the Middlesex Hospital Medical School in 1987 to form a large new Medical School incorporating also the Institute of Laryngology and Otology, the Institute of Orthopaedics and the Institute of Urology. In 1983 King's College Hospital Medical School reunited with King's College becoming the King's College School of Medicine and Dentistry. A third medical school integrated with a multi-faculty college has been envisaged by linking St Bartholomew's Hospital Medical College and the London Hospital Medical College with Queen Mary College, but this scheme – the notorious 'BLQ' project – has proved very difficult to achieve. Two large medical schools were created by amalgamation. In 1982 the medical schools of Guy's Hospital and St Thomas's Hospital were reunited, and in 1983 the Royal Dental Hospital of London School of Dental Surgery was amalgamated with Guy's Dental School to create the 'United Medical and Dental Schools of Guy's and St Thomas's Hospitals' (to which the Institute of Dermatology was added in 1985). In 1984 the Charing Cross Hospital Medical School and the semi-reprieved Westminster Medical School amalgamated to form the 'Charing Cross and Westminster Medical School'. Three schools remained as individual medical schools: St George's Hospital Medical School (rebuilt in Tooting in 1976–84), the Royal Free

352 The Australian Studies Centre established in 1982 at the Institute of Commonwealth Studies in Russell Square was opened in June 1983 by the Queen Mother in the presence of Bob Hawke, the Prime Minister of Australia, and Lord Home, the former British Prime Minister.

353 An aerial view of Queen Mary College in 1984 showing the extensive new building on the extended Mile End Road site around the original People's Palace (see **199**).

354 Lord Annan, Vice-Chancellor of the University, 1978–81, previously Provost of UCL, 1966–78, and Provost of King's College, Cambridge, 1955–66: photographed in a characteristically theatrical pose in the Vice-Chancellor's office, he brought decisiveness as well as style to the problems of the University at the beginning of the present era.

Hospital School of Medicine (rebuilt in Hampstead in 1978–83), and St Mary's Hospital Medical School, the one school essentially unchanged in the complex reorganization of medical education in the early 1980s.[17] The medical schools only took the University fully seriously after the late 1940s when their students all came to take its degrees rather than the easier 'conjoint' qualification of the Royal Colleges, mainly for reasons connected with the spread of local authority 'grants' for students taking degrees. Having for long pushed the University around, the medical schools now found themselves pushed around by the University. The effect, on the whole, was painful but beneficial.

355 The biting cuts in government expenditure on higher education announced in 1981 produced much anguish and outrage: in November 1981 a protest march to lobby Parliament set out from Queen Mary College.

356 The demise of Bedford as a separate college was wistfully noted in the national press in 1985: a college with the cumbersome but appropriate name of Royal Holloway and Bedford New College was to follow.

RIP
BEDFORD COLLEGE, ON July 31, 1985, aged 136, quietly, at home, after a brave fight against terminal apathy. Sadly missed, by some. The ashes have been scattered around London University.

Enough has been said to indicate that in the late 1970s and early 1980s the University of London moved into a new era. Too much has happened in the last ten years for comprehensive summary, and many of the new developments are still incomplete. The period since the retirement of Sir Douglas Logan as Principal in 1975 has seen a good deal of change in the shape and structure of the University, much of it a response to an increasingly bleak financial climate.[18] Before the end of the 1972–7 quinquennium, the system of quinquennial allocations by the UGC broke down under the pressure of inflation. Universities were obliged to exist on a year-to-year basis that often seemed hand-to-mouth. The UGC itself noted that 1975–6 'marked a decisive down-turn in a process of growth of resources which has continued for twenty years and is unlikely soon to be resumed'; the UGC admitted that 'the financial system which permitted and encouraged forward planning has been seriously damaged by successive short-term decisions. As a result there is a deep and damaging sense of uncertainty which can only be removed by the restoration of a longer-term planning horizon.'[19]

Uncertainty was to characterize the condition of universities in

357 The buildings of Bedford College in Regent's Park as photographed in 1963: originally acquired in 1913, the entire site was given up when the College was obliged to amalgamate with Royal Holloway College at Egham in 1985.

358 Sir Peter Swinnerton-Dyer, FRS, Professor of Mathematics at Cambridge from 1971, Master of St Catharine's College, Cambridge, 1973–83, and Chairman of the UGC since 1983: portrayed as a monster attacking the Senate House in a cartoon while he was chairman of an investigation into the academic organization of the University in 1980–81.

the following years, and of the University of London in particular. In the immediate aftermath of the Murray Report, the University attempted to improve its own planning machinery by establishing in 1973 a joint committee of the Court and the Senate for 'collective forward planning of the academic development of the University' and in particular 'to initiate, consider and co-ordinate proposals for rationalisation and inter-collegiate co-operation within the University'. It was increasingly evident that the University would have to cut its coat to a new pattern. Its share in Dillon's Bookshop was sold in 1977, as in 1979 was the Athlone Press, the publishing venture established in 1949, bearing the name of the then Chancellor, while the 'University of London Press' imprint was controlled outside the University. Sir Douglas Logan was succeeded by Dr Glenn Willson in 1975–8, and then by Dr J.R. Stewart, 1978–83, by Dr William Taylor, 1983–5, and since 1985 by Peter Holwell, who followed in the footsteps of Claughton, Logan and Stewart by having previously been Clerk of the Court. In 1972–6 Sir Cyril Philips, the Director of the School of Oriental and African Studies, was Vice-Chancellor, and in 1976 Sir Frank Hartley retired as Dean of the School of Pharmacy to become Vice-Chancellor in 1976–8. The demands on their time were heavy, and when Lord Annan retired as Provost of University College to become Vice-Chancellor in 1978–81, the post had become *de facto* full-time. Annan attempted to force the University to confront the need for structural change. The Flowers Report addressed itself to the third of the University concerned with medical education. In 1980 a new Committee on Academic Organization addressed itself to the non-medical two-thirds under the chairmanship of Sir Peter Swinnerton-Dyer, the

Cambridge mathematician who was later to become the Chairman of the UGC.

The 'Spin-Dryer Committee', as it became known, produced three discussion documents making a number of trenchant criticisms, some of them previously unproclaimed home-truths, some of them much resented in various parts of the University. The Swinnerton-Dyer Committee contended that 'there is nothing absurd about a University 10 per cent smaller and 15 per cent cheaper than London now is'. Many disagreed, but in 1981 the government imposed *force majeure* by announcing that funds for universities were not merely to be restricted, but were actually to be decreased. Most 'cuts' in government expenditure, in the increasingly difficult

359 The Easter 1985 number of the Westfield College student magazine – naturally entitled *WC* – portrayed a necromantic scene outside the Queen's Building, opened for accommodation of the expansion in science in 1962 and empty from the summer of 1985, since when the building's future has remained undecided.

360 Sir Randolph Quirk, FBA, Professor of English at UCL, 1960–81, and Vice-Chancellor of the University, 1981–5 – one of the most difficult periods in the history of the University, producing considerable 'restructuring', some of which was not welcomed, and all of which was painful.

WC EASTER ISSUE

VOLUME TEN NUMBER 6 NUMBER TEN VOLUME NUMBER

THE LAST SUPPER FOR WESTFIELD? CRUCIFICTION OR RESURRECTION? EDITORS: JULIA BRYAN & BILL HIGHAM

361 Dr William Taylor, Director of the Institute of Education, 1973–83, and Principal of the University, 1983–5. Formerly a schoolteacher who became a teachers' training college lecturer and Professor of Education at Bristol, 1966–73, now Vice-Chancellor of the University of Hull.

362 Peter Holwell, since 1985 the twelfth Principal of the University: previously Clerk of the Court, 1982–5, having joined the University administration in 1964 to develop its computing, management and financial systems.

363 The Joint Planning Committee of the Court and the Senate has played a crucial role in the difficult central decisions concerning the 'restructuring' of the University in the last few years. At its meeting in January 1986, the Vice-Chancellor, Lord Flowers, was in the chair, with to his right Dr B.B. MacGillivray, Dean of the Royal Free Hospital School of Medicine and one of the three new Pro-Vice-Chancellors; Peter Taylor, the Clerk of the Senate; J.S. Roderick, the Clerk of the Court, and Gillian Roberts, the Academic Registrar. On the left is Sir James Lighthill, the Provost of University College since 1979 and (second along) Professor S.R. Sutherland, the Principal of King's College since 1985.

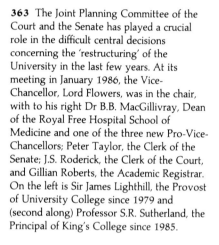

circumstances of the national economy, were cut-backs in projected increases, but universities were apparently to be singled out for real and evident reductions. The cuts hurt.

The new cuts coincided in 1981 with a number of other changes in the University of London. The Queen Mother retired as Chancellor after twenty-five years, and for the first time there was a contested election for the Chancellorship. Convocation chose Princess Anne rather than either Jack Jones or Nelson Mandela. On the effective rather than the formal level of governance, Professor Sir Randolph Quirk succeeded Lord Annan as Vice-Chancellor. The first phase of the new statutes came into operation, the result of the long process of agonized introspection since the Robbins Report and the Murray Report. The aims of the University were laid down in words which echoed back beyond 1929, to 1900, to 1858, to 1836 and back to 1826: 'The purposes of the University are to hold forth to all classes and denominations, both in the United Kingdom and elsewhere, without any distinction whatsoever, an encouragement for pursuing a regular and liberal course of education; to promote research and the advancement of science and learning; and to organise, improve and extend education of a university standard.'

Both the central bodies in the University's bicameral constitution were enlarged. The Court came to have twenty-four members. Besides the Chancellor, the Vice-Chancellor and the Chairman of Convocation, it had ten members appointed by the Senate, four by the Crown, two by the GLC, one after consultation with other local authorities and four co-opted members. The Senate was even larger than had been proposed in the Murray Report. It came to have over 120 members: all heads of Schools in receipt of grants from the Court, three heads of Schools not receiving such grants and of Senate Institutes, twenty-five teachers elected according to their membership of Boards of Studies, fifteen teachers elected according to the institutions at which they held their posts, ten other teachers, twenty Convocation members, twelve student members (including the President of ULU and the Immediate Past President), and five co-opted members. The 'democratised' Senate first met in the autumn term of 1981, and Sir Randolph Quirk became the first *de jure* full-time Vice-Chancellor. Quirk was an actively working scholar, still connected with the Survey of English Language Usage at University College, and producing while in office (with the collaboration of S. Greenbaum, G. Leech and J. Svartvik) his massive *Comprehensive Grammar of the English Language* (1985). His vice-chancellorship was marked by a number of painful 'restructurings' throughout the University. The refurbished ULU bar, agreeably named 'Quirks' originally in 1984, was soon renamed 'Mergers'.

By 1985 it was decided to amalgamate Bedford College with Royal Holloway College to become 'Royal Holloway and Bedford New College' on the Egham site. The fine if run-down premises of Bedford College in Regent's Park were given up. Chelsea College and Queen Elizabeth College were both amalgamated with King's College to create the enlarged 'KQC', initially operating on the three separate sites. Westfield College lost its science departments which were largely transferred to Queen Mary College. Westfield College itself considered several suitors, but nothing has been consummated. The 'Subject Area Review Committees' established in the wake of Swinnerton-Dyer made recommendations for significant changes in the disposition of resources between the Schools of the

364 In January 1986, while Princess Anne was taking part in the Presentation Day ceremony inside the Albert Hall (see **37**), picketing took place outside during the first national strike called by the Association of University Teachers to protest about poor salary levels and cuts in government expenditure on universities.

365 A cartoon by Colin Wheeler appearing in the *Daily Telegraph* in January 1986 at the time of the first official strike called by the AUT. Echoing the auto-icon of Jeremy Bentham (see **78**), it provides a sad comment on attitudes to the University in its sesquicentenary year.

University. There followed a number of redistributions of a sort not seen since the post-Haldane years when architecture was given up by King's and transferred to the Bartlett School of Architecture at University College in 1914 and the Tooke chair of Economic Science was transferred from King's to LSE in 1919. Dutch, Italian, and Algebra moved from Bedford to University College, for example, as did most of Geology from Queen Mary College. The intention was to slim the University and to concentrate the main science subjects in five centres at University College, Imperial College, King's College, Queen Mary College and Royal Holloway and Bedford New College. The mergers and concentrations in both the medical and the non-medical fields leave the future of some of the components of the University unsettled, including several of the Senate Institutes.

366 Lord Flowers, FRS, Vice-Chancellor of the University since 1985, the 44th to hold the office since 1836: formerly Professor of Physics at Manchester, 1958–72, Chairman of the Science Research Council, 1967–73, and Rector of Imperial College, 1973–85.

All ages, as Adam might well have pointed out to Eve, are ages of transition. There has been no real period of stability in the history of the University of London. The 150th anniversary of the 1836 Charter comes amidst a time of especial flux. The future for British universities appears unhappily uncertain; the future for the University of London in particular seems even more unpredictable than ever in 1986. By the time of the bicentenary in 2036, its history as an institution with any degree of unity could well be written entirely in the past tense. On the other hand, the University of London could well adapt and change and survive as it has shown a surprising capacity to do over the course of the last hundred and fifty years. Time will tell.

Notes

CHAPTER 1   The Federal
University

1 Counting universities is a
'specialized art'; see John
Carswell, *Government and the
Universities in Britain: Programme
and Performance, 1960–1980*
(1985), pp.3, 176.

2 F.M.L. Thompson in a review
in the *London Journal*, IV, 2 (1978),
p.270.

3 Sir Gregory Foster, *The
University of London: History,
Present Resources and Future
Possibilities* (1922), p.5; Lord
Beveridge, *Power and Influence*
(1953), p.185.

4 The two earlier meanings of
Bloomsbury are admirably dealt
with in Donald J. Olsen, *Town
Planning in London: The Eighteenth
and Nineteenth Centuries* (2nd edn,
1984) and Leon Edel, *Bloomsbury:
A House of Lions* (1979). The
history of the Senate House site is
chronicled in Eliza Jeffries Davis,
'The University Site, Bloomsbury'
in *London Topographical Record*,
XVII (1936).

5 Andrew Lewis, 'The College
and the University', *UCL Bulletin*,
V, 14 (1983), p.1.

6 Bennett quoted by Lord
Macmillan in *University of London
Union Magazine* (June 1936),
p.162; Wells in the *Standard* (31
January 1903) (in ULL ACO
[University of London
Library/Archives of the Central
Offices] VP 6/1).

7 Derived from *The University of
London: A Sketch of its Work and
History from its Foundation in 1837
[sic] to the Present Time* (1900);
University of London Calendar,
passim.

8 Counting students of the
University of London is a highly
specialized art. See *University of
London Calendar*, II (1972),
pp.114–18, and subsequent issues
of the *Calendar*, passim. There are
two types of definition, one
taking the number of registrations
of internal students whether full-
time or part-time at all institutions
forming part of the University,

and the other taking only full-
time students in the institutions
receiving UGC funds. The former
gives a better impression of the
scale of the University, and the
resulting series has been used
here; the latter is the one used by
the Universities' Statistical
Record, producing lower numbers
(40,514 for example, in 1983–4,
compared to 53,892).

9 H.G. Wells in the *Saturday
Review* (14 December 1895) (in
ULL ACO RO 1/13).

CHAPTER 2   Origins, 1123–1836

1 W.K. Jordan, *The Charities of
London, 1480–1600* (1960),
pp.252–67.

2 Sir Humphrey Gilbert, 'Queene
Elizabethes Achademy' in *Early
English Text Society, Extra Series*,
VIII (1869), pp.1, 10.

3 Sir Harold Hartley and Sir
Cyril Hinshelwood, 'Gresham
College and the Royal Society', in
Sir Harold Hartley (ed.), *The
Tercentenary Celebrations of the
Royal Society of London* (1961),
especially p.131.

4 S. John Teague, *The City
University: A History* (1980),
pp.194–5.

5 W.H.G. Armytage, *Civic
Universities: Aspects of a British
Tradition* (1955), pp.94–9, 105–7,
113–19.

6 Marquis of Lansdowne (ed.),
*The Petty Papers: Some Unpublished
Writings of Sir William Petty*, I
(1927), pp.36–7.

7 Andrew Moreton (i.e. Daniel
Defoe), *Augusta Triumphans: Or,
The Way to Make London the most
Flourishing City in the Universe*
(1728), pp.6–8.

8 See A. Osler, 'The London
University of 1742', *London
Journal*, VI, 1 (1980), pp. 67–9,
which suggests that the
'University' was a brief fantasy of
an Irishman, Thomas Sheridan, the
godson of Jonathan Swift and
father of Richard Brinsley
Sheridan.

9 William Harrison, *The
Description of England* (1st edn,

1577; 2nd edn, 1587; Folger
Shakespeare Library edn, 1968),
pp. 65–6, 75–7.

10 Wilfred R. Prest, *The Inns of
Court under Elizabeth I and the
Early Stuarts, 1590–1640* (1972),
pp.1–6, 115.

11 In John Stow and Edmond
Howes, *The Annales, or Generall
Chronicle of England* (1615),
pp.950, 958, 965–6.

12 S. Gordon Wilson, *The
University of London and its
Colleges* (1923), p.108.

13 E.M. McInnes, *St. Thomas'
Hospital* (1963), pp.14–16.

14 William Fitzstephen, *A
Description of London* (trans. H.E.
Butler, in F.M. Stenton, *Norman
London*, 1934), p.28.

15 McInnes, *St. Thomas' Hospital*,
pp.74–6, 79; J.L. Thornton, 'The
Medical College from its Origins
to the End of the Nineteenth
Century' in V.C. Medvei and J.L.
Thornton (eds.), *The Royal Hospital
of St Bartholomew, 1123–1973*
(1974), pp.43–5, 47–9.

16 H. Campbell Thomson, *The
Story of the Middlesex Hospital
Medical School, 1835–1935* (1935),
p.11; William Hunter, *Historical
Account of Charing Cross Hospital
and Medical School* (1914), p.15;
H.C. Cameron, *Mr Guy's Hospital,
1726–1948* (1954), pp.2, 89; A.E.
Clark-Kennedy, *London Pride: The
Story of a Voluntary Hospital*
(1979), pp.98–100; for the origin
of the London Hospital Medical
College I am indebted to Sir John
Ellis for a typescript copy of his
forthcoming history of the
College.

17 Hunter, *Historical Account of
Charing Cross Hospital and Medical
School*, pp.1–9, 11, 27, 38, 127.

18 See F.N.L. Poynter (ed.), *The
Evolution of Medical Education in
Britain* (1966); Charles Newman,
*The Evolution of Medical Education
in the Nineteenth Century* (1966);
M. Jeanne Peterson, *The Medical
Profession in Mid-Victorian London*
(1978).

19 C.C.F. Greville, *A Journal of
the Reigns of King George IV and*

King William IV, III (1875), p.82. The origins of what became University College and of King's College are amply described in H. Hale Bellot, *University College London, 1826–1926* (1929) and in F.J.C. Hearnshaw, *The Centenary History of King's College London, 1828–1928* (1929).

20 For the Commons debate on 26 March 1835, see *Hansard*, 3rd series, XXVII, cols.279–303.

21 Greville, *A Journal*, III, pp.260–3; W. Tooke, *University of London: Statement of Facts as to Charter* (1835); A.D. Kriegel (ed.), *The Holland House Diaries, 1831–40* (1977), pp.283, 301, 303, 306.

22 W.M. Torrens, *Memoirs of the Rt Hon. William, 2nd Viscount Melbourne*, II (1878), p.158.

CHAPTER 3   Metropolitan Degrees, 1836–1870

1 W.W. Rostow, *British Economy of the Nineteenth Century* (1948), pp.124–5; William Page (ed.), *Commerce and Industry* (1919), pp.99–101.

2 The full text of the 1836 Charter, and of the six subsequent Charters, is given in *University of London: The Historical Record, 1836–1912* (1912), pp.26–61.

3 ULL Airy Papers; see also Minutes of the Senate (ULL ACO ST 2/2/1), 29 May 1839, for a copy of a similar letter (dated 6 June 1836) to Sir Stephen Love Hammick.

4 G.M. Trevelyan, *Trinity College An Historical Sketch* (1943), pp.88, 94–5.

5 Quentin Bell, *The Schools of Design* (1963), p.74; see also pp.60–73; R.A. Needham and A. Webster, *Somerset House Past and Present* (1905), pp.214, 233, 235.

6 ULL ACO RO 1/2/1, Lubbock to Spring Rice, 25 February 1838.

7 F. Boase, *Modern English Biography*, III (1901); J.A. Venn, *Alumni Cantabrigiensis, 1752–1900*, V (1953); *Monthly Notices of the Royal Astronomical Society*, XVII (1856–7), p.103. I am

indebted to Sir Andrew Huxley of Trinity College, Cambridge, and the Librarian of the Royal Astronomical Society for confirming that neither of those institutions possesses a picture of Rothman, and to the National Portrait Gallery and the Science Museum for their help in establishing that one is not to be found elsewhere.

8 A.P. Stanley, *Life of Thomas Arnold* (1904 edn), pp.387, 388, 383, 459, 468–9, 485.

9 Minutes of the Senate, 31 January 1838 and 15 August 1838; ULL ACO RO 1/2/1, Rothman to the Royal Belfast Academical Institution, 17 August 1838.

10 Minutes of the Senate, 7 March 1838, 28 November 1838, 19 December 1838; C.E. Whiting, *The University of Durham, 1832–1932* (1932), especially pp.71–3.

11 Minutes of the Senate, 27 January 1841.

12 *London University College Magazine*, I (July 1849), pp.412–13.

13 See *DNB*; *Dictionary of Scientific Biography*, III (1971); *Lancet*, II (1885), p.928.

14 Derived from *The University of London: A Sketch of its Work and History from its Foundation in 1837 to the Present Time*, table at end.

15 Minutes of the Senate, 12 May 1858.

16 ULL ACO ST 3/4: *University of London: Report of Committee to Consider the Propriety of Establishing a Degree or Degrees in Science* (1858), p.65.

17 See Elaine Kaye, *A History of Queen's College, London, 1848–1972* (1972), especially pp.78–89; Margaret J. Tuke, *A History of Bedford College for Women, 1849–1937* (1939), especially pp.22–9.

18 ULL ACO RC 19/7, W.B. Carpenter to Lord Granville, 8 May 1868.

19 T.L. Humberstone, *University Representation* (1951), pp.38–40,

111–12. Lowe's 'intellectual mint' remark is recorded in the *Graphic* (21 May 1870).

CHAPTER 4   Examining versus Teaching, 1870–1900

1 Minutes of the Senate, 27 November 1867, 4 March 1868, 1 April 1868; *Survey of London, XXXII: The Parish of St James, Westminster, II, North of Piccadilly* (1963), pp.435–9.

2 Minutes of the Senate, 14 December 1870. See also Grote's letter and the official reply in ibid., 18 January 1871.

3 For the Brown Institution, see T. Le Marchant Douse in *The University of London: A Sketch of its Work and History* (1900) and Sir Graham Wilson in the *Journal of Hygiene* (1979).

4 Quoted in Jo Manton, *Elizabeth Garrett Anderson* (1965), p.255. Jenner's daughter was not dead; not surprisingly, she later became a militant suffragette.

5 Letter in the *Morning Post* (22 March 1912); ULL ACO VP 6/1/15.

6 See Eleanor Doorly in R.M. Scrimgeour (ed.), *The North London Collegiate School, 1850–1950* (1950), especially pp.71–91; Sophie Bryant, *1850–1922* (1922).

7 ULL ACO RC 19/7, W.B. Carpenter to Lord Granville, 8 May 1868. See above p.114.

8 C.B. Firth, *Constance Louisa Maynard: Mistress of Westfield College* (1949), pp.191–2.

9 N.B. Harte, *The Admission of Women to University College London: A Centenary Lecture* (1979); H.S. Solly, *The Life of Henry Morley* (1898), especially pp.267–89.

10 Hilda D. Oakeley, 'King's College for Women' in F.J.C. Hearnshaw, *The Centenary History of King's College London, 1828–1928* (1929), pp.489–509; see also ibid., pp.314–18, 377–8, 440–1 and 456–7, and the forthcoming history of Queen

Elizabeth College by Dr Neville Marsh.

11 Quoted in the 1888–9 *Royal Commission Report*, p.187.

12 The titles of the theses submitted for doctorates in all the faculties are listed in *The University of London: A Sketch of its Work and History*, pp.27–45. The first DSc by thesis was awarded in Zoology to W.B.S. Benham in 1887 for his 'Studies on Earthworms'; in 1890 there was not only the first DLit by thesis, but two: R.J. Lloyd in English for 'Vowel Sound', and John Taylor in Hebrew for 'The Massoretic Text and the Ancient Versions of the Book of Micah'. See also ULL ACO RC 3/18 and RC 4.

13 For the Queen's University of Ireland, see Graham Balfour, *The Education Systems of Great Britain and Ireland* (2nd edn, 1903), pp.267–70; for Toronto, see the Vice-Chancellor of Toronto's letter in Minutes of the Senate, 21 April 1869; for the Indian universities see Aparna Basu, *The Growth of Education and Political Development in India, 1898–1920* (1974), pp.14–16; for New Zealand, see J.C. Beaglehole, *The University of New Zealand: An Historical Study* (1937), especially pp.12, 102–6, 315.

14 Derived from *The University of London: A Sketch of its Work and History*, and Minutes of the Senate for 1900, tables at end.

15 Ibid.

16 Ibid.

17 W.H. Allchin, *An Account of the Reconstruction of the University of London*, I (1905), p.18.

18 Remarks of Playfair and Young quoted in ibid., pp.57, 63; resolutions of Convocation in P. Dunsheath and M. Miller, *Convocation in the University of London* (1958), p.66.

19 Stephen Paget (ed.), *Memoirs and Letters of Sir James Paget* (1901), pp.330–2.

20 *Report of Royal Commission to Inquire Whether Any and What*

Kind of New University or Powers is or are Required for the Advancement of Higher Education in London (1889), pp.x–xix.

21 Ibid., pp.115–23, 180.

22 Allchin, *An Account of the Reconstruction of the University of London*, II, p.161.

23 Ibid., III (1912), pp.124, 152, 238–9, 321.

24 *Report of the Commissioners Appointed to Consider the Draft Charter for the Proposed Gresham University in London* (1894), pp.xii, xiv, xv–xxviii, lvii, lix.

25 W.P. Wynne in *Nature* (5 December 1895); ULL ACO RO 1/13.

26 Beatrice Webb, *Our Partnership*, ed. B. Drake and M.I. Cole (1948), p.102; R.B. Haldane, *An Autobiography* (1929), pp.125–7. See also Sir Douglas Logan, *Haldane and the University of London* (1960), especially pp.3–8, and Eric Ashby and Mary Anderson, *Portrait of Haldane at Work on Education* (1974), especially pp.27–40.

27 *Survey of London, XXXVIII: The Museums Area of South Kensington* (1975), pp.220–6; Gavin Stamp and Colin Amery, *Victorian Buildings of London, 1837–87* (1980), p.168.

CHAPTER 5   The Reconstituted University, 1900–1929

1 The Statutes of 1900, together with the report of the Commissioners and the text of the University of London Act of 1898, are given in *University of London: The Historical Record* (1912), pp.62–113, and in editions of the *Calendar* during the period in which the Act and the Statutes applied.

2 The original 32 boards of studies are listed in *University of London: The Historical Record* (1912), pp.97–8.

3 Ibid., pp.111–13.

4 Treasury Minute of 21 February 1901, given in the Minutes of the Senate, 20 March

1901. The complexities of the old system of financing make the creation of a proper balance sheet for the University a virtually impossible task. See the exchanges in *The Times*, 16, 17 and 21 January 1896, correcting Silvanus Thompson's claim that the University was 'a mere examining board whose profits were seized by the government'.

5 For the full texts of the University College London (Transfer) Act, 1905, and the King's College London (Transfer) Act, 1908, see *University of London: The Historical Record* (1912), pp.114–68.

6 The bizarre story of the University of London Press is unravelled in a memorandum by Graham West (1980), ULL ULC 36/21.

7 Walter Seton, *William Howard Lister* (1919), p.25; see also Edward K. Ford, *The Brown Dog and his Memorial* (1908) and L.E. Bayliss, 'The "Brown Dog" Affair', typescript (1955) in UCL College Collection.

8 Sir Ray Lankester, 'Science from an Easy Chair', *Daily Telegraph* (11 March 1912).

9 ULL ACO CF 1 (1907–8), 707; A.D. Waller, *A Short Account of the Origins of the University of London* (1912), p.18. Waller's account is more interesting for what it says about contemporary disputes than for what it says about the origins of the University.

10 Treasury Minute of 16 February 1899, given in Minutes of the Senate, 22 February 1899. The Treasury Minute of 13 July 1899, given in Minutes of the Senate, 25 October 1899, was more specifically composed.

11 Letter in *The Times* (30 June 1933).

12 *Daily Telegraph* (5 April 1912); Campbell-Bannerman's remark quoted in E.M. Spiers, *Haldane: An Army Reformer* (1980), p.193; Lord Rosebery's correspondence with the Vice-

Chancellor and the Chairman of Convocation was published at his own expense in a pamphlet, *London University Site* – 'It seems desirable that the correspondence relating to the remarkable transactions herein recorded should be printed and preserved. R. April 1912'. See also ULL ACO CF 1 (1911–12), 707.

13 H. Campbell Thomson, *The Story of the Middlesex Hospital Medical School, 1835–1935* (1935), inserted at p.91.

14 *The Hospital* (23 August 1913); 'The Attempted Germanisation of London University', *Medical Press and Circular* (7 October 1914); *Haldane Commission Final Report* (1913), especially pp.107–22.

15 For the extraordinary consequences of this in connection with Greece in the 1920s, see the fascinating study by Richard Clogg, 'Politics and the Academy: Arnold Toynbee and the Koraes Chair', *Middle Eastern Studies*, 21 (1985).

16 Internal Students: *University of London Calendar*, II (1972), p.115. Internal students at institutions not in receipt of UGC grants – the theological schools and the institutions with recognized teachers – are excluded from these figures. Total number of candidates for all exams: *Calendar*, passim, and *Principal's Reports* (in Minutes of the Senate), passim. Degrees awarded: *Calendar*, passim.

17 *UGC Returns from Universities and University Colleges in Receipt of Treasury Grants* (1921).

18 Quoted in N.B. Harte, *One Hundred and Fifty Years of History Teaching at University College London* (1982), p.15.

19 The 'snarled and tangled' issues are discussed by Sir Ernest Barker, Principal of King's, 1920–8, in *Age and Youth: Memories of Three Universities* (1953), especially pp.112–17, 128–30.

20 Foster, *The University of*

London: History, Present Resources and Future Possibilities, p.9.

21 A. Taylor Milne, 'Notes on the History of the University: The Bloomsbury Site', *University of London Bulletin*, 4 (1972), p.11; *Vincula*, II, 10 (1926).

22. Beveridge, *Power and Influence*, p.192; Logan, *Haldane and the University of London*, p.4.

23 Transcript of the proceedings of the deputation to the Treasury, 17 June 1926 and 29 June 1926, in ULL ACO CF 1 (1925–6), 661. See also Beveridge, *Power and Influence*, pp.193–5.

24 Beveridge, *Power and Influence*, pp.192–3.

25 Ashby and Anderson, *Portrait of Haldane at Work on Education*, p.158; *The Times* (23 March 1926).

26 *Report of the Departmental Committee on the University of London* (1926), pp.6, 8, 23, 25, 38, 53–7.

CHAPTER 6   Bloomsbury and Beyond, 1929–1963

1 ULL ACO VP 1/4.

2 Sir William Beveridge, *The Physical Relation of a University to a City* (1928), p.15.

3 Beveridge, *Power and Influence*, p.206.

4 *University of London: New Buildings* (1932); see also the interview with Holden in *University of London Union Magazine* (centenary number, June 1936) and his own article in the *Journal of the Royal Institute of British Architects* (May 1938).

5 *Manchester Guardian* (4 June 1931); *Country Life* (2 July 1932) (in ULL ACO VP 6/3/1 and VP 6/3/2).

6 Nikolaus Pevsner, *The Buildings of England: London, Except the Cities of London and Westminster* (1952), p.211.

7 ULL ACO CF 1 (1932–3), 707; *Report of the Principal on the Work of the University during the Year 1933–34*, p.1.

8 See ULL ULC 32/3, and ULL ULC 34 and 35.

9 Sir Philip Manson-Bahr, *History of the School of Tropical Medicine in London, 1899–1949* (1956), pp.65, 167.

10 *Appeal for a University Sports Ground and Boat House* (1926); ULL ULC 2/10. See also *University of London Athletic Ground Jubilee, 1931–81, Programme* (1981).

11 Day-Lewis quoted in J.M. Richards, *Memoirs of an Unjust Fella* (1980), p.160; Evelyn Waugh, *Put Out More Flags* (1942), Penguin edn, p.61; Graham Greene, 'Men at Work', *Penguin New Writing*, 9 (1941) in John Lehmann and Roy Fuller (eds), *Penguin New Writing, 1940–50* (1985), pp.33, 35; Betjeman quoted in *Sunday Times* Colour Supplement (8 August 1965).

12 Sir Douglas Logan, 'David Hughes Parry – An Appreciation', *University of London Bulletin*, 7 (1973), p.10.

13 The whole time series is given in *University of London Calendar*, II (1972), pp.115–16, 118. The two sets of figures for internal students were compiled in accordance with different criteria which account for the apparent discrepancies. Numbers of external students are available only from 1932–3; they were not previously required to register as students of the University before entry to the examinations.

14 Up to 1938 statistics for all types of bachelor's and higher degrees both internal and external are given in detail in successive editions of the *Calendar*. Between 1939 and 1948 no published statistics are available, and the figures given here have been obtained by counting in the names given in the annual Pass Lists. From 1948 to 1965–6 the totals are given annually in the Minutes of the Senate.

15 See Eric M. Warburg, 'The Transfer of the Warburg Institute to England in 1933', in the Warburg Institute's *Annual Report* for 1952–3, pp.13–16.

16 The story is told in detail in Bruce Pattison, *Special Relations: the University of London and New Universities Overseas, 1947–70* (1984).

17 A. Temple Patterson, *The University of Southampton* (1962), pp.211–13.

18 Tuke, *A History of Bedford College for Women, 1849–1937*, pp.198, 247, 340.

19 UGC *Returns from Universities and University Colleges in Receipt of Treasury Grants*, conveniently summarized in the *University of London Calendar* for 1969–70, pp.107–16.

30 UGC *Returns from Universities in Receipt of Treasury Grants*, 1960–1, tables 11 and 11A.

CHAPTER 7   Robbins and After, 1963–1986

1 Carswell, *Government and the Universities in Britain*, p.38.

2 *Higher Education: Report of the Committee appointed by the Prime Minister under the Chairmanship of Lord Robbins, 1961–63* (1963), pp.223–4.

3 *University of London Reorganisation, 1964–66* (1966), pp.81, 87, 105.

4 Ibid., pp.74, 93, 95.

5 Lord Robbins, *Higher Education Revisited* (1980), p.50.

6 Dunsheath and Miller, *Convocation in the University of London*, pp.141–5.

7 *Final Report of the Committee of Enquiry into the Governance of the University of London* (1972), pp.28, 45, 48, vii, viii.

8 Ibid., pp.98, 131, 158–9, 162, and summary of recommendations, pp.171–90.

9 *University of London Calendar*, II (1972), pp.116–18; *University of London Calendar* (1985–6), p.263 (where the different bases of the figures for internal students are explained). Figures for 1984–5 kindly provided by Mr R.M. Cain and Mr S.B. Crooks.

10 S. John Teague, *The City University: A History* (1980), pp.132–5.

11 See *Report on the Future of the External System* (1972), including the Council for External Students' Report (1971) and the Interim Report of the Murray Committee on the External System (1971).

12 See *Report of the Academic Council Sub-Committee on the Review of Courses at Colleges Associated with the Institute of Education* (1979) – the Varey Report – adopted by the Senate, 12 December 1979.

13 *Report of the Royal Commission on Medical Education, 1965–68* (1968), pp.24–5, 178–82.

14 Balanced assessments of the difficulties of the Todd proposals were given by Sir Douglas Logan in the *University of London Bulletin*, 8 (May 1973) and by Professor F.L. Warren in ibid., 11 (October 1973).

15 *London Medical Education – A New Framework: Report of a Working Party on Medical and Dental Teaching Resources* (1980) – the Flowers Report – pp.11, 4.

16 Ibid., pp.41–7, 32.

17 The complexities of change in medicine are surveyed in Professor L.P. Le Quesne's Monckton Copeman lecture to the Society of Apothecaries on 'Medical Education in London: The Last Forty Years' in March 1986. I am indebted to Professor Le Quesne for a copy of his typescript.

18 The *University of London Bulletin* was published between 1972 and 1978, replacing the formal *University of London Gazette*. It contained much of interest that a full history would need to take into account, especially Sir Douglas Logan's 'The University of London – Retrospect and Prospect' (Special Issue, 10, October 1973), written after the Murray Report and before his retirement.

19 *UGC Annual Survey for 1975–76* (1976), para.24.

Illustrations: Sources and Acknowledgments

The illustrations are reproduced by courtesy of the following:

1 Guy's Hospital Medical School 2 From Foundation Day Programme, 13 Nov. 1985 3 *The Times*, 13 Nov. 1985, Times Newspapers Ltd 4 *London Student* 5 *Schoolmaster*, 9 July 1936, ULL ACO VP 6/4 6 School of Oriental and African Studies SOAS 7 As 4 8 Royal Holloway and Bedford New College RHBNC 9 *Sunday Times*, 11 Aug. 1985, Times Newspapers Ltd 10 As 4 11 Warburg Institute 12 London School of Hygiene and Tropical Medicine 13 Queen Elizabeth College QEC Archives 14 Drawing by W. Fairclough, 1947, Wye College Library 15 ULL ACO RC 40/21 16 St Bartholomew's Hospital Archives Misc. 45/102 17 *Graphic*, 16 May 1885 18 From *Graphic* 1884, in A. Bott (ed.), *Our Mothers* (1932) 19 *The Sphere*, July 1922, Westfield College Archives 20 Photograph by Gordon Rutter, through the kindness of Donald Mann, Warden of International Hall 21–2 Royal Free Hospital School of Medicine Archives 23 Photograph by C. Halfacre, Institute of Classical Studies 24 By courtesy of Miss Jean Fenton, London Secretary of the British Institute in Paris 25 ULL ACO VP/4/5/11 26 Courtauld Institute of Art 27 As 8 28 Petrie Museum of Egyptian Archaeology, University College London UCL 29 St Mary's Hospital Medical School 30 Percival David Foundation of Chinese Art 31 Royal Postgraduate Medical School RPMS 32 PhotoCERN, through the kindess of Dr Fred Bullock 33 Drawing by Paul Doherty, *Radio Times*, 8–14 March 1986 34 London Centre for Marine Technology, by courtesy of Dr Stephen Montgomery 35 Institute of Child Health 36 Photograph by Ken Barr, by courtesy of the *VCH* and Institute of Historical Research 37–41 Ian Coates Photography 42 From [H.J.T. Ellingham] *Centenary of the Imperial College of Science and Technology: A Short History* (1945) 43 Michael Barnett Photography, by courtesy of Professor J.P. Quilliam 44 As 1 45 Press advertisement 46 Imperial college IC Archives 47 As 4 48 UL Boat Club, through the kindness of the Captain, Iain Burnett 49 Westfield College Archives 50 ULL ULC 2/4 51

St Bartholomew's Hospital Dept of Medical Illustration 52 Society of Antiquaries 53 John Darley, *The Glory of Chelsey Colledge Revived* (1662) 54 UCL Library 55 B. Williamson, *Catalogue of the Paintings and Engravings in the Possession of the Hon. Society of the Middle Temple* (1931) 56 John Stow and Edmond Howes, *The Annales, or Generall Chronicle of England* (1615) 57 As 51 58 St Thomas's Hospital Medical School Library 59 Westminster Hospital Dept of Medical Illustration and Teaching Services 60 As 1 61 St George's Hospital Medical School 62 Engraving after portrait by Reynolds, as 61 63–4 As 1 65 Anon. etching, 1782, Wellcome Institute Library, London 66 Charing Cross & Westminster Medical School 67 London Hospital Medical College 68 Middlesex Hospital Medical School 69 Wellcome Institute Library, London 70 As 66 71 Engraving of portrait by Opie, as 67 72 Aquatint by Stadler, after Smollett, as 69 73 Royal Veterinary College Library 74 Portrait by Phillips hanging in ULL, photograph by courtesy of the Courtauld Institute 75 Portrait by Spiridione Gambardella hanging in the Court Room, as 74 76 Royal Institution 77 British Museum BM Dept of Prints and Drawings, George 14788 78 UCL Publications Dept 79 As 68 80–1 UCL 82–3 Birkbeck College 84 *Second Book: Lectures and Examinations for King's College Students* (1828), King's College London KCL Archives 85 *Saturday Magazine*, 21 Dec. 1833, ULL ULC 22/12 86 *First Book for the Instruction of Students in the King's College* (1828), as 84 87 As 84 88 *The Mirror of Literature, Amusement and Instruction*, 15 Oct. 1831, as 84, 89 UCL 90 KCH Library 91 Photogravure by LCC School of Photo Engraving from a painting by A. Legros, IC Archives 92 ULL ACO ST 1/1 93 Engraving by J. Linnell, 1836, as 77, C II, P5: 1868–8–8– 1932 94 Painted by Francis Grant, 1853, in Spencer Walpole, *Life of Lord John Russell*, II (1889) 95 Painting by William Tweedie hanging in the lobby to the Senate Room, as 74 96 Painting by Thomas Phillips hanging outside the Senate Room, as 74 97 As 77, Baugniet Portraits, VI, f. 40 98 As 1 99 Engraving after a daguerrotype by Jabez Hogg, NPG, negative no. 38444 100 As 77, C VII, P5:

1870–5–14–1444 101 As 77, C VII, P5: 1906–1–11–23–15 102 NPG, no. 402 103 Engraving by Sands in [E.J. Johnstone], *The Public Buildings of Westminster Described* (1831) 104 Engraving by J.H. Lynch after S. Laurence, NPG, negative no. 38443 105 As 77, C IV P5: 1868–12– 12–78 106 As 77, C VII, P5: 1865–6–10–1203 107 As 77, C III, P5: 52–11–16–343 108 ULL ACO ST 1/2 109 ULL ACO RC 44/15 110 Engraving after Thomas Phillips in A.P. Stanley, *Life of Thomas Arnold* (1904 edn) 111 Engraving by G.H. Adcock in V.A. Huber, *The English Universities*, ed. F.W. Newman, III (1843) 112–13 ULL, ACO UP 3/1, *Examination Papers, 1838–39* 114 In 111 115 As 112 116 ULL ACO AC 2/1/100 117 ULL ACO AC 2/1/2 118 ULL ULC 28/7 (i) 119 ULL ULC 28/7 (ii), see also ULC 2/16 120 ULL ACO RO 1/2/17 121 *Illustrated London News ILN*, 11 May 1850, ULL ULC 28/8 122 ULL ACO UP 1/1/1 123 UCL 124 ULL ACO RO 1/2/13 125 *Builder*, XII, 28 Oct. 1854 126 Painting by John Collier in store at Senate House, as 74 127 Painting by D. Laugee hanging outside the Senate Room, as 74 128 Painting of the Royal College in Port-Louis now at the Royal College in Curepipe, Mauritius, photographed by courtesy of the Rector 129 *ILN*, 1 July 1843, KCL Archives 130 *ILN*, 1846, UCL 131–2 IC Archives 133 As 77, C VII, P5: 1938–9–19–21 134 Huxley Papers, as 131 135 KCL Archives 136–7 Bedford College Archives 138 ULL ACO AC 2/1/1 139 Ape cartoon, *Vanity Fair*, 27 Feb. 1869, ULL ULC31 140 *ILN*, 14 May 1870 141 *ILN*, 21 May 1870 142 *Graphic*, 21 May 1870, ULL ULC 28/9 143 As 141 144 ULL ACO RO 2/19/7 145 Bust by Thomas Woolner in ULL, Photograph by F. Bosley 146 *ILN*, 24 Feb. 1872, photograph by M.D. Trace, with gratitude to the Minet Library, Lambeth 147 *Girl's Own Paper*, July 1882, by courtesy of Dr Janet Sondheimer 148 *Graphic*, 23 May 1891, ULL ULC 28/13 149 *Punch*, 19 Jan. 1884 150 North London Collegiate School 151–4 As 21 155–6 As 49 157 Royal Holloway College Archives 158 From H. Solly, *Life of Henry Morley* (1898) 159–60 As 157 161 Royal Borough of Kensington and Chelsea Library and Arts Services, Kensington

Local History Coll. **162** Painting by Millais hanging outside the Senate Room, as 74 **163** *Punch*, 19 Aug. 1882 **164** Ape cartoon in *Vanity Fair*, 13 March 1869, ULL ULC 3/1 **165** Portrait by John Collier hanging outside the Senate Room, as 74 **166** *Pictorial World*, 25 July 1874, as 51 **167** *ILN*, 29 Jan. 1859, KCL Archives **168** As 135 **169** *Cassell's Family Magazine* (1877), ULL ULC 23/11 **170** Drawing by H.W. Petherick, NPG, no. 2138 **171** Dept of Extra-Mural Studies, by courtesy of Mr John Burrows **172** As 58 **173** as 51 **174–7** ULL ACO RO 2/19/4, 9, 8, 6 **178** Drawing by the Duchess of Rutland, NPG Engravings Reserve **179** ULL ACO RC 13/2/5 **180** Ape cartoon in *Vanity Fair*, 26 June 1869, ULL ULC 3/1 **181** ULL ACO RO 1/13/1, f.27 **182** Spy cartoon for *Vanity Fair*, 19 March 1881, in NPG, 2721 **183** Photograph by G.C. Beresford, 1903, NPG, negative no. 29059 **184** KCHMS Photographic Dept **185** LSE **186** ULL ACO RC 44/12 **187** Ape cartoon, in *Vanity Fair*, 16 July 1869, ULL ULC 3/1 **188** ULL ACO RO 2/19/1 **189** ULL ACO FG 4/5/1 **190** From *The Imperial Institute of the United Kingdom, the Colonies and India* (1893), ULL ULC 29/7c **191** Engraving by Monk, 1909, ULL ULC 27/19 **192** From *Harper's New Monthly Magazine*, Oct. 1906, ULL ULC 24/3 **193** *Daily Graphic*, 10 May 1900, ULL ACO UL 3/3 **194** From *General Information for Internal Students* (1906) **195** From Report of Academic Council, 1910, ULL ACO RC 32/6 **196** Wye College Library **197** Cover of *South-western Polytechnic Prospectus* for 1895–6, Chelsea College Archives now in KCL Archives **198** Institute of Education **199** E.R. Robson's design for the People's Palace, 1891, Queen Mary College QMC Archives, by courtesy of Dr G.P. Moss **200** As 198 **201** ULL ACO VP, uncatalogued **202** *Daily Graphic*, 26 June 1903, ULL ACO VP 6/1/1 **203** *Graphic*, 4 July 1903, ULL ACO VP 6/1/1 **204** As 192 **205** Goldsmiths' College **206** *Mayfair*, 9 Oct. 1915, through the kindness of Dr Alan Sykes **207** ULL ACO CF 1(1913–14),364 **208** Painting by J.S. Sargent hanging in first-floor corridor at Senate House, as 74 **209** ULL ULC 9/34 **210** Certificate of Registration of

Design no. 508457, 31 July 1907, ULL ACO RC 13/4a **211** ULL Humberstone Papers **212** Cartoon by W.P. Starmer in Edward K. Ford, *The Brown Dog and his Memorial* (1908), by courtesy of Battersea Local History Library **213** *Daily Graphic*, 13 May 1909, ULL ACO ME 2/5, f.17 **214** ULL ACO ME 2/5, f.194 **215** As 214, f.124 **216** *Vanity Fair*, Jan. 1891, by courtesy of the City and Guilds of London Institute **217** From Cassell's *Old and New London* (1873–8), IC Archives **218** Drawing in The Architect, 14 Jan. 1882, IC Archives **219** *Graphic*, 18 May 1912, ULL ACO VP 6/1/15 **220** *ILN*, 3 Jan. 1914, ULL Humberstone Papers **221** *Graphic*, 24 Jan. 1914, ULL ACO VP 6/1/18 **222** *Estates Gazette*, 9 Nov. 1912, ULL ACO VP 6/1/15 **223** *The Undergraduate*, I,1 (1913), ULL **224** ULL ACO CF 1(1913–14), 2461 **225** *London Teacher*, 11 July 1914, ULL ACO VP 6/1/19 **226** Drawing by Helen Campbell hanging outside the Principal's office, Senate House **227** ULL ACO VP uncatalogued **228** As 16, Misc. 45/71 **229** *Illustrated Sporting and Dramatic News*, 6 Nov. 1915, QEC Archives **230** Drawing by Adams, Holden and Pearson in QEC Archives **231** Drawing in Masaryk Hall, School of Slavonic and East European Studies **232** SOAS **233** As 1 **234** Penson Papers in Bedford College Archives, by kind permission of Professor Hugh Lawrence **235** IHR **236** *Evening News*, 16 Sept. 1936, IHR **237–8** ULL ACO CF 1(1921–2), 2461 **239** *Vincula*, 3, Dec. 1922, ULL **240** *Vincula*, 1, Nov. 1922, ULL **241** *Vincula*, I, 23, 1924, ULL **242** ULL ACO CF 1(1922–3), 480 **243** ULL ACO CF 1(1923–4), 1219 **244** Painting by Sir William Nicholson, 1937, LSE **245** ULL ULC 28/18 **246** Holborn Local History Library, negative no. 3762, London Borough of Camden **247** As 12 **248** *Vincula*, II, 12, 1926, ULL **249** As 12 **250** *Vincula*, II, 7, 1926, ULL **251** *Vincula*, II, 11, 1926, ULL **252** As 29 **253** *ILN*, 21 Jan. 1933 (the original was presented to the University, but cannot now be traced) **254** As 228 **255** Painting by L. Campbell Taylor, hanging in first-floor corridor at Senate House, as 74 **256** ULL ACO FG 5/2 **257** Plaque in ULL **258** Portrait in Court and Senate Ante-Room at Senate House, as 74 **259** ULL ULC 27/1 **260** ULL ACO CT

3/4/1 **261** As 135 **262** *Daily Telegraph*, 30 May 1931, ULL ACO VP 6/1/30 **263** ULL ACO CT 3/4/1 **264–7** ULL ACO CF 1 (1932–3), 707 **268–9** ULL ACO CT 3/4/1 **270** ULL ACO SV 5/6 **271** ULL ACO CT 3/4/2 **272** ULL ACO SV 5/6 **273** Holden's re-design drawn by A. Bryett, *National Builder*, May 1939, ULL ACO VP 6/3/5 **274** ULL UCL 9/41 **275–6** ULL ULC 27/1 **277** *The Times*, 16 Dec. 1937, ULL ACO VP 6/3/5 **278** ULL ACO SV 5/8 **279–80** ULL ACO SV 27/1 **281** As 1 **282** As 278 **283** *Daily Telegraph*, 23 Jan. 1939, ULL ACO VP 6/3/5 **284** *Evening News*, 2 May 1938, ULL ACO VP 6/3/5 **285** As 278 **286** ULL ACO SV 5/35 **287** Courtauld Institute, negative no. B64/756 **288–9** Plaques by Paul Vincze and Ivan Metrović, SSEES **290–1** Institute of Archaeology **292** From *Appeal for a University Sports Ground and Boat House* (1926), ULL ACO UP 2/10 **293** By courtesy of Mr D.A.V. Morgan **294** As 135 **295** *Middlesex Hospital Journal*, XXXVI, 1936, MHMS **296** UCL **297** As 29 **298** ULL ACO CF 1(1929–30), 2426 **299** *Vincula*, II, 2, 1925 **300** Birkbeck College **301** ULL ULC 6/4 **302** BBC Hulton Picture Library **303** RPMS **304** ULL ACO SV 5/15 **305** As 10 **306** Portrait by John Gilroy hanging in the Court Room, as 74 **307** St Thomas's Hospital Medical School **308** ULL ACO UN 6/1 **309** ULL ACO SV 5/22 **310** Portrait hanging in Court and Senate Ante-Room, as 74 **311** Institute of Germanic Studies **312** LSE **313** RCV **314** As 135 **315** As 31 **316** ULL ACO UN 6/1 **317** ULL ACO UN 6/1 **318** As 289 **319** ULL **320** Pharmaceutical Society of Great Britain, photograph by courtesy of the School of Pharmacy **321** School of Pharmacy **322** Aerofilms Ltd **323** UCL **324** Times Newspapers Ltd **325** ULL ACO VP 4/5/1 **326** ULL ULC 27/8(ii) **327** Drawing by Murray Zanoni, by courtesy of the London Business School **328** *Financial Times* photograph, LSE **329** Drawing hanging in first-floor corridor at Senate House, as 74 **330** As 31 **331–2** Bloomsbury Conference Agency **333** Institute of Latin American Studies **334** LSE **335** By courtesy of Mr P.J. Griffiths **336** Marine Biological Station, Millport, through the

kindness of Mr P.M. Crossland **337** As 4 **338** As 6 **339–40** ULL Photographic Unit **341** Drawing by Derek Chittock hanging in first-floor corridor at Senate House, as 74 **342** Photograph by F.J. Bosley **343** As 67 **344** Penguin Books **345** Photograph by Pino Guidolotti, Warburg Institute. **346** Dept of Physiology, UCL **347** Camera Press **348** Dept of Chemistry, IC **349** As 61 **350** As 29 **351** As 4 **352** Institute of Commonwealth Studies **353** QMC **354** Vice-Chancellor's Office **355** As 353 **356** *Guardian*, 5 Aug. 1985 **357** As 322 **358** *Times Higher Education Supplement*, 5 June 1981 **359** As 49 **360** As 354 **361** As 4 **362** Principal's Office **363** As 37 **364** *Guardian*, 16 Jan. 1986 **365** *Daily Telegraph*, 20 Jan,. 1896 **366** As 354

Bibliography

ABSE, Joan (ed.), *My LSE* (1977).

ADAMSON, J.W., *A Short History of Education* (1919).

ALLCHIN, W.H., *An Account of the Reconstruction of the University of London* (3 vols: I *From the Foundation of the University to the Appointment of the First Royal Commission, 1825 to 1888* (1905); II *From the Appointment of the First Royal Commission to the Rejection of the Scheme of the Senate by Convocation, 1888 to 1891* [1911]; III *From the Rejection of the Senate's Scheme by Convocation to the Withdrawal of the Gresham Charter, 1891 to 1892* (1912)).

ALTER, Peter, *Wissenschaft, Staat, Mäzene: Anfänger moderner Wissenschaftspolitik in Grossbritannien, 1850–1920* (1982).

ANNAN, Lord, 'The University in Britain' in M.D. Stephens and G.W. Roderick (eds), *Universities for a Changing World* (1975).

ARGLES, M., *South Kensington to Robbins: An Account of English Technical and Scientific Education since 1851* (1964).

ARMYTAGE, W.H.G., *Civic Universities: Aspects of a British Tradition* (1955).

——, *Four Hundred Years of English Education* (1964).

ASHBY, Eric, *Community of Universities: An Informal Portrait of the Association of Universities of the British Commonwealth, 1913–1963* (1963).

——, *Technology and the Academics: An Essay on Universities and the Scientific Revolution* (1963).

ASHBY, Eric and ANDERSON, Mary, *The Rise of the Student Estate in Britain* (1970).

——, *Portrait of Haldane at Work in Education* (1974).

BALFOUR, Graham, *The Educational Systems of Great Britain and Ireland* (2nd edn, 1903).

BARKER, Sir Ernest, *Age and Youth: Memories of Three Universities* (1953).

BECKER, Bernard H., *Scientific London* (1874).

BELL, E. Moberly, *Storming the Citadel: The Rise of the Woman Doctor* (1953).

BELL, Quentin, *The Schools of Design* (1963).

BELLOT, H. Hale, *University College London, 1826–1926* (1929).

——, *The University of London: A History* (1969); also in *Victoria County History: Middlesex*, I (1969), with additions by J.S. Cockburn on 'The Constituent Colleges' (excluding the medical schools and those not in Middlesex).

BERDAHL, Robert O., *British Universities and the State* (1959).

BERMAN, Morris, *Social Change and Scientific Organization: The Royal Institution, 1799–1844* (1978).

BEVERIDGE, Janet, *An Epic of Clare Market: Birth and Early Days of the London School of Economics* (1960).

BEVERIDGE, William, *The Physical Relation of a University to a City* (1928).

——, *Power and Influence* (1953).

——, *A Defence of Free Learning* (1959).

——, *The London School of Economics and its Problems, 1919–1937* (1960).

——, 'The London School of Economics and the University of London' in Margaret Cole (ed.), *The Webbs and their Work* (1949).

BIBBY, C., *T.H. Huxley: Scientist, Humanist and Educator* (1959).

BIRD, D.T., *Catalogue of the Printed Books and Manuscripts (1491–1900) in the Library of St Thomas's Hospital Medical School* (1984).

BIRKBECK COLLEGE, *Centenary Lectures* (1924).

BLACKSTONE, Tessa, GALES, Kathleen, HADLEY, Roger and LEWIS, Wyn, *Students in Conflict: LSE in 1967* (1970).

BLOMFIELD, J., *St George's, 1733–1933* (1933).

BRITISH INSTITUTE IN PARIS, *L'Institut Britannique de l'Université de Paris* (1952): includes M.A. Desclos, 'La Fondation de l'Institut Britannique'; Maud Burt, 'La Guilde et l'Institut'; M.G. Harris, 'Les Années de guerre et d'après-guerre, 1939–50'.

BROOK, F.G., 'The University of London, 1820–1860, with special reference to its Influence on the Development of Higher Education' (London PhD thesis, 1958).

BURNS, C. Delisle, *A Short History of Birkbeck College* (1924).

BURNS, J.H., *Jeremy Bentham and University College* (1962).

BURROWS, John, *University Adult Education in London: A Century of Achievement* (1976).

CAINE, Sir Sydney, *The History of the Foundation of the London School of Economics and Political Science* (1963).

——, *British Universities: Purpose and Prospects* (1969).

CALNAN, James, *The Hammersmith: The First Fifty Years of the Royal Postgraduate Medical School at Hammersmith Hospital, 1935–85* (1985).

CAMERON, H.C., *Mr Guy's Hospital, 1726–1948* (1954).

CARDWELL, D.S.L., *The Organisation of Science in England* (2nd edn, 1972).

CARR-SAUNDERS, A.M., *New Universities Overseas* (1961).

CARSWELL, John, *Government and the Universities in Britain: Programme and Performance, 1960–1980* (1985).

CARUS-WILSON, E.M. (ed.), *Westfield College, 1882–1932* (1932).

CHAMBERS, R.W. (ed.), *University of London, University College: Centenary Addresses* (1927).

CHAPEL, Jeannie, *Victorian Taste: The Complete Catalogue of Paintings at the Royal Holloway College* (1982).

CHRIMES, S.B., 'Historical Account of the University of London Union Society', *University of London Union: Students' Handbook* (1929–30).

CITY AND GUILDS COLLEGE, *City and Guilds College, 1885–1985: Centenary Issue of 'The Central'* (1984).

CLARK, Catherine M. and MACKINTOSH, James M., *The School and the Site: A Historical Memoir to Celebrate the Twenty-Fifth Anniversary of the School* [London School of Hygiene and Tropical Medicine] (1954).

CLARK-KENNEDY, A.E., *The London: A Study in the Voluntary Hospital System* (2 vols, 1961, 1963).

——, *London Pride: The Story of a Voluntary Hospital* (1979).

——, 'The London Hospitals and the Rise of the University' in F.N.L. Poynter (ed.), *The Evolution of Medical Education in Britain* (1966).

CLAUGHTON, Sir Harold, 'The University of London: Past, Present and Future', *Universities Quarterly*, II (1948).

CLOGG, Richard, 'Politics and the Academy: Arnold Toynbee and the Koraes Chair', *Middle Eastern Studies*, XXI (1985).

COLLES, H.C. and CRUFT, John, *The Royal College of Music: A Centenary Record, 1883–1983* (1982).

COOK, J. Stewart, *Convocation: A Study in Academic Democracy* (1940).

COPE, Sir Zachary, *The History of St Mary's Hospital Medical School* (1954).

——, *Florence Nightingale and the Doctors* (1958).

——, 'The Private Medical Schools of London, 1746–1914' in F.N.L. Poynter (ed.), *The Evolution of Medical Education in Britain* (1966).

COPPING, Alice M., *The Story of College Hall, 1882–1972* (1974).

CORDER, F., *A History of the Royal Academy of Music* (1922).

CROUCH, Colin, *The Student Revolt* (1970).

CROWTHER, J.G., *Statesmen of Science* (1965).

DAVIS, Eliza Jeffries, 'The University Site, Bloomsbury', *London Topographical Record*, XVII (1936).

DENT, H.C., *Universities in Transition* (1961).

DOUIE, M.B., 'Women in Medicine' in Eleanor M. Hill (ed.), *Frances Mary Buss Schools' Jubilee Record* (1900).

DUNSHEATH, Percy and MILLER, Margaret, *Convocation in the University of London: The First Hundred Years* (1958).

DYMOND, Dorothy (ed.), *The Forge: The History of Goldsmiths' College, 1905–1955* (1955).

[EDWARDS, E.] *Metropolitan University: Remarks on the Ministerial Plan of a Central University Examining Board* (1836).

[ELLINGHAM, H.J.T.] *Centenary of the Imperial College of Science and Technology: A Short History of the College, 1845–1945* (1945).

FAITHFULL, Lilian M., *In the House of my Pilgrimage* (1924).

FELKIN, F.W., *From Gower Street to Frognal: A Short History of University College School from 1830 to 1907* (1909).

FIDDES, Edward, *Chapters in the History of Owens College and of Manchester University, 1851–1914* (1937).

FIRTH, Catherine B., *Constance Louisa Maynard: Mistress of Westfield College* (1949).

FITCH, Sir Joshua, Jubilee review article in *Quarterly Review*, 164 (1887).

——, 'History and Work of the University' in *The University of London: A Sketch of its Work and History from its Foundation in 1837* [sic] *to the Present Time* (1900).

FLEXNER, A., *Universities: American, English, German* (1930).

FODEN, Frank, *Philip Magnus Victorian Educational Pioneer* (1970).

FOSTER, Sir Gregory, *The University of London: History, Present Resources and Future Possibilities* (1922).

FRASER, Sir Francis, *The British Postgraduate Medical Federation: The First Fifteen Years* (1967).

GODWIN, George, *Queen Mary College: An Adventure in Education* (1939).

GOLLANCZ, Sir Hermann, *A Contribution to the History of University College London* (1930).

GOODLAD, Sinclair (ed.), *Education for the Professions: Quis Custodiet?* (1984).

HALL, A. Rupert, *Science for Industry: A Short History of the Imperial College of Science and Technology and its Antecedents* (1982).

HARRISON, J.F.C., *A History of the Working Men's College, 1854–1945* (1954).

HARTE, Negley and NORTH, John, *The World of University College London, 1828–1978* (1978).

HARTE, N.B., *The Admission of Women to University College London: A Centenary Lecture* (1979).

——, *One Hundred and Fifty Years of History Teaching at University College London* (1982).

HARTLEY, Sir Harold and HINSHELWOOD, Sir Cyril, 'Gresham College and the Royal Society' in Sir Harold Hartley (ed.), *The Tercentenary Celebrations of the Royal Society of London* (1961).

HARTOG, P.J., 'The Origins of SOS', *Bulletin of the School of Oriental Studies*, I (1917).

HAYEK, F.A., 'The London School of Economics, 1895–1945', *Economica*, n.s. XIII (1946).

HEARNSHAW, F.J.C., *The Centenary History of King's College London, 1828–1928* (1929).

HILL, Eleanor M., 'Women and the Universities' in idem (ed.), *Frances Mary Buss Schools' Jubilee Record* (1900).

HIMSWORTH, Sir Harold, *The Development and Organisation of Scientific Knowledge* (1970).

HOCH, Paul and SCHOENBACH, Vic, *LSE: The Natives are Restless. A Report on Student Power in Action* (1969).

HOLDEN, Charles, 'The University of London', *Journal of the Royal Institute of British Architects* (June 1938).

HOWARTH, O.J.R. (eds.), *London and the Advancement of Science* (1931).

HUBER, V.A., *The English Universities* ed. F.W. Newman (3 vols, 1843).

HUELIN, Gordon, *King's College London, 1828–1978* (1978).

HUGHES PARRY, David, *O Bentref Llanaelhaearn i Ddinas Llundain* (1972).

HUMBERSTONE, T.L., *University Reform in London* (1926).

——, *Torrington Square Saved!* (1938).

——, *Academic Adventures in Bloomsbury* (1951).

——, *University Representation* (1951).

——, *University Controversies* (1953).

HUMBLE, J.G. and HANSELL, P., *Westminster Hospital, 1716–1974* (1974).

HUNTER, M.I.A., *St George's, 1933–1983* (n.d.).

HUNTER, William, *Historical Account of Charing Cross Hospital and Medical School* (1914).

HUSSEY, Christopher, 'A Bloomsbury House To-day: The Institute of Commonwealth Studies, 27

Russell Square', *Country Life*, 4 May 1951.

HYAMSON, Albert M., *Jews' College, London, 1855–1955* (1955).

IMPERIAL COLLEGE, *The Royal Charter of the Imperial College of Science and Technology: Jubilee, 1907–57* (1957).

INSTITUTE OF EDUCATION, *Descriptive Booklet* (1939): includes 'Historical Sketch' by Sir Percy Nunn.

——, *Studies and Impressions, 1902–1952* (1952).

——, *Jubilee Lectures* (1952).

JEFFERY, G.B., *The Unity of Knowledge: Reflections on the Universities of Cambridge and London* (1960).

JENKINS, David and STANWAY, Andrew T., *The Story of King's College Hospital* (1968).

JOPSON, N.B., ROSE, W.J. and BOLSOVER, G.H., 'The School of Slavonic and East European Studies: The First Fifty Years', *Slavonic and East European Review*, XLIV (1966).

JUDGES, A.V., *The University of London* (1961).

KAMM, Josephine, *How Different from Us: A Biography of Miss Buss and Miss Beale* (1958).

KAYE, Elaine, *A History of Queen's College, London, 1848–1972* (1972).

KEARNEY, Hugh, *Scholars and Gentlemen: Universities and Society in Pre-Industrial Britain, 1500–1700* (1970).

KELLY, Thomas, *A History of Adult Education in Great Britain* (1962).

——, *George Birkbeck: Pioneer of Adult Education* (1957).

KER, W.P. (ed.), *Notes and Materials for the History of University College London* (1898).

KIDD, Harry, *The Trouble at LSE, 1966–67* (1969).

KING'S COLLEGE, *Documents relating to King's College London* (2nd edn, 1933).

KOGAN, Maurice and David, *The Attack on Higher Education* (1983).

LANG, Jennifer, *City and Guilds of London Institute: Centenary, 1878–1978* (1978).

LANGDON-DAVIES, John, *Westminster Hospital: Two Centuries of Voluntary Service, 1719–1948* (1952).

LAWSON, John and SILVER, Harold, *A Social History of Education in England* (1973).

LIGHTHILL, Sir James, 'Academic Innovation', *Journal of the Royal Society of Arts* (May 1980).

LINSTEAD, Sir Patrick, *The Prince Consort and the Founding of Imperial College* (1961).

LISTENER, THE, 'University of London Centenary Number' (1 July 1936).

LOGAN, Sir Douglas, *The University of London: An Introduction* (1st edn 1955, 2nd edn 1962, 3rd edn 1971).

——, *Haldane and the University of London* (Haldane Memorial Lecture, 1960).

——, 'University of London: Retrospect and Prospect', *University of London Bulletin*, 10 (1973).

LONDON SCHOOL OF ECONOMICS, *LSE Register, 1895–1932* (1934).

LYLE, H.W., *King's and Some King's Men: Being a Record of the Medical Department of King's College London from 1830 to 1909 and of King's College Hospital Medical School from 1909 to 1934* (2 vols, 1935, 1950).

MacLEOD, Roy (ed.), *Days of Judgement* (1982).

MACLURE, Stuart, *One Hundred Years of London Education, 1870–1970* (1970).

McDOWELL, R.J.S. and GURNEY, D.M., *The Story of the University of London: What and Where it is* (1952) [unreliable].

McINNES, E.M., *St Thomas' Hospital* (1963).

McLACHLAN, H., *English Education under the Test Acts* (1931).

MANSELL, A.L., 'Examinations and Medical Education: The Preliminary Sciences in the Examinations of London University and the English Conjoint Board, 1861–1911' in R. Macleod (ed.), *Days of Judgement* (1982).

MANSON-BAHR, Sir Philip, *History of the School of Tropical Medicine in London, 1899–1949* (1956).

MANTON, Jo, *Elizabeth Garrett Anderson* (1965).

MARRIOTT, S., *A Backstairs to a Degree: Demands for an Open University in Victorian England* (1981).

MARSH, Neville, *The History of Queen Elizabeth College: One Hundred Years of University Education in Kensington* (1986).

MASSON, David, 'London University and London Colleges and Schools of Science', *Macmillan's Magazine* (Oct. 1867).

MAURICE, Sir Frederick, *Haldane, 1856–1928: The Life of Viscount Haldane of Cloan* (2 vols, 1937, 1939).

MEDVEI, V.C. and THORNTON, J.L. (eds), *The Royal Hospital of St Bartholomew, 1123–1973* (1974).

MERRINGTON, W.R., *University College Hospital and its Medical School: A History* (1976).

MILES, Frank and CRANCH, Graeme, *King's College School: The First 150 Years* (1979).

MILNE, A. Taylor, 'Notes on the History of the University', *University of London Bulletin*, 2, 3 and 4 (1972).

MONTGOMERY, R.J., *Examinations: An Account of their Evolution as Administrative Devices in England* (1965).

MOODIE, G.C. and EUSTACE, Rowland, *Power and Authority in British Universities* (1974).

MOORE, Sir Norman, *The History of St Bartholomew's Hospital* (2 vols, 1910).

MORGAN, J.M., *Address to the Proprietors of the University of London* (1833).

MORLEY, Henry, *An Account of the Evening Classes at King's College, London* (1861).

——, *University College London, 1828–78* (1878).

MOSS, G.P. and SAVILLE, M.V., *From Palace to College: An Illustrated Account of Queen Mary College* (1985).

NEEDHAM, R. and WEBSTER, A., *Somerset House, Past and Present* (1905).

NEWMAN, Charles, *The Evolution of Medical Education in the Nineteenth Century* (1957).

O'DAY, Rosemary, *Education and Society, 1500–1800* (1982).

PAFFORD, J.H.P., 'The University of London Library' in Raymond Irwin and Ronald Staveley (eds), *The Libraries of London* (2nd edn, 1961).

PARLIAMENTARY PAPERS, *London University: Returns to an Address of the Honourable the House of Commons dated 19 May 1840* (1840).

——, *Report of Royal Commission to Inquire Whether Any and What Kind of Powers is or are Required for the Advancement of Higher Education in London* (1889).

——, *Report of the Commissioners Appointed to Consider the Draft Charter for the Proposed Gresham University in London* (1894).

——, *Royal Commission on University Education in London: Final Report of the Commissioners* (1913).

——, *Board of Education: Report of the Departmental Committee on the University of London* (1926).

——, *Report of the Royal Commission on Medical Education, 1965–68* (1968).

PARSONS, F.G., *The History of*

St Thomas's Hospital (3 vols, 1932, 1934, 1936).

PATTERSON, A. Temple, *The University of Southampton, 1862–1962* (1962).

PATTISON, Bruce, *Special Relations: The University of London and New Universities Overseas, 1947–1970* (1984).

PERCIVAL, Janet (ed.), *A Guide to Archives and Manuscripts in the University of London* (1984).

PERKIN, Harold, *Key Profession: The History of the Association of University Teachers* (1969).

PETERSON, M. Jeanne, *The Medical Profession in Mid-Victorian London* (1978).

PHILLIPS, C.H., *The School of Oriental and African Studies, 1917–1967: An Introduction* (n.d.).

POWELL, M.J. (ed.), *The Royal Holloway College, 1887–1937* (1937).

POYNTER, F.N.L. (ed.), *The Evolution of Medical Education in Britain* (1966).

PREST, W.R., *The Inns of Court under Elizabeth I and the Early Stuarts, 1590–1640* (1972).

PUGH, L.P., *From Farriery to Veterinary Medicine, 1785–95* (1962).

RANGER, Sir Douglas, *The Middlesex Hospital Medical School: Centenary to Sesquicentenary, 1935–1985* (1985).

READER, W.J., *Professional Men: The Rise of the Professional Classes in Nineteenth-Century England* (1966).

REEKS, Margaret, *Register of the Associates and Old Students of the Royal School of Mines and History of the Royal School of Mines* (1920).

ROBBINS, Lord, *The University in the Modern World* (1966).

ROBERTS, Gerrylynn K., 'The Establishment of the Royal College of Chemistry: An Investigation of the Social Context of Early-Victorian Chemistry', *Historical Studies in the Physical Sciences*, VII (1976).

RODERICK, G.W. and STEPHENS, M.D., *Scientific and Technical Education in Nineteenth-Century England* (1972).

ROYAL COLLEGE OF SCIENCE, *One Hundred Years of the Royal College of Science* (1981).

ROYAL VETERINARY COLLEGE, *The Royal Veterinary College and Hospital* (1937).

RUSSELL-WELLS, Sir Sydney, 'The University of London: An Introduction' in S. Gordon Wilson, *The University of London and its Colleges* (1923).

RUTLAND, Harold, *Trinity College of Music: The First Hundred Years* (1972).

SANDERSON, Michael, *The Universities and British Industry, 1850–1970* (1972).

——, (ed.), *The Universities in the Nineteenth Century* (1975).

——, *Education, Economic Change and Society in England, 1780–1870* (1983).

SILVER, Harold and TEAGUE, S. John, *The History of British Universities, 1800–1969: A Bibliography* (1970).

——, (eds.), *Chelsea College: A History* (1977).

SIMMONS, Jack, *New University* [Leicester] (1958).

SIMPSON, Renate, *How the PhD Came to Britain: A Century of Struggle for Postgraduate Education* (1983).

SINGER, Charles and HOLLOWAY, S.W.F., 'Early Medical Education in England in Relation to the Pre-history of London University', *Medical History*, IV (1960).

SKEAT, W.O., *King's College London Engineering Society, 1847–1957* (1957).

SONDHEIMER, Janet, *Castle Adamant in Hampstead: A History of Westfield College, 1882–1982* (1983).

STONE, Lawrence (ed.), *The University in Society* (2 vols, 1975).

——, 'Literacy and Education in England, 1640–1900', *Past and Present*, 42 (1969).

SYKES, J.D., *A Short Historical Guide to Wye College* (1984).

TAYLOR, David, *The Godless Students of Gower Street* (1968).

TEAGUE, S. John, *The City University: A History* (1980).

THOMSON, H. Campbell, *The Story of the Middlesex Hospital Medical School, 1835–1935* (1935).

TILDEN, Sir William A., *Sir William Ramsay, KCB, FRS: Memorials of his Life and Work* (1918).

TREVOR-ROPER, P. (Intro.), *Westminster Medical School, 1834–1984* (n.d.).

TUKE, Dame Margaret J., *A History of Bedford College for Women, 1849–1937* (1939).

UNIVERSITY OF LONDON, *Calendar*, issued annually from 1844 (apart from 1940–7); between 1891–2 and 1969–70 contains a periodically revised 'Historical Note'.

——, *General Register* (3 vols, 1890, 1899, 1901).

——, *University of London: The Historical Record, 1836–1912* (1912).

——, *University of London: The Historical Record, 1836–1926* (1926).

——, *University of London: New Buildings* (1932).

——, *The Bloomsbury Site* (1933).

——, *University of London, 1836–1936* (1936).

——, *University of London, 1836–1936: Centenary Commemorative Volume* (1936).

——, *The Senate House and Library* (1938).

——, *The Federal University of London* (1983).

USHER, H.J.K. (ed.), *An Angel without Wings: The History of University College School, 1830–1980* (1981).

VENABLES, Sir Peter, *Higher Education Developments: The Technological Universities, 1956–1976* (1978).

WALLER, A.D., *A Short Account of the Origins of the University of London* (1912).

WALLIS, T.E., *History of the School of Pharmacy* (1964).

WARBURG, Eric M., 'The Transfer of the Warburg Institute to England in 1933', Warburg Institute *Annual Report, 1952–53*.

WARMINGTON, E.H., *A History of Birkbeck College during the Second World War* (1954).

WEBB, Sidney, *London Education* (1904).

——, 'London University: A Policy and a Forecast', *Nineteenth Century* (1902).

WESENCRAFT, Alan, 'Enter the Ladies', *University of London Bulletin*, 7 and 8 (1973).

——, 'Gresham College', ibid., 15 (1974).

——, 'Sir Joshua Girling Fitch, 1824–1903' ibid., 32 (1976).

——, 'Sir George Biddell Airy, 1801–1892', ibid., 35, 38 and 42 (1976–7).

WESTON, Timothy, *And Now at Gordon Square: The History of the University of London Careers Advisory Service, 1909–1984* (1984).

WILSON, S. Gordon, *The University of London and its Colleges* (1923).

YOUNG, Sir Frank, 'The Origin and Development of the University of London with particular reference to Medical Education', Appendix to *Report of R.C. on Medical Education, 1965–68* (1968).

Acknowledgments

The University of London is too large and diverse a collection of institutions for its history to be easily or satisfactorily written. Any attempt must be either sketchily superficial or highly selective. This work is both. It has been produced at the request of the former Vice-Chancellor, Professor Sir Randolph Quirk, with the aim of seizing the opportunity of marking the 150th anniversary of the first Charter which falls in November 1986. The size and complexity of the task will readily – it may he hoped – excuse the shortcomings of the attempt.

It is a history of controversy and compromise, a story in which educational and scientific achievement of genuine distinction can all too conveniently be constrained into a chronology of successive constitutional and administrative arrangements. Such themes figure necessarily large. But the aim has been to compose an overview of the total history of the University, touching on a wide variety of aspects. The illustrations are a crucial component, attempting to encapsulate as much as possible about the changing life and work of the University as a whole. It has not been thought necessary to burden the text with a full apparatus of references. Footnotes have been used sparingly, and have been avoided where the source can without too much difficulty be traced in the central archives of the University or in the various publications on the constituent parts listed in the bibliography.

I am grateful to Sir Randolph Quirk for the opportunity of undertaking this work, daunting as it frequently seemed, and for permitting me to have unrestricted access to the University's central archives up to 1975. I received much help and encouragement from Dr William Taylor and Peter Holwell, successive Principals of the University, from Mrs Pauline Charnock and Jane Jones, successive Administrative Assistants to the Vice-Chancellor, and from Peter Taylor, the Clerk of the Senate. Further encouragement, much needed at times, has come from Professor F.M.L. Thompson, to whom I am especially indebted, and from Professor Douglas Johnson, Sir James Lighthill, Andrew Lewis, Dr John North, Professor T.C. Barker, Dr Penelope Corfield, and Dr David d'Avray. Wise advice was given by Sir Douglas Logan, Dr J.R. Stewart, Professor M.J. Wise, Arthur Tattersall, John Carswell, Sir Bryan Thwaites, Professor C.D. Cowan and Lord Flowers. In an apostolic gesture, A. Taylor Milne kindly passed on some notes of the late Professor H. Hale Bellot. Kind help on particular points has been given by Professor J.P. Quilliam, Dr W.F. Bynum, Professor Paul Samet, Dr Alan Sykes, Dr A.D. Johnstone, Dr W. Stephenson and Dr M.J. Daunton. In work undertaken on an overtime basis, in periods snatched from other commitments over the last three years, I owe much to the tolerance of many colleagues and more students. They are too numerous to name, but they are known in my heart.

The staff of the Palaeography Room of the University Library, where the archives of the central offices of the University are kept, have been a constant source of enlightenment as well as encouragement. Joan Gibbs presided over my early efforts to come to terms with the bulk of the University's central archives, and her successor Simon Bailey has been unfailingly helpful: I am much in his debt. I am grateful too to Piers Cain, Helen Young, Pamela Baker and Erika Panagakis for lightening my burdens there. In 1918 reference was made to 'the shameful condition of the archives in the basement, which has for a long time been a happy hunting-ground for mice and beetles and a standing danger to the lungs of the clerks who have to go down there from time to time to search for old documents ...' (ULL ACO CF 1 (1917–18), 736). The University's central archives are now being put in order. Proper hand-lists are being prepared, and can be consulted in the Palaeography Room.

Throughout the University many others have helped. All Schools and Institutes provided liaison contacts who guided me through the separate and complex histories of the various constituent parts of the University. My visits were invariably fascinating voyages of discovery, for which I am grateful to all of the following: R.E. Swainson, Secretary of Birkbeck College; Sir David Innes Williams, Director of the British Postgraduate Medical Federation; Ian Middleton, Secretary of the Institute of Child Health; Alan Ingle, Secretary of the Institute of Psychiatry; G.K. Buckley, Secretary of the Charing Cross and Westminster Medical School, Professor Sydney Selwyn of the Dept. of Medical Microbiology, and Mrs Pamela Bentley of the Dept. of Medical Illustration; Mrs J. Pingree, Archivist of Imperial College; Patricia Methven, Archivist of King's College, G.M. Pentelow, Librarian of the King's College School of Medicine and Dentistry, and Dr Neville Marsh of the Department of Physiology, historian of the former Queen Elizabeth College; Sir John Ellis, the former Dean of the London Hospital Medical College and Jonathan Pepler, the District Archivist; Dr Angela Raspin, Archivist of the LSE and Paula Kendal of the Information Office; Dr C.E. Gordon Smith, Dean of the London School of Hygiene and Tropical Medicine and Mary Gibson, Assistant Librarian; William Slack, Dean of the Middlesex Hospital Medical School and Janet Cropper, Librarian; G.G. Williams, Secretary of Queen Mary College and Dr G.P. Moss of the Dept. of Chemistry; Dr Edith Gilchrist, Hon. Archivist of the Royal Free Hospital and Professor Ruth Bowden of the School of Medicine; Mrs Elizabeth Bennett, Archivist of Royal Holloway and Bedford New College (formerly of Bedford College), Dr Francis Robinson of the Dept. of History, and Mrs Caroline Bingham, historian of Royal Holloway College; Alan N. Smith, Deputy Secretary of the Royal Postgraduate Medical School; Professor E. Cotchin, Hon. Archivist and former Vice-Principal of the Royal Veterinary College and Linda Warden, Librarian; D.J. Brown, Secretary of St Bartholomew's Hospital Medical College and Janet Foster, District Archivist; Dr Richard West, Dean of St George's Hospital Medical School; K. Lockyer, Secretary of St Mary's Hospital Medical School; E. O'Connor, Secretary of the School of Oriental and African Studies, Paul Fox, Photographer, and Rosemary Scott, Curator of the Percival David Foundation of Chinese Art; Linda Lisgarten, Librarian of the School of Pharmacy; A.W. Baker, Registrar of the United Medical and Dental Schools of Guy's and St Thomas's Hospitals, D.G. Bompas, Secretary, Jerry Rytina of the Guy's Dept. of Audio-Visual Services and Yvonne Hibbott, Librarian of St Thomas's Hospital Medical School; Gillian Furlong and Mrs Janet Percival of the University College London Library; Dr Janet Sondheimer, Archivist (and historian) of Westfield College; Mrs Mary Lucas, Librarian of Wye College and Donald Sykes of the Dept. of Environmental Studies and Countryside Planning; Francis X. Walker, SJ, Principal of Heythrop College; Jean Fenton, London Secretary of the British Institute in Paris; Professor Michael Kitson, Deputy Director of the Courtauld Institute of Art; W.A. Steiner, former Librarian of the Institute of Advanced Legal Studies; Belinda Barratt, Deputy Librarian of the Institute of Archaeology; Alicia Totolos, Secretary of the Institute of Classical Studies and Professor J.P. Barron, Director; Margaret Beard, Assistant Secretary of the Institute of Commonwealth Studies; Denis Baylis, Information and Publications Officer of the Institute of Education; Dr John L. Flood, Deputy Director of the Institute of Germanic Studies; Dr Alice Prochaska, Secretary of the Institute of Historical Research and Cynthia Hawker, the Director's Secretary; Professor John Lynch, Director of the Institute of Latin American Studies; Dr Howell Daniels, Secretary of the Institute of United States Studies; Dr J.E.O. Screen, Librarian of the School of Slavonic and East European Studies; Professor J.B. Trapp, Director of the Warburg Institute; Moira Rees, Senior Assistant Registrar of Goldsmiths' College; Esra Kahn, Librarian of Jews' College; Brian L. Dodridge, Secretary and Treasurer of the London

Graduate School of Business Studies; R. Golding, Registrar of the Royal Academy of Music; O. Davies, Keeper of Portraits and Ephemera at the Royal College of Music; C.A. Cork, Vice-Principal of the Trinity College of Music.

Help in connection with various aspects of the central activities of the University was given by John Burrows, formerly of the Extra-Mural Department, Peter Newsham of ULU, Donald Mann of International Hall, D.A.V. Morgan of Motspur Park, Malcolm Smith of the Bloomsbury Conference Agency, Dr G.R. Field of the Computer Centre and P.F. Dawson of the School Examination Board. Others in the Senate House who willingly coped with my needs in various ways include P.J. Griffiths, Deputy Clerk of the Court, P.M. Crossland, Central Projects Officer, Mrs Gillian Roberts, Academic Registrar, Louisa Smith and Judith Maynard of the Academic Division, A.C. Millns, the Public Relations Officer, S.B. Crooks, Secretary for External Students, Mrs E. Upham, Secretary of Convocation, Vasanta Synge of the Principal's Office, Joan Robins of the Clerk of the Senate's Office, Susan Small of the Vice-Chancellor's Office, Graham West of the Vice-Chancellor's Office, and P.G. Goodall, the Secretary for Services. I am especially grateful also to R.M. Cain of the Court Department and to A.J. Fryer, Head of Domestic Services.

In the Department of History at University College Nazneen Razwi performed word-processing miracles and helped in all manner of ways. For eighteen months Dr Kevin Jefferys, now of St Mary's College, Twickenham, was a part-time research assistant of rare ability: I owe a good deal of thanks to him. Ruby Way kindly provided typing assistance at a crucial moment. F.J. Bosley of the University Library's Photographic Section laboured enthusiastically over the taking of many photographs. Some photographic tasks were also undertaken by the Central Photographic Unit of University College. Many acknowledgments in connection with obtaining particular items are made in the list of sources of illustrations. The two graphs in chapter 1 were kindly drawn by Alick Newman of the Department of Geography at UCL.

I have tested the patience of the Athlone Press to the limit. Brian Southam has been an incomparably sympathetic and tolerant publisher, and his colleagues Helen Lefroy and Della Couling have coped heroically with the last-minute delivery of text and illustrations. The designer, Roger Davies, rose admirably to the challenge of all the difficulties I created.

With such impressive help of all sorts, the failings that result must inescapably be mine. Any opinions expressed are also, of course, mine, and not in any way those of the University of London. No attempt has been made to influence the independence of my judgment at all. At the end of so long a list I have to inadequately record my appreciation of those who have suffered most: Eva Harte, my wife, and Pendle Harte and Piran Harte, my children. But for them, I would not have survived the course.

NBH

Index

Bold figures refer to illustration numbers and not to pages.